Psychological
Perspectives
on
Literature

Psychological Perspectives on Literature:
Freudian Dissidents
and
Non-Freudians

A Casebook

Joseph Natoli, Editor

1984
Archon

Design and Composition by Mim-G Studios, Inc.
9 Elm St., Westerly, R.I. 02891

Library of Congress Cataloging in Publication Data

Main entry under title:
Psychological perspectives on literature.

Includes index.
1. Literature—History and criticism—Addresses,
essays, lectures.   2. Psychology and literature—Addresses,
essays, lectures.   I. Natoli, Joseph P., 1943-
PN56.P93P7   1984   809   83-22452
ISBN 0-208-01989-8

The authors and editor gratefully acknowledge the following permissions:

Clifton Snider chapter adapted and revised from "C.G. Jung's Analytical Psychology
and Literary Criticism (I)," *Psychocultural Review I*, i (Winter 1977): 96-108 and from
"C. G. Jung's Analytical Psychology and Literary Criticism (II)," *Psychocultural Review
I*, ii (Spring 1977): 216-242. Published by Redgrave Publishing Company, P.O. Box 67,
South Salem, NY 10590.

Frederik L. Rusch chapter adapted and revised from "Marble Men and Maidens, The
Necrophilous People of F. Scott Fitzgerald: A Psychoanalytic Approach in Terms of
Erich Fromm," *Journal of Evolutionary Psychology III*, 1-2 (1982): 28-40.

Bernard J. Paris chapter adapted and revised from *The Literary Review*, Vol. 24, No. 2,
Winter, 1981. Published by Fairleigh Dickinson University.

R.J. Huber chapter adapted and revised from R.J. Huber and G. Ledbetter, "Holden
Caulfield, Self-Appointed Catcher in the Rye: Some Additional Thoughts," *Journal
of Individual Psychology* 33 (1977): 250-56., Now published by The University of Texas
Press.

Contents

Contributors

Arthur Efron, Department of English/Center for the Psychological Study of the Arts, State University of New York at Buffalo

Sam B. Girgus, American Studies Department, University of New Mexico

Henry D. Herring, Department of English, Wooster College

R. J. Huber, Department of Psychology, Meredith College

David J. Kann, Department of English, California Polytechnic State University

Martin S. Lindauer, Department of Psychology, State University College of New York at Brockport

Joseph Natoli, English and American Literature Bibliographer, Michigan State University

Bernard J. Paris, Department of English, University of Florida, Gainesville

Ellie Ragland-Sullivan, Department of French, University of Illinois, Chicago

Frederik L. Rusch, Department of English, John Jay College, City University of New York

Clifton Snider, Department of English, California State University, Long Beach

Sara van den Berg, Department of English, University of Washington

Introduction

Joseph Natoli, Editor

D ear reader — what you have in your hands is a collection of "unorthodox" psychological perspectives on literature. Each contributor has not only seized the opportunity to present the perspective dear to his or her heart but has followed a certain format in presentation (exposition of the psychological approach and an application of that approach to a literary text) in the hope of expanding the literary world's sense of orthodoxy.

Ten years ago the editors of a broadly titled journal, *Literature and Psychology*, refused to publish an essay I had done on Jung and Blake because they had concluded that Jung's view of such a basic concept as the unconscious was radically different from Freud's. I supposed then that a Jungian inclusion might have jeopardized psychoanalysis's own precarious position in conventional literary circles. As a point of fact, no psychological approach to literature has had a warm reception by the Formalist critics, the arbiters of convention during all the years that I was student. In 1973, Tennenhouse, in an introduction to a collection of psychoanalytic essays selected from *American Imago* and *Criticism* (including a Jungian essay!) felt the need to do a two-page explanation/defense of the psychoanalytic perspective.[1] As the editor of "unorthodox" psychological perspectives, perspectives twice removed from a "consensually validated literary universe," I feel the need of making a double defense — one to all those antideterminists who yet maintain the insular sovereignty of the literary text, and one to all those psychoanalysts who doggedly pursue that same text in the footsteps of Freud.

1

Joseph Natoli

The aura of antideterminist criticism has not vanished, although we have been conscious for a long time that we are, in the present, decidedly after the new criticism, to use the title of Frank Lentricchia's recent book.[2] Some have indeed severed all the old connections and have plunged into the worlds of Structuralism and Deconstruction, or have followed the mercurial trail of Harold Bloom or Stanley Fish or René Girard or Wolfgang Iser or — fill in your special choice. But many a literary interpreter has just dropped out, no longer openly espouses Brooks or Warren, but goes about literary interpretation as he or she "knows it." Minds here molded by New Criticism, forever in its grip, face a Continental theory-onslaught that does not relate in the same way New Criticism related to Anglo-American "metaphysics."

Happily, the minds of today's students are after-the-new-criticism minds. I do not mean that the real contributions of that mentality should be ignored, but simply that the political hold, if you will, of New Criticism no longer extends to today's students. Such minds have no historical bias against a consideration of "structural" determinants operating upon literature-as-discourse, or against considerations of the *Lebenswelt* (the human life-world) of an author or the identity theme of a reader or the ways language subverts meaning in a literary text. A criticism that ignores the affective element of literature and plays up the role of form over chaos, of genre conventions, of a ". . . self-fathered, self-nurturing, self-referential . . ." text — is now finally seen, taking a term from Frederick Crews, as an Anesthetic Criticism.[3]

We are, I believe, aware that we have been anesthetized as literary critics, and that awareness, though it replaces what Gerald Graff calls "ideological peace and harmony," is a stimulating awareness, an awareness that indicates growth, however unsettling the pains of that growth may be.[4] The stimulating theories generating a stimulating awareness (which in turn generate pain and growth) are those of the Structuralists, Deconstructionists, Phenomenologists, and "Mercurial Individualists." But somewhere in between our anesthetized and our present lives in which "both logocentric metaphysics and nihilism are jostling irreconcilably with one another," are an ever-increasing variety of psychological approaches to literature.[5] And some of these approaches are based on the work of "dissident" Freudians and non-Freudians. Before we were all stimulated by Barthes, Derrida, Foucault, Iser, Bloom et al., some were being stimulated by Jungian, Adlerian, Reichian, Rankian, Horneyan perspectives on literature, perspectives that could

2

be found occasionally in psychological journals and in a potpourri of "little magazines," but seldom if at all in the traditional literary lists. Of course, I think there is a fundamental difference between aesthetic and linguistic theories directed toward literary interpretation and theories of consciousness and behavior not directed toward literary interpretation. I am also mindful of the fact that the authors of the following essays do not fail to transform the ore of their various perspectives into illuminating literary interpretation. Derrida, Foucault and others have not been mined with any less effort.

To the early, classic Freudian dissidents, I have added perspectives that contain within them seeds of independence from Freud the Father. In some cases these seeds have already borne fruit.

I believe Jacques Lacan and Roy Schafer are in the latter category. William Kerrigan, in an article titled "Psychoanalysis Unbound," speaks of Schafer as demonstrating a Freud-liberated ego psychology, and of Lacan as demonstrating a "dauntless anti-ego psychology."[6] Both, however, wreak havoc, from a traditional Freudian view, on the Freudian metapsychology. And I would say that Karen Horney and Erich Fromm have achieved even greater independence. I have chosen Norman Holland's approach to literature because I feel it is in itself a "dissident" Freudian view and because it represents audience-oriented criticism, a widely controversial criticism whose roots are psychological. Among the non-Freudian perspectives, I have chosen the phenomenological because I think its psychological dimensions provide a fine entrance into literature and have been somehow passed by.[7] I have chosen cognitive psychology because it is presently in its heyday in this country and I think there is much interest in perceiving its usefulness in literary interpretation. And, finally, the empirical methodology based on the natural sciences is but a fair counterbalance to the phenomenological method.

In his preface to *Deconstruction and Criticism*, Geoffrey Hartman defended Deconstructive criticism's base in philosophy by saying that ". . . without the pressure of philosophy on literary texts, or the reciprocal pressure of literary analysis of philosophical writing, each discipline becomes impoverished."[8] Doesn't this reciprocal relationship exist between literature and psychology? Perhaps psychology owes even more to literature than does philosophy when we consider both Freud's and Jung's expressed debts to literature, when we consider Lacan's return to *Hamlet* in order to complete, in his view, the work of Freud.

3

And have not our ties as readers to *Hamlet*, for example, been multiplied by Ernest Jones's efforts as well as by Lacan's? Why shouldn't mutual probing of our human-world be mutually beneficial? Why shouldn't the psychologist refer to literature as a canvas not only of human behavior and intentions displayed in full panoply, but also as a canvas in which he or she can discover his or her own identity by interacting with a literary text? And — final question — why shouldn't a reader of a literary work take advantage of the broadest spectrum of contemporary psychology in the hope of constructing a significant relationship between himself/herself and the literary work?

It seems to me, then, that presenting a casebook of unrecognized and/or controversial and/or "unthought-of-in-this-context" psychological perspectives on literature encourages a nonrestrictive dialogue between psychology and literature. Secondly, it puts on display in the clear light of day an assorted dozen essays not always joined on either latent or manifest levels. And, thirdly, it reaches out, one hopes, to the after-the-new-criticism minds of students currently reading literary criticism, literature, and psychology. I only believe, as Robert Coles does, that ". . . psychiatrists and psychoanalysts . . . ought for a good while to stop poking into homes next door, if not those located on an entirely different street . . . ," in regard to armchair diagnosis of authors.[9] When I think of the way Arthur Efron has led me to re-see *Wuthering Heights* by drawing upon the perceptions of Reich, or the way Frederik Rusch has used Erich Fromm to illuminate a particular kind of death-in-life in contemporary literature — pick any one of these twelve essays — I know then that there is merit in seeing literature and psychology residing on one block, that there is something quite right about placing imaginative portrayals of human consciousness and action, and formal psychological studies of human consciousness and action in a reciprocal relationship.

In writing of audience-oriented criticism, Susan Suleiman says that it is ". . . not one field but many, not a single widely trodden path but a multiplicity of criss crossing, often divergent tracks that cover a vast area of the critical landscape in a pattern whose complexity dismays the brave and confounds the faint of heart."[10] I realize dismay and confoundment are the probable results of trying to track Iser, Fish, Holland and others on the subject of audience-oriented criticism. However, I believe another level of dismay and confoundment may face the reader who attempts to trace a clear, simple map, with all intersecting, divergent, parallel points and lines highlighted, of the twelve essays herein presented. We have Jung, Adler, Fromm, and Reich wiping their feet on the Freudian mat — each going to a different portion of it and applying themselves with varying force and determination. Lacan perceived himself as something of a reincarnated French Freud. Schafer seems to believe that Freud anticipated him. Holland sees his work as not necessarily work Freud would have given his approval to, but as a natural continuation — from id to ego to identity — of Freud's thought. R. D. Laing reverses Freud's "politics of experience," and the phenomenologists ignore Freud's metapsychology as just so much metaphysics to be "bracketed out." Third Force and cognitive psychologists disdain the Freudian view that man is a biologically and socially determined animal, and emphasize the existence of constructive forces in man, in the case of Third Force, and the constructive aspects of thought, in the case of the cognitive view.

Freudian psychology is thus a reference point on our map. Even the non-Freudians expound and interpret with Freud on their horizon. The relation of one approach to another is less trackable. Divergent tracks do not converge north, south, east, or west of Freud, either here at the very beginning or upon completion of the last essay in the collection. No one perspective resolves the dilemmas of all others. No one perspective seems pertinent to all literary texts. What we do find is some parallel action at certain points. This casebook, therefore, advocates a true critical pluralism, a pluralism whose constituency is here only partially presented. Even a critical pluralism, however, can be aided by some appropriate introductory comments, ones that it is hoped will block out with a few brush strokes an "horizon" for the reader.

Carl Gustav Jung (1875–1961) earns his title of Freudian dissident with some ease:

> Of all possible accusations, "Jungian" is still probably the most devastating among Freud's intellectual descendants. Every subculture has its villains, and Jung is a particularly odious figure, partly because Freud had placed such high hopes in him. His later contact with the Nazis only put the final seal of disapproval on a man Freud's pupils had learned to detest. Jung is still dismissed today, following Freud's lead, as a "mystic," supposedly as unscientific as the Socialist Adler.[11]

In essence, Jung's model of psychic growth via a dialectic of conscious and unconscious energies leading to the creation of a Self has definite ties to Third Force psychology. His view that much of the energy of the unconscious must be assimilated if a fully "individuated" human self is to be achieved foreshadows to some degree Laing's perception of virtue in psychosis. It is this process of individuation that Clifton Snider uses as his entrance into Carson McCullers's *The Member of the Wedding*.

Alfred Adler (1870–1937) "desexualized" Freudian psychoanalysis (as did Jung), and Freud responded accordingly:

> The view of life which is reflected in the Adlerian system is founded exclusively on the aggressive instinct; there is no room in it for love.[12]

In actuality, Freud's notion of "love" here is "libido," a concept that Adler saw as subordinate to ego functioning. And, interestingly enough, Adler's views in this area were taken up by Anna Freud. Adler's "instinct of aggression" was based on feelings of inferiority, feelings that led to "a will to power." However, Adler's later view of "social interest" is, in R. J. Huber's view, ". . . a term which is one of the cornerstones of Maslow's description of the self-actualized individual." In his concern for developing a view that encompassed man at every stage, and with the development of a "normal psychology," Adler paralleled Jung and Third Force psychology. And his concern with societal determinants anticipated Fromm and Reich. Huber presents a succinct summary of Adler's views and an application of those views to Holden Caulfield of Salinger's *Catcher in the Rye*. The Adler who has been summarily dismissed as the "drive-for-power" theorist is presented by Huber as a psychologist sensitive to the creative, evolving aspects of "being."

Wilhelm Reich (1897–1957) joined Adler and Jung in a concern with a psychology that would encompass the total personality. In an essay that I am sure will reawaken interest in Reich's potential for literary study, Arthur Efron lists and discusses ten basic Reichian perspectives on the human body and its contexts. What one discovers surprisingly is Reich's link with Fromm and Laing in a concern for modern society's destructive effect on individual human life. Reich's descriptions of society's destructiveness, its creation of "armored" lives, and the human body's ties with Orgone, a pervading, cosmic, vital energy, are descriptions vitalized by, and that in turn vitalize, Efron's reading of *Wuthering Heights*.

Introduction

Erich Fromm (1900–) is so wide-ranging, so eclectic that such eclecticism has discouraged an early development of a "Frommian" perspective on literature. In surveying Reichian criticism, Efron refers to Frederik Rusch as a pioneer in Reich-Whitman studies. Rusch's essay in this collection applying Fromm's social psychology to literature is, as far as I know, also a pioneering effort. Fromm's breadth has positive repercussions on literary interpretation. Characters are considered within the total ambiance of the literary work, and the interaction between character and literary ambiance replaces considerations of the psychic deficits of one character. Thus, Rusch does not simply analyze Prufrock, Gatsby, or Willy Loman but discusses the relationship of those characters to the modern society they find themselves in.

> Confronted with Jacques Lacan's (1901–1981) radical thought and impenetrable style, the general reaction of American intellectuals tends to be either one of curiosity and frustration or one of anger and disgust.[13]

In this same review essay, Ellie Ragland-Sullivan announced her intention to "speak clearly about Lacan." I think American readers are equally determined to find a clear exposition of Lacan, a man who sought to ". . . bring about a return to the 'true' meaning of Freud's texts through a study of the theoretical contradictions in them."[14] Lacan not only challenged the terminology and meaning of Freudian metapsychology, but replaced Freud's instinctual stages with a theory of "symbolic representation in the psyche as the source of drive and libido. . . ."[15] Although Lacan alters Freudian terminology, he does not reduce the intricacy of the scaffolding. Ragland-Sullivan's discussion of Genet's *The Maids*, however, not only glosses Lacan's terms but also gains entrance, in a provocative fashion, into Genet's enigmatic drama.

Norman Holland (1927–) has been chosen as a prominent representative of audience-oriented criticism. Susan Suleiman points out the interest and extent of this type of criticisms:

> Today, one rarely picks up a literary journal on either side of the Atlantic without finding articles (and often a whole special issue) devoted to the performance of reading, the role of feeling, the variability of individual response, the confrontation, transaction, or interrogation between texts and readers, the nature and limits of interpretation — questions whose very formulation depend on a new awareness of

7

the audience as an entity indissoluble from the notion of artistic texts.[16]

Indeed, while Holland opts for the term "transactive," in which the reader or literent begins and creates the response to the text, Wolfgang Iser, who finds his base in phenomenological rather than psychoanalytic theory, opts for a "bi-active" theory in which each text "constitutes its own reader." Even though Michel Grimaud includes Holland in his 1976 survey of psychoanalytic trends while excluding those who ". . . have given up adherence, or never adhered, to the basic principles of Freudian psychology . . . ," I think now in 1984 it is clear that Holland's is a "dissident" Freudian view of literature, one that places both the core unconscious fantasy and the defenses against it in the reader and not in the text, where they have traditionally been viewed as the sublimated products of the author.[17] David Kann's reading of "Rip Van Winkle" is one in which he, as reader, is enmeshed in the events of the story, in the narration. He describes to us the various ways he feels and perceives the text manipulating his own particular reading.

Roy Schafer's action language, according to a recent assessment, is ". . . actually a proposed substitution for psychoanalytic metapsychology . . . (and) should not be taken lightly."[18] Another reviewer declares that Schafer's is ". . . clearly the most radical recasting of the theory (psychoanalysis) in years. . . ."[19] Sara van den Berg expresses the view that no complex terminology attached to a metapsychology clutters Schafer's methods, methods that, she feels, should form the "native tongue of literary, as well as, psychoanalytic interpretation." In van den Berg's discussion of sonnets by Milton and Keats, our attention is on multiple levels of action, residing in the poems themselves, in the interaction of reader and poem, in the act of creating the poems, and in the criticism ensuing.

"There are many works," Bernard Paris writes in his essay on Third Force psychology, "about which I can say very little from a Horneyan perspective; but there are others with which it seems highly congruent." Third Force psychologists are those psychologists who recognize a force operating in man other than that presented by Freudians and Behaviorists, "an evolutionary constructive force." Paris leans most on Karen Horney's (1885-1952) theory of self-alienation and Abraham Maslow's (1908-1970) theory of the hierarchy of basic needs. There are certainly ties here with Jung's theory of individuation, that is, the development of the full human personality, the cognitive view that "emphasizes the constructing capacities and processes of human thought," and the existential brand of phenomenology wielded by Carl Rogers and Rollo May. In his discussion of Hamlet, Paris reveals the changing relationships among Hamlet's natural inclinations, his self-perceptions, and the world around him. We see Hamlet as a man torn between self-effacement and aggression, between a need to reconcile the two, and a need to be punished if he fails. The use of the Third Force perspective is itself performed so "self-effacingly" that the staunchest formalist would not, I think, object.

R. D. Laing's (1927-) dissidence goes well beyond Freud and indeed psychoanalysis. He is "a psychiatrist in rebellion against the authority of his own professional power."[20] Thus, he is non-Freudian in fact and nonpsychiatrist in intention. Sam Girgus's essay on Laing and literature gives us his view of both the assets and deficits of the Laing perspective on literature. One of the assets of Girgus's own discussion is his use of Freud, both as contrast to Laing's view and as a perspective that conjoins with Laing's in an interpretation of Kate Chopin's *The Awakening* and Hawthorne's *The Scarlet Letter*. Girgus perceives a certain relevance in Laing's view of a self divided by a sick society and the plight of women, victims of society's own divisions on both social and personal levels. I think it is important to note that Laing's perspective on literature, although deriving to some extent from a phenomenological base, does not partake of phenomenological method but is rather an indictment of contemporary society fashioned from an existential perspective.

Robert Magliola has clearly distinguished existentialism's concern with ontological and ethical notions and phenomenology's metaphysical neutrality.[21] Such a distinction applies to a Laing perspective on literature and the kind I have attempted in my own discussion of phenomenological psychology and literature. Rather than refer to the phenomenological aesthetics of Roman Ingarden, Mikel Dufrenne, Georges Poulet or others, I have followed Paul Brodtkorb's lead and turned to the work of the phenomenological psychiatrist, Jan van den Berg. I have also referred to Ludwig Binswanger, and to Merleau-Ponty rather than Sartre or Heidegger. Although my work leans heavily on the work of psychiatric clinical practitioners, such an orientation is by no means fully representative of the wide-ranging expression "phenomenological criticism." I do believe that it is the psychological brand of phenomenology that is most relevant to literary interpretation and that has not received due attention. An interesting use of phenomenology's tenet of an intentional consciousness, an indivisible relationship between object and perceiver, text and reader, is Wolfgang Iser's contribution to audience-oriented criticism.

Henry Herring identifies the literary work as a "construction of reality," an artefact that not only reveals in an imaginative setting the ways in which people construct their own lives but that is itself ". . . a deliberately constructed expression in which design and subject function as an ensemble." When this ensemble is portrayed as collapsing, as in Berryman's *Dream Songs*, both the cognitive acts of the poet and the language and form of the poem are portrayed as simultaneously collapsing. In considering the "cognitive act" of reading as well as the cognitive act of the writer writing, the cognitive aesthetic enters the domain of audience-oriented criticism. In the first sentence of his essay, Herring recognizes that ". . . the dominant mode of psychological interpretation in literature has continued to be psychoanalytic . . . ," and appropriately throughout his essay, Herring contrasts a psychoanalytically based aesthetic and a cognitive one. His comparative critique of a Holland and a cognitive view of the "Tomorrow and tomorrow and tomorrow" speech from *Macbeth* is both illuminating and balanced. What is also implicit throughout the essay are the points at which a cognitive view coincides with other views in this collection. There is a phenomenological touch in the following:

> . . . a constructivist criticism brings its focus to the cognitive strategies in the work . . . to assessing the effectiveness of a character or speaker's construct from within his conception of his world.

And there is an unmistakable cognitive touch in Bernard Paris's description of Third Force as "an evolutionary constructive force."

The essays in this collection do divide roughly into dissident Freudian (although some are more dissident than others, and each displays a different and perhaps, in the case of Holland, an arguable brand of dissidence) and non-Freudian. A more particular division might align perspectives in which a self interacting with its environment and not totally determined either by it or by biological mechanisms, and perspectives in which no recognizable self, integrated or moving toward integration, has as much or indeed any significance in contrast with biological and/or environmental dynamics. In this collection such a division leaves out two perspectives — the phenomenological and the empirical, both "metaphysically neutral," both concerned with methodology, and both able, in spite of such neutrality, to encompass what Martin Lindauer terms the "psychology of literature" — the literary work, the reader, and the author. While Freud saw himself as working inductively and empirically, Jung, declared a mystic by Freud and ever since, defended the empirical nature of his own work. Both, however, fashioned an elaborate "metapsychology" based on clinical observations that, in the case of Freud, Schafer has set out to purge.

These metapsychologies, be they Jungian, Reichian, Laingian, etc., are worlds themselves applied to both real people and literary texts. And to the degree to which they do not seek to reduce, resolve, or replace the text, they are illuminating, as I believe the essays in this collection are. Although it may initially appear that phenomenology possesses an attendant metapsychology, at least when compared with an empirical methodology as described by Lindauer (in other words, one based on the natural sciences), phenomenology's acceptance of a Husserlian intentional consciousness is no more a "metaphysical" tenet than empiricism's acceptance of a Cartesian consciousness, an epistemological dualism. However, I have used the work of Jan van den Berg, a clinical practitioner, and have employed certain categories — self, others, objects, and time — as an entrance into literature. Although these categories are, as Paul Brodtkorb says, ". . . primarily existential categories rather than metaphysical ones (such as id, superego, and so forth) . . . ," they are yet more of a classifying schema than Lindauer brings to his discussion of how literature may best be approached from an empirical view.[22] The virtues of empiricism are not restricted to psychology, but Lindauer finds an empirically based psychology to be the most suitable entrance to the totally human enterprise of literature. He succeeds in demonstrating a purely empirical approach to literature, an approach whose assets and limitations are revealed when glossed by a reading of the other essays in this collection. It is my hope that these essays will be read comparatively, that each will gloss each, and that the unorthodox twelve will serve to gloss the conventional psychoanalytic interpretation of literature.

Jungian Theory, Its Literary Application, and a Discussion of *The Member of the Wedding*

by Clifton Snider

> *We are such stuff*
> *as dreams are made on, and our little life*
> *Is rounded with a sleep.*
> (Shakespeare, *The Tempest*)

Although Freud's psychoanalysis remains the most influential psychology in literary criticism, Jung's analytical psychology has exerted, within the last decade or so, a growing force among literary critics. Part of this renaissance of interest in Jung has been due to negative responses to the Freudian view of literature as the expression of the artist's neurosis; but the rise of Jungian criticism also parallels the rise of "archetypal criticism," which is, itself, influenced heavily by Jungian thought. Indeed, Jungian literary criticism is sometimes placed as a subcategory of archetypal or "myth" criticism. René Wellek lists six major kinds of criticism "new in this last half-century"; one of these is "psychoanalytic criticism," while another is "myth criticism appealing to the results of cultural anthropology and the speculation of Carl Jung."[1] Jung's influence on archetypal or myth criticism may be seen in the wealth of recent anthologies of literature that are concerned wholly or at least in part with works of an archetypal nature. In addition, an increasing number of dissertations and articles are using Jungian psychology to illuminate literature.[2]

The most thorough treatment of Jungian ideas about art is Morris Philipson's *Outline of a Jungian Aesthetic*. Philipson points out that it would appear that of Jung's literary modes only the visionary is worth considering from a psychological point of view because the psychological mode is already clearly intelligible. Yet "Jung has oversimplified his scheme for the modes of art and their interpretation" (p. 160), for there is an unconscious element in the seemingly conscious psychological mode and a conscious shaping in the apparently unconscious visionary mode. If Jung is a bit inconsistent in his classification of literary types, his justification for studying art ("visionary" art in particular) is clear: "Jung believes symbolical [i.e., visionary] art-work serves the same purpose for a society that an individual symbolic experience [as in a dream, for example] serves for a patient in therapy" (pp. 127–28). Thus, the questions Jungian literary criticism attempts to answer are: "What *purpose* does the symbolic work of art fulfill in the psychic life of a society? What is its psychic significance?" (p. 127). We may also say that once we have answered these questions we shall have a greater appreciation for how a particular piece of literature *works*. Further, as Philipson writes,

> Jung offers a basis for an historical analysis of psychically significant works of art. "The nature of the work of art (Jung says) permits conclusions to be drawn concerning the character of the period from which it sprang." Consequently, a psychological interpretation can be offered in answer to such questions as: "What was the significance of realism and naturalism to their age? What was the meaning of romanticism, or Hellenism? They were tendencies of art which brought to the surface that unconscious element of which the contemporary mental atmosphere had most need. The artist as educator of his time — much could be said about that today." (p. 130)

Strictly speaking, the psychology of Carl Gustav Jung should be called "analytical psychology" in order to distinguish it from Sigmund Freud's "psychoanalysis" and Alfred Adler's "individual psychology." Jung, who was associated as a young man with Freud, feels that the theories of both Freud and Adler are reductive. Freud reduces neurosis to sexual repression (the "pleasure principle"); Adler reduces mental illness to the drive for power (stemming from the "inferiority complex").[3] Jung posits a theory of human psychology that essentially traces mental problems to an imbalance of psychic forces within the individual. His theory is as applicable to "normal" human development as it is to the "abnormal"; it rests on a concept of stadial development, each stage of which is determined by a particular instinctual "archetypal" constellation.

Like Freud, Jung believes in a personal unconscious that contains all the repressed and forgotten or even subliminal perceptions of the individual. But Jung goes a step beyond Freud to postulate the collective unconscious. The collective unconscious contains the archetypes that are, like physical instincts, the innate ability and tendency to create forms and images. These images are symbols of the archtype. Archetypes are, by definition, common to all mankind, and their number is immeasurable. In the same way, archetypal images are infinitely varied. In this sense Jung's theory is not reductive.

The archetype is only a hypothesis. It cannot be proved; nor can we ever fully know the meaning of an archetype. We do know, however, that the central characteristic of the archetype is its duality: it can always have a positive or a negative effect. Within the individual the archetype is stirred to produce images or symbols whenever an imbalance in the psyche is struck. Thus, the archetype exhibits a peculiar autonomy. The individual may then have archetypal (as opposed to merely personal) dreams and fantasies that are trying to compensate for the imbalance. The same applies to communities (which always have a collective consciousness). If a large group of people have an imbalance in their collective consciousness or their collective unconsciousness, then archetypal images will appear in myths, in folk tales, and in more formal literature.

Literary criticism based on Jungian analytical psychology can add a new dimension to literary art. It can show, as I have indicated, how literature contributes to the psychic balance of a community. In doing this, it demonstrates how an individual poem works. Examining a literary work in Jungian terms can show why the piece is structured as it is. For example, the passage in Swinburne's longest and most ambitious poem, *Tristram of Lyonesse*, where Tristram jumps naked into the sea, has been criticized for being "an especially long digression."[4] From a Jungian point of view, however, this passage is crucial to the poem, for it represents Tristram's last realization of the Self (psychic wholeness) before he dies. In the sea Tristram is at one with nature and himself.

The naked dip in the sea is the third time that Tristram is able to unite the opposing parts of his psyche.[5] The fourth, and most complete, realization of wholeness for Tristram is his death; and, since in Jung's theory four is the number of wholeness, the sea-dip episode is absolutely essential and necessary from a Jungian point of view. The structure of the poem would not be complete without it.

It may be objected that some inferior works are archetypal and, like great art, also compensate for imbalance. This is quite true, but a Jungian literary critic will not give such works much attention.[6] The critic who employs Jungian psychology cannot operate in isolation. He needs the tools of other schools of criticism to determine the value of a piece of art. What Ronald Crane has to say about his neo-Aristotelean school of criticism expresses exactly my sentiments in regard to Jungian criticism: "I should not want to leave the impression . . . that I think it the only mode of criticism seriously worth cultivation at the present time by either teachers of literature or critics, but simply that its development, along with the others, might have many fruitful consequences for our teaching and criticism generally."[7] The value of Jungian criticism is that it sets literature in its proper place in a human context as a representative of the psyche without, at the same time, getting away from literature's intrinsic worth as an art form.

Since I am dealing with Jungian theory as a tool of literary criticism, perhaps it is advisable to distinguish first Jung's concept of the archetype from that of the major "archetypal" literary theorist, Northrop Frye. Frye defines archetype as "a symbol which connects one poem with another and thereby helps to unify and integrate our literary experience" (*Anatomy of Criticism*, 99). By limiting archetypes to literature, Frye reduces their universality. A Jungian critic, on the other hand, recognizes that the archetypal image found in literature also forms part of a huge complex of images and symbols that have psychic meaning for all mankind. He does not, however, have to go outside the literature itself, except for his terms and his theory — and this is what any critic does anyway, including Frye. Frye's theory of literary modes is as much "outside" of literature, in that it is Frye's own creation, as is Jung's theory of literary modes. This fact does not in the least diminish the validity or the utility of either theory. The Jungian critic looks at an archetype in a particular piece of literature *in the context of the work in front of him,* just as a Jungian psychiatrist interprets his patient's dream in the context of the patient's individual experience, situation, and psychological condition.

16

Jung has used the terms "motifs" and "primordial images" to stand for "archetypes." For Jung, "primordial" means "archaic," or "in striking accord with familiar mythological motifs" (*CW*, 6:443). He says that the archetype is always collective; that is, "it is at least common to entire peoples or epochs. In all probability the most important mythological motifs are common to all times and races. . . ." (p. 443). Elsewhere, Jung has said that "the archetypes appear in myths and fairytales just as they do in dreams and in the products of psychotic fantasy" (*Essays*, 72). And they also appear in formal literature. Furthermore, Jung writes, "contents of an archetypal character are manifestations of processes in the collective unconscious. Hence they do not refer to anything that is or has been conscious, but to something essentially unconscious. In the last analysis, therefore, it is impossible to say what they refer to. . . . The ultimate core of meaning may be circumscribed, but not described" (p. 75). If the archetype itself is not conscious, its symbols (which may be called archetypal images) are brought to consciousness in myths, dreams, and so forth.

Jung continually revised his idea of the archetype as new evidence presented itself. For a good review of this development I suggest Jolande Jacobi's *Complex/Archetype/Symbol*. Jung's essay in *Man and His Symbols* represents his final statement on the archetype:

> The term "archetype" is often misunderstood as meaning certain definite mythological images or motifs. But these are nothing more than conscious representations; it would be absurd to assume that such variable representations could be inherited.
>
> *The archetype is a tendency to form such representations of a motif* — representations that can vary a great deal in detail without losing their basic pattern. There are, for instance, many representations of the motif of the hostile brethren, but the motif remains the same. (p. 67, italics mine)

Jung goes on to defend himself against critics who "assumed I am dealing with 'inherited representations.'" Archetypes are, indeed, "an instinctive *trend*, as marked as the impulse of birds to build nests, or ants to form organized colonies" (pp. 67–69). One contemporary Jungian, Edward F. Edinger, has said: "An archetype is to the psyche what an instinct is to the body" ("An Outline," p. 6). Although archetypal criticism has been called reductive by some critics who are largely unfamiliar with it, in fact it recognizes the infinite possibilities for the expression of archetypes (which are themselves unlimited). If the shadow is an archetype of the unconscious, there are at least as many varieties of its archetypal image as there are human individuals; and the likelihood of a similar diversity of "motifs" is just as great.

Even though the number of archetypes is limitless, they can be classified to some extent. Jung says that the shadow, the anima, and the animus are "the archetypes most clearly characterized from the empirical point of view," and that they "have the most frequent and the most disturbing influence on the ego" (*Aion*, 8). Elsewhere, he has listed as major archetypes: the wise old man, the child, the mother, the maiden, as well as the three just mentioned (*Essays*, 157). As we shall see, there are also archetypal themes or patterns.

At this point, however, I would like to discuss Jung's theory of creativity and the artist and how it relates to his theory of the archetype and to literary criticism. For Jung, the artist, or at least the superior artist, does not, as Freud believes, create from the repressed contents of his own personal unconscious; rather, he gives form (or image) to the archetypes of the collective unconscious. The poet "lifts the idea he is seeking to express out of the occasional and the transitory into the realm of the ever-enduring. He transmutes our personal destiny into the destiny of mankind, and evokes in us all those beneficent forces that ever and anon have enabled humanity to find refuge from every peril and to outlive the longest night" ("On the Relation of Analytical Psychology to Poetry," in *CW*, 15:82). Just as the archetypal, as opposed to the merely personal, dreams of an individual are compensatory, so great art "is constantly at work educating the spirit of the age, conjuring up the forms which the age is most lacking" (p. 82). Great literature, then, speaks to its era to correct the latter's psychic imbalance.

When he talks about the artist and literature, Jung makes it clear that he speaks from a psychologist's point of view, not from a literary critic's standpoint. He is most interested in the creative process, and his views on this are not wholly unique, having been suggested as far back as Plato (in his theory of inspiration in *Ion*). The creative act is, essentially, an "autonomous complex," and it springs from the unconscious: "The unborn work in the psyche of the artist is a force of nature that achieves its end either with tyrannical might or with the subtle cunning of nature herself, quite regardless of the personal fate of the man who is its vehicle" ("On the Relation of Analytical Psychology to Poetry," p. 75). Therefore, it is a mistake to analyze a work of art strictly on the basis of the artist's biography or personal psychology, for if these ever fully explain the work of art, then it is reduced merely to a symptom ("Psychology and Literature," in *CW*, 15:86) and is not worth further study. This, of course, is contrary to the view of Freud's school of psychoanalysis.

In "Psychology and Literature" (1930), Jung classifies literature into two modes: the "psychological," which springs from the conscious mind, and the "visionary," which springs from the collective unconscious. The first mode requires little psychological interpretation, for it is readily explainable in itself, its "raw material" having been "derived from the contents of man's consciousness, from his eternally repeated joys and sorrows, but clarified and transfigured by the poet." In this group belong "all the novels dealing with love, the family milieu, crime and society, together with didactic poetry, the greater number of lyrics, and drama both tragic and comic" (p. 89). Jung is, of course, speaking as a psychologist, and has earlier stated that sometimes psychologists are most interested in works "of highly dubious merit" (p. 88). His classification is, then, a little naive from the literary critic's point of view.

This is Jung's definition of the visionary mode: "It is something strange that derives its existence from the hinterland of man's mind, as if it had emerged from the abyss of prehuman ages, or from a superhuman world of contrasting light and darkness. It is a primordial experience which surpasses man's understanding and to which in his weakness he may easily succumb" (p. 90). Jung uses Goethe's *Faust* to illustrate the difference between his modes. The first part of *Faust* is psychological, the second visionary. Other examples of works in the second category are: the *Shepherd of Hermes*, Dante; Wagner's *Ring*, *Tristan*, and *Parsifal*; William Blake's paintings and poetry; E. T. A. Hoffman's *The Gold Bowl*; and James Joyce's *Ulysses* (though in his essay on *Ulysses*, Jung expresses some reservations — p. 91 and " 'Ulysses': A Monologue," in *CW*, 109–34).

In "Psychology and Literature," Jung refutes the Freudian method of analyzing literature as the expression of neurosis, or at least of the artist's own repressions, by saying something that most critics would agree with (except for, perhaps, the Romantic-critic who emphasizes the role of the artist's personality): "The essence of a work of art is not to be found in the personal idiosyncrasies that creep into it — indeed, the more there are of them, the less it is a work of art — but in its rising above the personal and speaking from the mind and heart of the artist to the mind and heart of mankind" (p. 101). Jung goes on to echo the Platonic view: "Art is a kind of innate drive that seizes a human being and makes him its instrument" (p. 101). The artist is really two people: the man himself and the artist. Sometimes the creative energy of the artist alters the personal ego of the man so that such things as "ruthlessness, selfishness ('autoeroticism'), vanity, and other infantile traits" may result. The artist "must pay dearly for the divine gift of creative fire"; he is "a man upon whom a heavier burden is laid than upon ordinary mortals" (pp. 102–3).

The creative process itself has something of the "feminine" in it, arising as it does from the unconscious, "from the realm of the Mothers." The artistic work is organic; "it grows out of . . . [the artist] as a child its mother" (p. 103). Thus it is that the literary artist creates symbols and archetypal images from the collective unconscious.

Finally, Mario Jacoby, in "The Analytical Psychology of C. G. Jung and the Problem of Literary Evaluation," implies that it is "the archetype of the highest good with its unconscious call to action" that motivates the literary critic (p. 124), who is himself a kind of artist — or at least, as Matthew Arnold suggests, a kind of creator. Even if literary critics are not aware of it, they are moved by archetypes. In modern literature the technique of "stream of consciousness" attempts, as M. H. Abrams says, to "reproduce the raw flow of consciousness, with its perceptions, thought, judgments, feelings, associations, and memories. . . ." (*A Glossary of Literary Terms*, 60). It should be noted, however, that much of what (in the work of James Joyce and Virginia Woolf, for example) is called "stream of consciousness" is really concerned with the threshold of consciousness, and the contents presented are often below that threshold. That is, the ego often has nothing to do with the "stream" of impressions. The "interior monologue," such as Joyce uses at the end of *Ulysses*, is closer to consciousness in the sense Jung defines the term because the ego is directly involved; it is "conscious" of what is going on.

For Jung the ego must be directly attached to consciousness. In *Psychological Types*, he defines the term "consciousness" as the

> function or activity which maintains the relation of psychic contents to the ego. Consciousness is not identical with the psyche . . . because the psyche represents the totality of all psychic contents, and these are not necessarily all directly

connected with the ego, i.e., related to it in such a way that
they take on the quality of consciousness. (pp. 421–22)

Just as there is a collective unconscious, so there is a collective consciousness common to large groups of people.

Jung defines ego "as the complex factor to which all conscious contents are related. It forms, as it were, the centre of the field of consciousness; and, in so far as this comprises the empirical personality, the ego is
the subject of all personal acts of consciousness" (*Aion*, 3). He is careful
to point out that the ego is not the same as the Self, "since the ego is
only the subject of my consciousness, while the self is the subject of my
total psyche, which also includes the unconscious " (*CW*, 6:425). The
ego acts as a sort of filter between the unconscious and the conscious,
for, as Jacobi says, "all our experiences of the outer and inner world
must pass through our ego in order to be perceived" (*Psychology of
Jung*, 8). Thus, Jung declares that "the ego rests on the *total field of consciousness* and . . . on the *sum total of unconscious contents*," and that "although its bases are in themselves relatively unknown and unconscious,
the ego is a conscious factor par excellence" (*Aion*, 4–5). Jung also notes
that the ego is not the same as the fields of consciousness and unconsciousness, but that it is the former's "point of reference."

Related also to consciousness is the individual's "persona." Jung's
persona should not be confused with the literary definition of persona as
the speaker of a poem or as an identity assumed by an author. Jung's
persona is "a functional complex that comes into existence for reasons
of adaptation or personal convenience, but is by no means identical with
the individuality" (*CW*, 6:465). In *Two Essays on Analytical
Psychology*, Jung further defines this concept:

> Fundamentally the persona is nothing real: it is a com-
> promise between individual and society as to what a man
> should appear to be. He takes a name, earns a title,
> represents an office, he is this or that. In a certain sense all
> this is real, yet in relation to the essential individuality of
> the person concerned it is only a secondary reality, a pro-
> duct of compromise, in making which others often have a
> greater share than he. (pp. 167–68)

Later Jung makes the point that individuals often use their personae to
impress others or to hide their real natures (p. 203). The psychological

task is to realize that the persona is merely a "mask" worn for society, and not the true identity. This mask should be variable according to the social milieu the individual finds himself in. This, as Dr. Jacobi observes, requires that the individual be "relatively conscious" of his persona, just as he is conscious of his clothes, which symbolize his persona. If a person identifies too long with his persona, he may be susceptible to "psychic crises and disorders" (*Psychology of Jung*, 29–30).

In a large measure, the persona is imposed upon an individual by society (and often the family as well). An example is Victorian England, where single, middle-class women, for instance, were extremely limited in the "respectable" roles they could play; usually they had a choice between being a teacher or a governess. Becky Sharp, in Thackeray's *Vanity Fair*, begins as a governess. She does not, however, identify with the persona that has been largely imposed upon her. The difficulty in the later nineteenth century of a man's choosing his persona may be seen in Thomas Hardy's *Jude the Obscure* or even in his *The Mayor of Casterbridge*. Jude is never able to fully adjust to society's prescribed role for him; instead of a stonemason he would much prefer to go to college and become a minister. And part, though only part, of Michael Henchard's psychic disintegration comes as a result of the loss of his exalted persona as the mayor of Casterbridge.

The unconscious includes all psychic activity not related directly to the ego. Unlike Freud, who acknowledges only a *personal unconscious*, Jung postulates a *collective unconscious*. The personal unconscious contains "all the acquisitions of personal life, everything forgotten, repressed, subliminally perceived, thought, felt." The collective unconscious has "contents which do not originate in personal acquisitions but in the inherited possibility of psychic functioning in general, i.e., in the inherited structure of the brain. These are the mythological associations, the motifs and images that can spring up anew anytime, independently of historical tradition or migration" (*CW*, 6:485). If the conscious is functioning too one-sidedly (for instance, emphasizing thinking at the expense of feeling), the unconscious will function in a *compensatory* manner, trying to balance the misplaced emphasis. It does this by producing archetypal images in dreams and in fantasies. On a collective scale, the images appear in myths, fairy tales, and formal literature.

Symbols that stand for the unconscious are closely related, as I indicated earlier, to the feminine, chthonic world. The earth itself, caves, bodies of water, mazes, and nearly anything that encloses may be considered as symbols not only of the Great Mother, but also of the unconscious. The traditional hero always has to go through what Joseph Campbell calls "the belly of the whale" (*Hero with a Thousand Faces*, 90–94). For the ordinary man, the heroic experience means confronting the unconscious and its symbols in the process of individuation. The symbolism of the confrontation varies: for Jonah, it is a whale; for Theseus, a labyrinth; for Beowulf, the underwater world of Grendel's mother; and, for Gawain, both the wasteland he passes through to find the castle of the Green Knight, and the castle itself.

The process of individuation, in which the conscious confronts the unconscious, is the central concept of Jung's psychology of the unconscious. Individuation is one of the most important goals of human life and, therefore, of analytical psychology. In *Two Essays on Analytical Psychology*, Jung defines the term: "Individuation means becoming a single, homogeneous being, and, in so far as 'individuality' embraces our innermost, last, and incomparable uniqueness, it also implies becoming one's own self. We could therefore translate individuation as 'coming to selfhood' or 'self-realization'" (p. 182). The true hero-journey for modern man, as W. H. Auden implies in his poems, "The Quest" and "Atlantis," is a phase in the internal search for self-realization or individuation. As Auden suggests in "The Quest," one must admit, if necessary, that one is not heroic in the traditional sense: "And how reliable can any truth be that is got / By observing oneself and then just inserting a Not?" In order to start the road to individuation it is necessary to separate the ego from the world of the mother (the womb), and later to distinguish the identity of the individual ego from the collective norm. Individuation does not, however, require separating oneself from and disdaining society; rather, it helps the person to realize his own particular uniqueness in his own particular environment. "Individuation," Jung says, ". . . leads to a natural esteem for the collective norm," instead of either a separation from or a melting into the norm (*CW*, 6:449).

The role of the ego is crucial to the process of individuation, for it is through the ego that the symbols of the unconscious become conscious. And, if the conscious successfully assimilates the contents of the unconscious, the change is brought about by the *transcendent function*. Violet S. de Laszlo calls individuation a "religious experience . . . because it means to live one's own existence creatively in the awareness of its participation in the stream of an eternal becoming" (*Psyche and Symbol*, xxix). Indeed, for the many who have lost their faith in traditional religion, individuation can provide a satisfactory alternative (*An Introduction*, 76). High levels of individuation can be, and are, achieved by some people without their even knowing it, though some Jungians claim that conscious growth is necessary. Others complete it, or a stage of it, through analysis, but it must be kept in mind that individuation is, strictly speaking, never a finished state of being;[8] rather, it is a continuing process, in fact, a struggle. Finally, it goes without saying that most people never come to self-realization or "wholeness."

The individuation process is divided into two parts. The first part is limited to the first half of life. The goal is adaptation to one's outer environment. As Jolande Jacobi puts it, the task is "consolidation of the ego, differentiation of the main function and the dominant attitude type, and development of an appropriate persona" (*Psychology of Jung*, 108). Jung concentrated mainly on the second half of life, and of the individuation process, where the job is to look inward to develop one's inner unique personality. Each new level of consciousness, or phase of individuation, that is achieved is characterized by a symbolic *death* and *rebirth*.

As with the quest of the hero, the process of individuation starts with a "call," possibly in the form of an injury to the personality or a mental boredom, like existential dread (von Franz, *Man and His Symbols*, 166–67). The next step is realization of the shadow, then of the anima or the animus, and finally of the Self (ibid., 168–229; and *Aion*, chaps. 2–4). I shall discuss each of these archetypal symbols separately. Suffice it to say at this point that, in general, the analysis of literature from the Jungian point of view explores the stages in the process of individuation. Some works, such as the epic, the drama, and the novel, are long enough to portray the success or failure in reaching wholeness; others, including the short lyric, the short play, and the short story, can encompass only part of the process.

The encounter with the shadow is the first major stage in the process of individuation. Although the shadow is an archetype of the collective unconscious, "its nature," Jung writes, "can in large measure be inferred from the contents of the personal unconscious" (*Aion*, 8). It is the dark opposite side of ourselves that we usually prefer to hide from others, and even from ourselves. The shadow is always personified by a member of one's own sex. It is easier to recognize and understand than the anima or the animus because with the shadow, we have the advantage of being prepared in some sort by our education, which has always endeavoured to convince people that they are not one-hundred-per-cent pure gold. So everyone immediately understands what is meant by "shadow," "inferior personality," etc. And if he has forgotten, his memory can easily be refreshed by a Sunday sermon, his wife, or the tax collector. (*Aion*, 17)

An individual can avoid recognition of his shadow, or its "assimilation" into his "conscious personality," by projection. He may perceive certain of his shadow traits, but he will not fully admit them to himself because the emotion of those traits "appears to lie, beyond all possibility of doubt, in the *other person*" (p. 9). Shakespeare's Caliban, who fits Jung's definition of the shadow exactly ("the adverse representation of the dark chthonic world," *Aion*, 34), projects his own shadow onto Prospero and thus remains oblivious of his true self. Prospero, on the other hand, is psychologically mature, what Jung would call individuated; he has come to terms with his shadow and does not feel threatened by it.[9]

The shadow is not always negative; dark may connote the unknown as well as the menacing. Dr. Edinger writes that "in many cases unconscious positive potentialities of the personality reside in the shadow. In such cases we speak of a *positive shadow*" ("An Outline," 5). In literature there are many examples of contrasting pairs of the same sex. Often one is "evil" while the other is "good." Such a pair are Fielding's Blifil and Tom Jones. Each may be considered the shadow of the other. Blifil, in particular, has projected his shadow onto Tom so that the former does not confront his own evil nature. Although Fielding probably would deny that either has the potentialities of the other, psychologically we know that they do. Another case of shadow projection is Oscar Wilde's *The Picture of Dorian Gray*. In order to avoid facing it, Gray, whose very name suggests his dark nature, projects his "inferior personality" onto his hidden portrait. The psychological danger of carrying such projection to the extreme is demonstrated by Gray's destruction at the end of the novel. Perhaps the clearest example in literature of the split nature of man is the one Jung himself cites in *Man and His Symbols:* Stevenson's *Dr. Jekyll and Mr. Hyde* (58).[10]

After recognizing and accommodating his shadow, the next step in the process of individuation is, for a man, the accommodation of the anima; for a woman, it is the accommodation of the animus, which I shall discuss more fully later. The anima is the feminine side of a man's psyche, just as the animus is the masculine side of a woman's psyche. As Jolande Jacobi writes in *The Psychology of C. G. Jung*:

> The archetypal figure of the soul-image [i.e., the anima or the animus] always stands for the complementary, contrasexual part of the psyche, reflecting both our personal relation to it and the individual human experience of the contrasexual. It represents the image of the other sex that we carry in us as individuals and also as members of the species. (p. 114)

Another Jungian psychologist, Marie-Louise von Franz, further defines the anima as "a personification of all feminine psychological tendencies in a man's psyche, such as vague feelings and moods, prophetic hunches, receptiveness to the irrational, capacity for personal love, feeling for nature, and — last but not least — his relation to the unconscious" (*Man and His Symbols,* 177). Yet another Jungian, Barbara Hannah, explains the role of the contrasexual image in the individuation process: "The struggle between ego and shadow . . . can seldom or never be solved without the intervention of the following phase, the struggle between the human being and animus or anima, just as the latter can never be solved without the intervention of the Self" (*Striving Towards Wholeness,* 55). The anima and the animus stand, as it were, in the middle of the second half of the individuation process.

The anima and the animus are harder to acknowledge than the shadow, for they are rooted deep in the collective unconscious. The anima, is, indeed, as Dr. von Franz points out, the "personification of a man's unconscious" (p. 178). Furthermore, whether the anima takes a negative or a positive shape in an individual is largely determined by the man's relationship with his mother. Once the parental "imago" has been split off from man's consciousness, the anima assumes the form of a woman. She may be an inner manifestation, as in dreams or fantasies; or she may be projected onto an actual woman. Jung writes that, "she is . . . a very influential factor, and, like the parents, she produces an imago of a relatively autonomous nature — not an imago to be split off like that of the parents, but one that has to be kept associated with consciousness" (*Two Essays,* 198). The psychological danger is disassociating the anima from the consciousness. If a man does not come to terms with the anima he may not be able to "distinguish himself from her" (p. 205). When this happens to a married man, his wife may exercise "an illegitimate authority over him" (p. 208). He runs the risk of becoming overly effeminate and succumbing to the "moods" of his "soul-image" that are buried in his unconscious. Jung says that "the repression of feminine traits and inclinations naturally causes these contrasexual demands to accumulate in the unconscious" (p. 199). This can be a very real danger, especially since in Western culture, unfortunately, "a man counts it a virtue to repress his feminine traits as much as possible" (p. 199).

As with all archetypal symbols, the anima may have either a negative or a positive influence. Or it may be a mixture of both in any of its manifestations. In *Man and His Symbols*, Dr. von Franz succinctly outlines the four stages of the anima as it can be realized in a man:

> The first stage is best symbolized by the figure of Eve, which represents purely instinctual and biological relations. The second can be seen in Faust's Helen: She personifies a romantic and aesthetic level that is, however, still characterized by sexual elements. The third is represented, for instance, by the Virgin Mary — a figure who raises love (*eros*) to the heights of spiritual devotion. The fourth type is symbolized by Sapientia, wisdom transcending even the most holy and the most pure. Of this another symbol is the Shulamite in the Song of Solomon. (p. 185)

Dr. von Franz goes on to point out that modern man seldom reaches the final stage.

What the anima is for a man, the animus is for a woman. Just as the initial image of the anima in a man stems from his mother, so the image of a woman's animus starts in her father. When a woman succumbs to the negative animus, she becomes opinionated instead of reflective; she is not logical. As Jung writes, ". . . the animus is partial to argument, and he can best be seen at work in disputes where both parties know they are right" (*Aion*, 15). An animus-possessed woman is concerned with power. When anima and animus meet, the "relationship is always full of 'animosity,' i.e., it is emotional, and hence collective" (p. 16). Some of the more negative characteristics of the animus are "brutality, recklessness, empty talk, and silent, obstinate, evil ideas" (von Franz,

Man and His Symbols, 193). On the positive side, "in the same way that the anima gives relationship and relatedness to a man's consciousness, the animus gives woman's consciousness a capacity for reflection, deliberation, and self-knowledge" (*Aion*, 16). In *Man and His Symbols*, Dr. von Franz points out that the animus can also "personify an enterprising spirit, courage, truthfulness, and in the highest form, spiritual profundity" (p. 195).

Like the anima, the animus also has four levels of development. Dr. von Franz lists them:

> He first appears as a personification of mere physical power
> — for instance, as an athletic champion or "muscle man."
> In the next stage he possesses initiative and the capacity for
> planned action. In the third phase, the animus becomes the
> "word," often appearing as a professor or clergyman. Final-
> ly, in his fourth manifestation, the animus is the incarnation
> of *meaning*. On this highest level he becomes (like the
> anima) a mediator of the religious experience whereby life
> acquires new meaning. He gives the woman spiritual firm-
> ness, an invisible inner support that compensates for her
> outer softness. (*Man and His Symbols*, 194)

Just as the anima, according to Jung, represents the "maternal Eros," so the animus "corresponds to the paternal Logos" (*Aion*, 14).

We can see the compensatory power of the animus in D. H. Lawrence's short story, "The Horse Dealer's Daughter." In that story, Mabel Pervin is alienated from the animus; she has no consciousness of her masculine side. She has so given herself over to the feminine that she tries to drown herself in a pond (itself a symbol of the feminine, as well as of the unconscious) in order to join her dead mother. Jack Fergusson, a local doctor, rescues her, and she realizes that she loves him. He represents her rational animus, which hitherto she had not encountered. Together they start on the road to psychic wholeness.

Henry James's Isabel Archer, in *The Portrait of a Lady*, on the other hand, is too much possessed by the animus. She rejects two men, Caspar Goodwood and Lord Warburton, who are combinations of the first two animus stages. In order to keep her independence and freedom, she marries a dilettante, Gilbert Osmond, who is himself anima-possessed. The marriage is, predictably, a disaster.

The negative aspect of the animus is also embodied in the dark men who are the subjects of many of Sylvia Plath's poems, poems such as "Full Fathom Five," "Man in Black," and "Daddy." The failure to come to terms with the animus in such poems also forebodes disaster. There is not much hope of psychic health for the speaker who declares: "Daddy, daddy, you bastard, I'm through." While it is psychically necessary for a woman to declare her independence from her father, she must also accommodate the animus, the image of which stems from her father.

The culmination — indeed, the goal — of the individuation process is the realization of the Self.[11] Full knowledge of the Self is never reached in life, but various degrees of self-knowledge can be achieved, especially in the second half of life. For Jung, the Self "designates the whole range of psychic phenomena in man. It expresses the unity of the personality as a whole." Since we can never fully know, or be conscious of, the unconscious part of ourselves, "the self is, in part, only *potentially* empirical and is to that extent a *postulate*" (*CW*, 6:460). The archetype of the Self, as Dr. Edinger notes, "often appears as a process of centering [i.e., balancing] or as a process involving the union of opposites" ("An Outline," 7). Thus, as we shall see, the *hieros gamos* and the hermaphrodite are symbols of the Self. Furthermore, what Jung calls a "supraordinate personality" (for example, a hero, king, prophet, or savior) may also symbolize the Self. Geometrical figures such as the mandala stand for the Self, as may many other symbols, including animals, stones, and jewels.

The paradoxes of Keats's "Ode on a Grecian Urn," which Cleanth Brooks has explicated, may be considered as betraying a desire for the wholeness that the Self represents and also the wish for stasis once that wholeness is won. It is questionable, however, whether psychic wholeness is achieved in the poem. The libido, or psychic energy, is frozen, as it were, for the lovers of stanza two will never be able to embrace each other; nor will they ever move any farther apart. But the urge toward unity, or totality, is there in the last stanza with the coupling of the opposites suggested by the "Cold Pastoral!" (which is the urn itself) and the famous line: "Beauty is truth, truth beauty.'" The urn itself speaks this line, and the urn itself may be considered a symbol of the Self. As I indicated earlier, there are infinite possibilities for the expression of an archetypal symbol. I would like now to examine some of the symbols of the Self that Jung has discovered. These include: the mandala, the *hieros gamos*, the hermaphrodite, the Wise Old Man and Woman, and the God-image.

Mandala is a Sanskrit word meaning a "circle" (*Mandala Symbolism*, 3). Often it will be squared; that is, it will contain a square, the four points of which usually touch the circumference of the circle. Jung calls the mandala the *"archetype of wholeness,"* and declares: "The 'squaring of the circle' is one of the many archetypal motifs which form the basic patterns of our dreams and fantasies" (ibid, 4). Mandalas have appeared throughout history, and they are *"symbols of unity and totality"* (*Aion*, 31). Mandalas are also symbols of order as is shown by the ancient swastika, a symbol which, as Jung points out, was adopted by a people badly in need of order — Germany of the 1930s (*CW*, 10:220–21). In 1918–19, while drawing his own mandalas, Jung came to realize that his "mandalas were cryptograms concerning the state of the self . . . I acquired through them a living conception of the self." He also came to see that "the mandala is the center. It is the exponent of all paths. It is the path to the center, to individuation" (*Memories, Dreams, Reflections*, 196).

When they appear in literature, mandalas can mean a need or desire for wholeness or Selfhood, especially if the mandala is imperfect; or they can symbolize the current psychic state, which may have reached a new stage of self-realization or even the completion of individuation. King Arthur's round table is an obvious mandala, standing for, as Merlin initially intended in Malory's *Morte Darthur*, "the rowndenes signyfyed by ryght." When it disintegrates, it symbolizes the end of wholeness — the fall of the court of Arthur. Another symbolic mandala is found in Henry Vaughan's poem, "The World," which begins: "I saw Eternity the other night / Like a great *Ring* of pure and endless light." The ring is connected with Christ, who is also a symbol of the Self (*Aion*, chap. 5) at the end of the poem: "*This Ring the Bride-groome did for none provide / But for his bride.*" We have here a *hieros gamos*, another symbol of wholeness: Christ, the "Light of the World," married to his bride, the earthly Church; so that the poem ends with a cluster of three archetypal symbols — the mandala, Christ, and the *heiros gamos* — all standing for psychic wholeness.

The term *hieros gamos* means "sacred wedding" (*CW*, 8:156) and stands for the wholeness achieved by the union of opposites, especially by coming to terms with the contrasexual, the anima in man, the animus in woman. The *coniunctio* signifies essentially the same thing. Of it, Jung says in *Mysterium Coniunctionis*, "The factors which come together . . . are conceived as opposites, either confronting one another in enmity or attracting one another in love" (p. 3). In alchemy the opposites range from moist / dry to Sol / Luna. In modern literature, as in analytical psychology, the union of the opposites need not be divine in the Christian sense, but it is religious as Jung uses the term. Much of the fiction of D. H. Lawrence ("The Horse Dealer's Daughter" or "The Virgin and the Gipsy," for instance) illustrates the need of the *hieros gamos* in the twentieth century.

The hermaphrodite is closely related in its symbolism to the *hieros gamos*. In a discussion of the hermaphroditism of the divine child, Jung says: "The hermaphrodite means nothing less than a union of the strongest and most striking opposites" (*Essays*, 92). Like the *hieros gamos*, the hermaphrodite shows a completeness illustrated by a man's coming to terms with the anima or a woman with the animus, what Jung calls the *syzygy (Aion*, 11). The syzygy is the *sine qua non* for the achievement of Selfhood; and the hermaphrodite as a symbol of Selfhood is an image of wholeness that itself "consists in the union of the conscious and the unconscious personality" (*Essays*, 94). In Shakespeare's comedies, such as *The Merchant of Venice* or *Twelfth Night*, when the hermaphroditic theme is suggested by women dressed as men, the outcome is always one of wholeness or a return to balance. The marriages with which *Twelfth Night* ends, for instance, symbolize the union of both sexes.[12]

As symbols of the Self, the Wise Old Man and the Wise Old Woman are "supraordinate personalities." They are helpers and guides for the hero or for the common man in his quest for individuation. As Jung says of the masculine image of this archetype, "The old man knows what roads lead to the goal and points them out to the hero" ("The Phenomenology of the Spirit in Fairy Tales," in *Psyche and Symbol*, 76). The Wise Old Man and the Wise Old Woman stand for the highest spiritual wisdom and the wholeness represented by the Self. Sometimes, for older people, the Self may appear as a youth (von Franz, *Man and His Symbols*, 196–98). Literature is filled with examples of the Wise Old Man in particular, but it has cases of the Wise Old Woman also–Naomi, in the Book of Ruth, for instance. Naomi helps guide Ruth to spiritual renewal in a new land. The sage and mage of King Arthur's court, Merlin, is a symbol of the whole man and an archetypal image of the Wise Old Man (*The Grail Legend*, 365). And the old man in Chaucer's "The Pardoner's Tale" symbolizes the self-realization that the youthful rioters reject.

I have saved the "God-image" for last because it is the highest order of "supraordinate personalities," and because it is a major concern of literature from the Victorian era to the present. Aniela Jaffe succinctly defines this archetypal image in her glossary for Jung's *Memories, Dreams, Reflections:*

> (The God-image is) . . . derived from the Church Fathers, according to whom the *imago Dei* is imprinted on the human soul. When such an image is spontaneously produced in dreams, fantasies, visions, etc. it is, from the psychological point of view, a symbol of the self . . . of psychic wholeness. (p. 394)

The God-image is not itself a supernatural being but the image of what might be called the "God archetype," as well as the archetype of the Self. Jung believes that there is an innate spiritual dimension in man that requires fulfillment before he can be psychically healthy. If he cannot experience the God-image — a representation of spiritual wholeness — by means of traditional religion, he can do it through the process of individuation. Even a cursory glance at the literature of the last one hundred and fifty years will reveal a need for spiritual gratification. Tennyson in particular reflects this need in the face of nineteenth century scientific discoveries that seemed so inimical to religious faith. *In Memoriam* begins with a hopeful assertion of faith in the God-image:

> Strong Son of God, immortal Love,
>   Whom we, that have not seen thy face,
>   By faith, and faith alone, embrace,
> Believing where we cannot prove. . . .

Here Christ is the image of God, just as a son often may be considered the image of his father. At the end of his life, the God-image again reveals its power in Tennyson's poem, "Crossing the Bar": "I hope to see my Pilot face to face / When I have crost the bar." All that the speaker of the poem can offer is hope that the self-realization offered by the symbol of the God-image, his "Pilot," is real and will sustain him after death.

In the twentieth century the possibility of a firm hope is even more difficult. One way of viewing the problem posed by Samuel Beckett's *Waiting for Godot* is that modern man lacks a viable God-image. Nowhere is the difficulty of establishing a firm hope in the image of

God more clear than in T. S. Eliot's "The Hollow Men": the loss of religious faith and the implicit need for an image of God are suggested by the unfinished Lord's Prayer at the end of the poem. Eliot's later poetry expresses a much closer relationship to and knowledge of the spiritual, indicating that he, as artist, and probably as man, came to realize the God-image.

I have attempted to elucidate Jung's psychology of the conscious and the unconscious and his theory of creativity and to show how these can be used as effective tools in criticizing literature. As I have indicated, I do not feel Jungian criticism is the only kind worth practicing, but I do feel that it can discover many hitherto unexplored treasures in literature.

A relatively recent example of literature in Jung's "visionary" mode is Carson McCuller's *The Member of the Wedding* (1946).[13] Written during World War II, when the world was collectively split, *The Member of the Wedding* is an unconscious attempt — an attempt, indeed, from the collective unconscious — to compensate for that split. Just as the world badly needed wholeness, so does Frankie Addams, the lonely imaginative twelve-year-old protagonist of the novel and the play (which opened on Broadway on 5 January 1950). A Jungian examination of *The Member of the Wedding* will demonstrate new levels of meaning and elicit, I hope, a greater appreciation of McCullers's art.

The genesis of the novel illustrates nicely Jung's theory of creativity. In fact, McCuller's beliefs about creativity are similar to those of Jung. In reference to the creative process, she writes: "After months of confusion and labor, when the idea has flowered, the collusion is Divine. It always comes from the subconscious and cannot be controlled."[14] McCullers had been working on *The Member of the Wedding* for some time without finding a clear direction for the novel. Then, on Thanksgiving Day 1940, she and the other members of the artistic ménage at 7 Middagh Street, Brooklyn Heights, were having coffee and brandy when they heard the sound of a fire engine siren. McCullers and Gypsy Rose Lee went out to follow it. After running a few blocks, McCullers received her spark of illumination. Grabbing Lee by the arm, McCullers burst out: "Frankie is in love with her brother and his bride, and wants to become a member of the wedding." Later McCullers said that "Gypsy . . . stared at me as though I had lost my mind."[15]

In writing *The Member of the Wedding*, McCullers created archetypal images to compensate for contemporary imbalance. In other words, she made a myth for our time, for today, as in the forties, humanity is in need of wholeness and growth, just as Frankie is in need of psychic wholeness and growth. The plot is very simple. Her mother being dead, Frankie lives alone in a large house with her father, but she spends most of her waking hours in the kitchen with her six-year-old cousin, John Henry West, and the middle-aged black cook, Berenice Sadie Brown. Frankie has an older brother, a soldier named Jarvis, who comes home from Alaska with Janice, a young woman from a town farther north, Winter Hill. Jarvis announces his plans to marry Janice. Frankie, who is sick of her environment, is struck by the idea that she will join Jarvis and Janice in the wedding and thereafter depart with them for unknown and exciting regions. The idea transforms her life, and she becomes obsessed by it, ignoring the advice of Berenice.

Both her names and her appearance ("her hair had been cut like a boy's," p. 601) indicate her androgynous personality, but this fusion of opposites is on the surface only: she is not whole psychologically. Her last name also suggests her case is primal; she is an "everyperson." Jung believes that every person has a personal myth, and Frankie's myth is that she and her brother Jarvis and his bride Janice are to be united:[16]

> *They are the we of me.* Yesterday, and all the twelve years of her life, she had only been Frankie. She was an *I* person who had to walk around and do things by herself. All other people had a *we* to claim, all other except her. When Berenice said *we*, she meant Honey and Big Mama, her lodge, or her church. The *we* of her father was the store. All members of clubs have a *we* to belong to and talk about. The soldiers in the army can say *we*, and even the criminals on chain-gangs. But the old Frankie had had no *we* to claim, unless it would be the terrible summer *we* of her and John Henry and Berenice — and that was the last *we* in the world she wanted. Now all this was suddenly over with and changed. There was her brother and the bride, and it was as though when first she saw them something she had known inside of her: *They are the we of me.* (p. 646)

Just as the soldiers of the United States had traveled to war around the world, so Frankie planned to travel with her brother and sister-in-law after the wedding.

What has happened is that Frankie has become possessed by the archetype of the *hieros gamos*, or "sacred wedding," an archetype of wholeness, symbolizing the union of opposites. Thinking about the wedding, Frankie sees "a silent church, a strange snow slanting down against the colored windows" (p. 600). Jung writes: "When a situation occurs which corresponds to a given archetype, that archetype becomes activated and a compulsiveness appears, which, like an instinctual drive, gains its way against all reason and will. . . ."[17] These words describe Frankie's situation exactly. After seeing her brother and his bride, after coming to the compulsive realization that she was "going off with the two of them to whatever place that they will go" (p. 650), Frankie is convinced she knows who she is, and her goal is undivided: she will be a member of the wedding; she will go with the married couple. No longer do the old questions, "who she was and what she would be in the world" (p. 651), bother her. She is no longer unconnected. She is going someplace, and never mind what reason — available to her in the words of Berenice — says to the contrary.

The stage of the individuation process (the process wherein one becomes a whole individual) in which the individual's task is to accommodate the contrasexual (the anima in a man, the animus in a woman) comes in the second half of life. In the first half, the task is "consolidation of the ego, differentiation of the main function and of the dominant attitude type, and development of an appropriate persona, it aims at the adaptation of the individual to the demands of his environment."[18]

In traveling with Jarvis and Janice, Frankie would be escaping her environment: the hot summer, which "was like a green sick dream, or like a silent crazy jungle under glass," the "black and shrunken" town, her "old ugly house," and the "sad and ugly" kitchen where she spends most of her time with John Henry and Berenice. First, the wedding would take place in Winter Hill, a hundred miles to the north. Frankie associates Winter Hill with Alaska, where her soldier brother had been stationed. Winter Hill is connected "with dreams of Alaska and cold snow" (p. 604). Second, Frankie imagines "bright flowered islands . . . China, Peachville, New Zealand, Paris, Cincinnati, Rome. . . . But still she did not know where she should go" (p. 640).

Although she doesn't know where she will go, her fervent wish is to go, as it were, to an Eden of her imagination. That her world is governed by the unconscious is indicated by the many references throughout the novel to dreams and craziness — both expressions of the archetypes, as is fantasy, in which she freely indulges.[19] The desire to journey from the dull but real world of her own town to unknown Edens is in fact an evasion of the task before her: to achieve inner growth and maturity. As Laurens van der Post shows, Jung came to believe that often travel "for sheer travel's sake" was a substitute, *Ersatz* journey for a far more difficult and urgent journey modern man was called upon to undertake into the unknown universe of himself" (*Jung and the Story of Our Time*, 51).

Frankie is quite unhappy with her environment. She has only begun the process of becoming a whole person psychologically. Indeed, McCullers subtly shows this in several ways. One of the ways is the unfinished scale of the piano tuner (p.700), which hints that Frankie is not to achieve wholeness in the novel. Another of the subtle indications that wholeness is not to be achieved is also vaguely connected with music. Sitting in the dark kitchen after their last meal together (there is a resemblance to the Last Supper, for Frankie, like Christ, will soon be transformed and both meals are enactments of ritual), Berenice, John Henry, and F. Jasmine each spontaneously begins to cry, just as in the past they would automatically begin to sing, each in a separate voice "until at last the tunes began to merge and they sang a special music that the three of them made up together" (p. 743). Such music they are not to make again. The wholeness and harmony of the womblike kitchen is to be broken, and the crying is both a lament for the loss of their secure world, whatever its limitations, and an indication that the nature of their experience is spiritual.

Frankie has yet to consolidate her ego: it is clearly unstable. Her "attitude type" is extraversion, for her libido (that is, her psychic energy) flows outward, but she has not differentiated her main function. I refer to Jung's functions of consciousness: thinking, feeling, sensation, and intuition (Jacobi, 10–23). Frankie has developed a little of each of these: she asks fundamental questions about her life, thus using the thinking function; she makes judgments as to right and wrong (as in her conception of the ideal world, pp. 713–14), thus using the feeling function; she relates to the world through her senses (her knife throwing is an example), thus using the sensation function; and she shares with Berenice an ability to recognize "signs" and, as in her fears for Honey, potential danger, thus using the intuition function.

But none of these functions has she developed yet as her main function. She is "trying" them out; her personality is still forming. When she has developed a main function, she will need to integrate the other functions into her consciousness as fully as possible. Last, Frankie is far from developing "an appropriate persona." The persona is the "mask" or conscious public identity an individual takes on. Frances, the name Frankie prefers after the shattering experience of the wedding, cannot decide whether she will be "a great poet — or else the foremost authority on radar" (p. 787).

Though Frankie has masculine aspects in her personality (she is the "best knife-thrower in this town," p. 639, and the knife is an obvious masculine symbol), she has yet to accommodate the masculine in her psyche. That task will come in later life. To grow up, she has to break with her father and her foster mother. The previous April her father, with whom she had been sleeping, decides she is now "too big" to sleep with him, and "she began to have a grudge against her father" (p. 625). The break with her father was necessary, and now she is ready for a symbolic rebirth from the womblike kitchen. That the kitchen is symbolic of the womb — and hence the unconscious — is suggested by "the queer drawings of Christmas trees, airplanes, freak soldiers, flowers" (p. 606) on its walls. These childish drawings, drawn by John Henry and Frankie herself, give the room "a crazy look, like that of a room in the crazy-house" (p. 602). It was his experiences at a "crazy-house," the Burghölzli Mental Hospital in Zürich, that gave Jung some of his first evidence of the collective unconscious and the archetypes. As the summer wears on, the drawings begin to "bother" Frankie: "The kitchen looked strange to her, and she was afraid" (p. 606). To paraphrase Saint Paul, she is ready to put away childish things.

Lonely and afraid, she is not fully aware of this. Without any adolescent friends, she clings to her six-year-old cousin, John Henry, inviting him to spend the night, as she has done frequently since she has been unable to sleep with her father "I thought you were sick and tired of him, " says Berenice upon being told Frankie has invited John Henry again to spend the night.

> "I am sick and tired of him," said Frankie. "But it seemed
> to me he looked scared."
> "Scared of what?"
> Frankie shook her head. "Maybe I mean lonesome," she
> said finally. (P. 606)

Frankie is, of course, projecting — attributing to John Henry her own problems. The following day she again asks John Henry to spend the night. This time he is reluctant, and Frankie responds by screaming: "Fool jackass! . . . I only asked you because I thought you looked so ugly and so lonesome" (p. 647).

Frankie's problem is at root a spiritual one; indeed, McCullers herself has written: "I suppose my central theme is the theme of spiritual isolation."[20] Here the role of John Henry as the archetype of the Child becomes significant. Jung refers to the "numinous character" of the child, and maintains " 'Child' means something evolving towards independence."[21] In John Henry, Frankie unconsciously sees the child in herself evolving toward independence, and quite naturally, she is afraid. All archetypes, however, have a dual nature, and, paradoxically, the child symbolizes "both beginning and end, [he is] an initial and a terminal creature." Furthermore, Jung states:

> Psychologically speaking, this means that the "child" symbolizes the pre-conscious and post-conscious essence of man. His pre-conscious essence is the unconscious state of earliest childhood; his post-conscious essence is an anticipation by analogy of life after death. In this idea the all-embracing nature of psychic wholeness is expressed. (*Essays*, 97)

John Henry's making of a "perfect little biscuit man" that reminds Frankie of John Henry himself (p. 607) suggests his symbolic wholeness. His consciousness is still in a nascent state, not fully differentiated yet. His death near the end of the novel is not only symbolic of the death of Frankie's childhood (see Oliver Evans, 124), but also an adumbration of the wholeness possible for Frankie.

While John Henry symbolizes the archetypal Child, Berenice, the middle-aged black cook with the blue glass eye, symbolizes two archetypes: the Mother and the Wise Old Woman. Frankie's biological mother had died just after Frankie was born. Berenice, as one scholar has put it, "is as responsive to Frankie as a mother would be."[22] Berenice fits into the archetypal motif of the dual mother, wherein the hero is raised by a foster mother (Oedipus and Moses are examples). "The dual-mother motif," writes Jung, "suggests the idea of a dual birth. One of the mothers is the real, human mother, the other is the symbolical mother . . . she is distinguished as being divine, supernatural, or in some way extraordinary" (*Symbols of Transformation,* 322). While Frankie is hardly a hero of the stature of Oedipus or Moses, she is symbolic of the individual, the "everyperson," in the twentieth century and his/her needs. Indeed, she is an anti-hero like Holden Caulfield, an older version of herself.

My calling Berenice an example of the dual-mother motif may appear farfetched because she does not seem "divine, supernatural, or in some way extraordinary," but actually she is numinous in a way uncommon to most women in her position. Like Tiresias, the blind prophet of Thebes, the one-eyed Berenice has, in the words of Frank Baldanza, "spiritual vision . . . the more intense for her physical handicap" ("Plato in Dixie," 158). When she recites the history of her marriages, she makes "each sentence like a song . . . in a chanting kind of voice" (p. 708). The recitation is a kind of primitive ritual, and, when Frankie becomes possessed by the archetype of the wedding, she is for the first time able to believe in love and be "included in the conversation as a person who understood and had worth-while opinions" (p. 716).

Throughout the novel Berenice is both the symbolic mother and the Wise Old Woman to Frankie. She gives both Frankie and John Henry the love and nourishment of a mother, but to Frankie she gives more — her advice and experience as a woman. To Berenice, Frankie's obsession with the wedding is a "mania" that is "pure foolishness" (p. 692). Her advice frequently comes in the form of "known sayings," folk wisdom such as "Two is company and three is a crowd. And that is the main thing about a wedding" (p. 690). However, it is Berenice's experience that is potentially of most benefit to Frankie, though Frankie chooses to pursue her obsession with the wedding despite Berenice's warning. Most people who are possessed by archetypes do choose to pursue their obsessions.

In telling Frankie about her past, Berenice has a purpose — to warn Frankie about the danger of her obsession with the wedding, "the saddest piece of foolishness I ever knew" (p. 725). Although Frankie is rapidly growing away from her child ego state, she is unable to heed Berenice's warning. Frankie has to act out her obsession with the archetype in order to learn the lesson Berenice has been trying to teach her. The Wise Old Woman has traveled a similar road, but the hero — or anti-hero — must travel her own road; she must fulfill her own destiny.

Frankie's problem is that she is isolated, afraid, "a member of nothing in the world" (p. 599). She fears the older girls who have excluded her have been "spreading it all over town that I smell bad" (p. 610), and she is certain if her present rate of growth continues she will be nine feet tall by the time she is eighteen (p. 618). She will be a freak, like the ones she has seen each year at the Chattahoochee Exposition — the freaks who try "to connect their eyes with hers, as though to say: we know you. She was afraid of their long Freak eyes" (p. 619). These freaks (which include the Wild Nigger, the Pin Head, and the Half-Man Half-Woman) are personifications of archetypes. She sees something of herself in them through her own eyes, symbolic of a growing consciousness (see *The Archetypes and the Collective Unconscious*, 337). Because she does not understand the symbolism of the freaks, she is afraid. Finally, Frankie has become "a criminal. If the Law knew about her, she could be tried in the courthouse and locked up in the jail" (p. 622).[23]

An important part of the novel that McCullers merely alludes to in the play is Frankie's encounter with the soldier at the Blue Moon Hotel. Though she has learned a little about sex, Frankie does not accept what she has learned. The older girls who do not admit her to their club, she tells John Henry, "were talking nasty lies about married people" (p. 610). So F. Jasmine, despite her new status as indicated by her name, is not at all prepared psychologically or physically, I suspect, for a "date" with a grown man. Archetypally this means she is not ready for an encounter with the animus, the archetype of the male in the female. This encounter will come in later life, if she reaches that stage of individuation.

All of her fears are symptoms of a deep psychic unrest, and none of them is unusual for a twelve-year-old. Frankie is ready for a change, and she is ripe for an archetype of wholeness — the *hieros gamos* — when it presents itself to her personified by her brother and his bride. She quickly becomes a victim of psychic inflation, which, in the words of Jungian psychologist Frieda Fordham, is "possession" by an archetype, "indicating that the person so possessed has been, as it were, blown up by something too big for himself, something that is not really personal at all, but collective."[24] Thus, Frankie imagines she and the wedding couple will be asked "to speak over the radio some day" (p. 710). "Things will happen so fast," she says, "we won't hardly have time to realize them. Captain Jarvis Addams sinks twelve Jap battleships and decorated by the President. Miss F. Jasmine Addams breaks all records.

Mrs. Janice Addams elected Miss United Nations in beauty contest"
(pp. 737–38). Frankie feels "the power of the wedding; it was as though
. . . she ought to order and advise" (p. 754). Specifically, she feels she
should warn Honey, Berenice's foster brother, so she advises him to go
to Cuba or Mexico — in other words, to travel, as she plans to do, and
thereby avoid looking inward, where the real problem and solution lie.
Fordham says the "feeling of godlikeness . . . which comes through inflation is an illusion, " and Frankie is to suffer severely for the illusion.

Having failed to persuade Jarvis and Janice to take her with them,
Frankie decides to run away that night by herself. John Henry is again
sleeping in her bed, and it is he who, albeit inadvertently, alerts Royal
Addams that his daughter has run away. Out on the street by herself, in
a last vain attempt to evade personal growth, Frankie finds she does not
know how to escape: "If there was only somebody to tell her what to do
and where to go and how to get there!" (p. 780). She still needs a guide,
yet, as her decision not to shoot herself with her father's pistol indicates,
she has chosen to continue the struggle that eventually leads to individuation or Selfhood — psychic wholeness. But at this moment she
seems caught in the world of the unconscious:

> She was back to the fear of the summertime, the old feelings
> that the world was separate from herself — and the failed
> wedding had quickened the fear to terror. There had been a
> time, only yesterday, when she felt that every person that
> she saw was somehow connected with herself and there was
> between the two of them an instant recognition. (P. 784).

Back in the Blue Moon Hotel, she feels "queer as a person drowning"
(p. 785), and then her father arrives to take her home.

The image of someone drowning is appropriate, for she might well
have been permanently and pathologically possessed by the archetype.
Luckily, though Frankie has not achieved wholeness, she has been
reborn into a more mature psychic state. As the death of the child John
Henry symbolizes, Frankie has grown. She is leaving the womb of the
summer kitchen and breaking away from Berenice, her symbolic
mother, who has served her purpose. This breaking away is a necessary
transition for the adolescent. Frankie has yet to come to terms with the
masculine in her psyche, symbolized by her father, but she has begun to
accommodate the shadow, that other unrecognized part of the psyche
personified by a member of the same sex. Her earlier, "criminal" career

41

had been an expression of her shadow, which is now symbolized by her new friend, the Catholic Mary Littlejohn, who, unlike Frankie, has "lived abroad." Frankie still indulges in fantasy, planning to travel around the world with Mary (p. 790), but she is "mad about Michelangelo" (p. 786), who as a supraordinate personality is symbolic of the Self and therefore foreshadows a new awareness for Frankie.

One might say the reader and/or the spectator has also gained new awareness. If we recognize and respond to Frankie's emotions, problems, and needs, we do so because these are universal — that is, archetypal. We may not ourselves have been victims of psychic inflation or had dual mothers, yet these and the other archetypal conditions and images in the novel are not alien to us, for they are buried deep in our collective psyches. McCullers shows the completion of a cycle of growth for one adolescent, and in so doing she illuminates a problem for our time — the need for collective balance and personal growth.

Adlerian Theory
and Its Application to
The Catcher in the Rye —
Holden Caulfield

by R.J. Huber

Alfred Adler felt that observations of the great writers were invaluable assets to the contemporary psychologist, and, in particular, he found the Bible, Goethe, and Shakespeare extremely helpful in his understanding of human nature.[1] He also engaged in literary interpretation through his comments on the works of Alfred Berger, Dostoevsky, and the diary of the Russian ballet great, Nijinsky.[2] Contemporary Adlerians have shown a sustained interest in literary analysis in articles over the past several years that have appeared in their principle English language journal, *The Journal of Individual Psychology.*[3] In a recent book Leon Edel has stressed the cogency of Adlerian psychology to understanding literature.[4] The compatibility between literature and Adlerian psychology exists because the writer and the Adlerian psychologist are about the same task, as Phyllis Bottome, a novelist and one of Adler's biographers, states: "Not what happens to people, but how people take what happens to them has always been the chief part of the novelist's task to reveal."[5] The Adlerian psychologist, similarly, is most interested in how one interprets his or her environment. The world view of the individual is a proper beginning for a discussion of Adlerian literary analysis; however, before this topic can be pursued it is necessary to paint a minature sketch of Adlerian theory.

While it is true that Adler was a member of the original Vienna Psychoanalytic Society, one should not regard him as a disciple of

Freud. There is a great deal of evidence indicating that Adler's ideas differed significantly from those of Freud before the two men were acquainted. In his first publication Adler emphasized social factors in the occupational diseases of tailors; this emphasis dominated his thought before, during, and after his association with Freud.[6] It is this difference and others that nurtured the split of Adler from Freud in 1911 because Freud insisted on orthodoxy of thought. In 1911 Adler and his co-workers founded the school of Individual Psychology, which adhered to principles that are the cornerstones of many contemporary theories of personality. Carl Rogers and Abraham Maslow accepted the concept of the creative self and the individual frame of reference as fundamental postulates for their theories.[7] These writers as well as others accepted the idea that the human is a continually evolving, striving being. Indeed, Adler's approach to motivation suggests that the prime human motive is not biological in the traditional sense; certainly he felt that the desire to grow, to be more, and to be significant transcended physiological desires such as hunger, thirst, and sex. From this perspective, the death-inviting exploits of someone like Evil Kneivel become readily understandable.

To the lay person, Adler is most famous for his complementary concepts of the inferiority and superiority complexes. When Adler spoke of the human striving for superiority, he was, however, actually speaking of something that can be more properly labeled a growth urge. That anyone can always be more than they are is clearly summarized in Adler's statement, "I would like to stress that the life of the human soul is not a 'being' but a 'becoming'."[8] Striving for completion, therefore, is a lifelong process that is never accomplished. The growth urge is differentiated from a pathological striving. Many literary characters are examples, par excellence, of the type of striving that involves an attempt on the part of the individual to achieve an almost godlike state to compensate for felt feelings of inferiority. George Orwell's depiction of a wretched albino who attempts to rule the world by becoming invisible, and Albert Camus's description of a Parisian lawyer who tries to be superhuman are good examples of this inferiority complex.[9] It is unfortunate that fewer literary works have depicted the self-actualized individual.[10] Not all compensatory striving rests on deep-seated feelings of inferiority. Some strivings are more normal types of adjustment that are the result of a temporarily induced feeling of inferiority. An example here would be Thomas Aldrich's depiction of the moody behavior of a young boy who finds that his ardent love is not reciprocated by a mature young woman.[11]

Adler's psychology is known as Individual Psychology, yet there is nothing in his description of striving for superiority to account for the uniqueness of the individual. To account for individual differences, we must describe what Adler called one's scheme of apperception, or one's world view. One's world view gives direction to striving. There are myriads of ways in which one can assert oneself in the world. As William James noted, the individual selects the sphere in which he or she tries to exert influence.[12] The stamp collector may care little if he or she is a miserable chess player, and similarly the chess player may care little for stamps. There are even people who achieve feelings of self-worth by arranging words on pages and then covering them with cloth or paper covers. Others, perhaps rightfully so, cannot fathom how this could be a satisfying pursuit. Thus, the world view gives direction to the striving. The world view also influences how one interprets so-called objective events. Adlerian psychologists, therefore eschew causal explanations of human behavior. Having a snake placed on one's lap, for example, is open to a variety of interpretations. To most this would be a revolting event, and the perpetrator of this deed would be viewed as unfriendly. The same act, nevertheless, may be viewed by a budding herpetologist as a token of interest and friendship. From this perspective no behavior is psychologically nonsensical, and thus behavior is in accord with the individual's world view. What, then, separates psychological functioning that is commonly viewed as nonsensical from that usually viewed as normal? To answer this question, which has been considered the most significant aspect of Adlerian theory, we must consider social interest.[13]

Social interest is the common English translation of the German term *gemeinshcaftsgefuhl*, a term that is one of the cornerstones of Maslow's description of the self-actualized individual. I have described social interest as an empathic cooperative style of living where empathy is the cognitive aspect and cooperation is the behavioral aspect of social interest.[14] Adler felt that the socially interested individual saw with the eyes of another, heard with the ears of another, and felt with the heart of another. Social interest is the criterion for assessing one's world view and consequent behavior. On the one hand, if one's behavior springs from a world view imbued with empathy and a cooperative spirit, it is easily understood. While on the other hand, if one's behavior springs from a world view that is private and egocentric, it appears illogical. John Hinckley, for example, tried to assassinate the President in order to show his love for the movie star Jodie Foster and to achieve fame. This act from his perspective was most logical. It does not, however, evoke a responsive note in the world view of others; he can thus be viewed as insane, and indeed a jury ruled him innocent by reason of insanity.

Adler did indeed feel that humans were inextricably social creatures.[15] He often stated that he "... refused to recognize the isolated human being." This contention has its roots in a biological theory that holds that most species live better in aggregate than in isolation.[16] The implications of this view for Adler were that the person must be considered as part of a social situation involving what he regarded as the three life problems: love, occupation, and community.[17] Thus, Adler was interested in the psychological development of the individual insofar as that development either fostered or hindered the development of social interest. And he considered five factors that he believed affected the development of social interest in the individual: pampering, neglect, organ inferiorities, birth order, and creativity.[18] The first four of these factors may adversely affect the development of social interest. The pampered individual like Nellie Olson in Laura Ingalls Wilder's *Little House* books for children is ill prepared for the reciprocity necessary for social living, while the neglected child such as Smike in Dickens's *Nicholas Nickleby* is never introduced to the world of love and social interest.

Physical deformities can predispose one to feel inferior and thus cause one to strive for superiority in a socially useless manner. Shakespeare vividly describes this in Richard III, who is portrayed as the ugly yet successful seducer of women he seeks for conquest rather than love. Adler also believed that birth order can affect one's view of the world. The firstborn is more likely to feel dethroned and neglected, while the youngest is most likely to be pampered. McLaughlin describes these dynamics in relation to the tragedy of *King Lear*.[19] And, finally, it is an individual's possession of creative power that relegates the first four factors to a nondeterministic level. Objective events provide probabilities only of what *may* be, since all events are answered by the styled creative power of the individual as expressed in his or her world view.

Adler believed that each person was, to a large extent, the author and actor of his or her own play of life. The individual, therefore, can never be explained. He or she can only be understood by accurately assessing his or her world view. Literature, similarly, is not to be explained; it is to be understood from the psychological viewpoint of its characters. An Adlerian approach to literature is mutually beneficial. In Adler's words,

> We have no desire to tamper with the marvellous outpourings of our poets and thinkers and shall therefore attempt merely to determine, through their creations to what extent we are on the right path and how much of their work can be understood by reference to the working methods of Individual Psychology.[20]

An Adlerian View of Holden Caulfield

The word "analysis" is not appropriate from an Adlerian frame of reference, since the goal of literary interpretation from this point of view is a holistic understanding of a character's world view and consequent style of living in relation to his or her social situation. "Creative synthesis" would be a more appropriate description of the Adlerian approach to literature. In essence, an Adlerian psychologist, whether dealing with a client or a literary character, attempts through keen observation of behavioral minutiae to understand the individual's frame of reference. If the psychologist understands the frame of reference, a consistent psychological depiction of a character can be formed. If a character's prime goal is social victory at all costs, he or she may be a veritable Uriah Heep in one instance and a Simon Legree in another; the contradictory behaviors may serve the same ends.

To aid them in their understanding, many Adlerian literary interpreters have evaluated issues that are embodied in the following query: Is the individual striving for growth and fulfillment in a beneficient way with his fellow humans? Or is the individual striving for useless superiority because of feelings of inferiority in a manner that is inconsiderate of others and ultimately destructive of self? In short, the Adlerian is always interested in knowing whether one feels competent or inferior, and whether one strives with or without social interests in mind.

A wide range of literature has proved itself amenable to Adlerian interpretation — Shakespeare (including Philip Mairet's essay on Hamlet), German medieval and romantic literature, existential literature, science fiction, autobiography, and contemporary American literature.[21] This wide spectrum underscores the validity of the Adlerian approach in its applicability to many cultural contexts over a great expanse of time. Readers of the post-World War II era, the Eisenhower era, the Vietnam era, and the present have all been able to identify with the pangs of Holden Caulfield as he attempts to come of age in America. As many critics have indicated, Holden Caulfield has served as more than a character many adolescent readers can identify with. He has become an adolescent folk hero.[22] In one sense, he can be seen as a valiant knight struggling against an evil society. In another sense, Holden's cynical world view can be seen as much more than the typical view of a typical rebellious adolescent. In fact, from an Adlerian perspective, Holden is more prototypical of maladjustment in general than of normal adolescence. Even a cursory inspection of Salinger's classic character reveals deep-seated inferiority feelings and a compensatory striving for grandiosity.

If Holden Caulfield is a prototype of a maladjusted person, why has he so often been considered an adolescent hero? The Adlerian response is that one's schema of apperception, one's world view, is never *completely* mistaken. The neurotic is right up to a point. In some instances, Holden aptly describes flaws in our society. For example, he indicates the callousness of a headmaster who dotes on wealthy parents and ignores parents of less affluent students. Similarly, many would agree with Holden that the Radio City Christmas pageant is only quasi-religious in nature. One must, however, take a look at Holden's total life context. The question to be asked is: Are the above instances parts of an empathic and cooperative life-style, or are they parts of a life-style filled with inferiority feelings and self-seeking grandiosity? As one describes Holden's style of living in detail, it is obvious that the latter is true. It seems that Holden selectively attends to and retains the negative aspects of his world, and then depreciates others and his surroundings in order to compensate for deep-seated feelings of inferiority. One would expect to find egocentricity and not social interest in such an individual. A closer look at Holden's world view, his schema of apperception, will reveal Holden's maladjustment rather than his folk-hero proportions.

Since one's world view pervades all one's life, Holden's every action and attitude should be closely integrated parts of his total personality. Adler connects actions and meaning:

> If we close our ears to his words and observe his actions, we shall find that he has his own individual 'meaning' of life and that all his postures, attitudes, movements, expressions, mannerisms, ambitions, habits, and character traits accord with this meaning.[23]

Holden's world view is permeated with feelings of inferiority, and his self-perception mirrors these feelings. At various points in the novel, Holden depicts himself as a "moron," "yellow," "quite illiterate," "not too tough," "a liar," "the only dumb one," and "weak." He perceives himself as a "loser in life." When one of his former professors, Mr. Spencer, states that life is a game, Holden retorts with the following:

> Game, my ass. Some game. If you get on the side where all the hot-shots are, then it's a game, all right — I'll admit that. But if you get on the other side, where there aren't any hot-shots, then what's a game about it? Nothing — No game.[24]

Clearly, as Adler would put it, Holden sees himself in a minus situation. He definitely is not a hotshot. Holden describes himself as extremely slender, abnormally tall, prematurely gray, very weak. He has respiratory problems and a disfigured hand. But there is an even more dramatic congruence between Holden's world view and his physical life, physical expressions of his psychic state. His intense feelings of inferiority are manifested in a somesthetic awareness. Toward the end of the novel, Holden has a psychotic episode when he steps off a curb and feels he will descend "down, down, down," and be lost forever. The downward direction is indicative of his intense feeling of failure and inferiority.

Given Holden's negative interpretation of his life position, it is logical to find a negative behavioral counterpart. Holden adopts a hesitating attitude, one in which he attempts to avoid life's problems and yet preserve his frail self-esteem. The hesitating attitude "offers an alibi to the neurotic."[25] The neurotic lives according to the formula "yes-but." The goal to be attained is the "yes," and the "but" is the fictive excuse that arrests the individual's goal-oriented strivings. Holden exemplifies this hesitating "yes-but" attitude when dealing with members of the opposite sex. When Jane Gallagher, a friend from the previous summer, is in the lobby of his dorm, Holden avoids meeting her by saying he is not "in the mood," even though it is more than obvious that he would like to see her. Similarly, having hired a prostitute, Holden once again uses the fictive excuse of not being in the mood to avoid a sexual encounter. However, Holden does not merely avoid members of the opposite sex. He avoids most social contact. He excludes others from his social sphere by adopting an "all or nothing" attitude. This "all or nothing" attitude is characteristic of the individual who feels he is living in "enemy territory" and shows the oversensitivity of one threatened by defeats. Holden's oversensitivity is seen when he is driven "damn near crazy" when he sees "fuck you" written on the wall of his sister's school. This to him is proof positive that the entire world is an evil place and that the plight of man is hopeless. Holden uses his oversensitivity to exclude himself from society, and therefore he is able to cleverly protect his self-esteem. Adler terms this the exclusion tendency:

> . . . anything that does not fit in with his early adopted attitudes is more or less excluded; or it is wholly or in part stripped of its intellectual content and objective meaning and is interpreted, always in accordance with the individual's view of the world.[26]

Inferiority and superiority feelings work in a dialectical fashion, that is, the greater the feelings of inferiority the more grandiose the goal. ". . . an increased insecurity feeling in childhood causes a higher and more unalterable goal setting, a striving which goes beyond human measure . . ."[27] This active upward striving to overcome inferiorities always includes maintenance of the self-esteem. Given Holden's avoidance of the problems of life, he employs, as one would expect, other safeguarding mechanisms in addition to hesitating and all-or-nothing attitudes as means of achieving a sense of grandiosity and godlikeness. Holden uses his unrealistic imagination to place himself over others and thus succeeds in enhancing his self-esteem. Fantasy helps to give a neurotic ". . . an illusory view of enhancement of his self-esteem, usually spurring him on . . ."[28] When Holden's grandiose self-image is threatened, he imagines himself as a dying hero, similar to those seen in

Saturday matinees, to achieve a sense of grandiosity. He often sees himself wounded and ". . . holding onto my guts, blood leaking all over the place." Thus, Holden's fantasies give him an illusory view of increased personal worth, and compel him to view himself as a hero in the manner of John Wayne, a manner Adler describes as masculine protest.

Means of safeguarding the self-esteem through "masculine protest" follows the schematic formula "I want to be a real man." Instead of a dashing hero, however, Holden is a caricature of a "real man." Consider, for example, his frequent offer to buy cocktails for those he meets. In an attempt to be suave, he asks numerous people to join him for a drink, but they are people who have no time for a drink — cabdrivers, waitresses, etc. The inappropriateness of his offers reveals their overdriven quality. Similarly, Holden's repetitive use of profanity is indicative of his masculine protest, an empty protest serving a useless goal. Adler emphasizes that to understand an individual, one must understand his or her goals, an important part of one's world view, one's line of direction. Holden's goal is one of useless grandiosity — to be a catcher in the rye — to be the person who catches small children running through a field of rye before they go over a cliff. Holden sees himself as a savior of the children of the world. This unique sort of striving for godlikeness is characteristic of the compulsive neurotic, who ". . . tries to represent himself . . . as a demigod, who exalts himself above humankind."[29] Appropriately, Holden states that there would be "nobody big . . . except me . . . ," indicating his wish to be superior in every way.

In addition to his godlike image, Holden strives for superiority in a most ungodlike manner, namely through depreciation. Like the neurotic ". . . who exalts himself above mankind and depreciates everyone else and puts them in the shade . . . ," Holden repeatedly belittles his environment.[30] A key word in his vocabulary is "phony," a word that reflects his general view of society. His school ". . . was a terrible school no matter how you looked at it." The hotel he stayed in had "vomity looking chairs," and was "full of perverts." This depreciatory attitude blends well with Holden's hesitating attitude. He feels it is not worthwhile to get involved with the world he sees. Considering this negative view, it is comprehensible that his social interest is low.

It is, in Adler's view, always a lack of social interest that causes insufficient preparation for all of the problems of life—love, society, and occupation. Life's problems are of a social nature and therefore demand social interest for their successful solution. Holden inadequately copes with the problems of life by hesitating and avoiding love and communal relationships and striving for a useless goal. His low social interest is further indicated by his desire to isolate himself from the rest of mankind. He attempts to do so through language, " . . . a common creation of mankind. . . ."[31] Holden wishes, in fact, to be a deaf-mute, to be cut off from mankind's common base, language. He prefers to seek the company of a dead brother, and through this positive orientation with someone dead, reveals his tendency to isolate himself. He can have an idealized but not ideal (socially interested) relationship. He is in enemy territory, mute and sure only that his safest social relationship is with a dead brother. This kind of estrangement is poignantly revealed at the beginning of his narration. He depicts himself as alone, on a hill above others, watching the homecoming football game of his school. He literally feels that others are his enemies, a feeling that is evident when he describes his red hunting hat, bought on a recent trip to New York City, as a "people shooting hat." This aggressive attitude is one Adler would expect from someone with a low degree of social interest and a high degree of activity, that is, a choleric type.

And truly Holden's adventures are indicative of someone with a great deal of energy. In the span of two days, he goes to a movie, leaves school, checks in and out of a hotel, goes to several bars, attends a Broadway show, goes ice skating, visits home, visits a former teacher, and takes several long walks. Even when he is in one place, he is constantly moving — dancing, shouting, drumming on the table, striking matches. And he even wants to jump out the window. In an Adlerian view, suicide is a real possibility when someone has a low social interest and a high degree of activity. Holden's ultimate end is what Mr. Antolini, a former teacher, tries to warn Holden about. He quotes Wilhelm Stekel: "The mark of the immature man is that he wants to die nobly for a cause while the mark of a mature man is that he wants to live humbly for one." Mr Antolini seemed to realize, as did Adler, that those who have contributed little to the general good and have not given life meaning cannot endure into the future. It is interesting to note that Adler felt that any work of art was a reflection of the life-style of its creator. In one famous passage in *The Catcher in the Rye*, Salinger has Caulfield state at length how he would like to live in a cabin in Vermont where he would rarely have to speak to anyone. This has been the fate of J. D. Salinger himself.

Reichian Criticism:
The Human Body in
Wuthering Heights

by Arthur Efron

P robably the best rule of thumb for anyone attempting a Reichian approach to literature is: *Pay attention to the body*. Reich's theories of the body, when traced not merely to the point of his expulsion from the International Psychoanalytic Association in 1934, but through his later work, even including his ideas on desert formation in 1955, show the body in a number of perspectives that are not attainable within other psychological frameworks. These perspectives fit within an over-all Reichian world view, but describing that view in brief compass is inevitably to do it some violence. It has been said that no accurate "summary" of Freud could ever be compiled, given the complexity of his development and the radical meanings of his central concepts. The same is true of Reich. Two good guidebooks exist,[1] but there is no sub-stitute for thorough immersion in his writings. I will offer an introduc-tory list here, with only slight elaboration, of ten basic Reichian perspectives on the human body and its contexts. This will introduce a good part of what we must attend to, if we pay attention to the human body in Reichian ways:

1. The quality, not merely the fact, of the sex act.
2. Recognition of the special value of adult sexuality, including the orgasm, which cannot be reduced to the psychoanalytically familiar notions of infantile sexuality, or Oedipal relations, nor to object relations.

Early in his work as a therapist, Reich noticed that a great deal of nonsense is spoken by people who report their sexual experiences. Often the quality of the experience and the feeling of contact with the sexual partner were omitted entirely. The reasons for such reticence were not those of modesty; there has never been any shortage of claims that sexual experience has been earth-shattering or lovely or "great." Reich found upon inquiry that very often the sex was made possible only by keeping the mind occupied with fantasies about the sexual partner. Some of these fantasies were hostile ones; others were idealizations of the partner's body to imagine that it conformed to some pattern held in the mind of the lover. In either case, Reich maintained that the *function* of the adult orgasm is *blocked* when part of the mind goes on apart from the act, refusing to surrender to the full force of energy that is potentially there.

In Reichian terms, the sexual embrace is said to involve contact for the very good reason that it requires the superimposition of two energy systems, that of the man and the woman. Reich took seriously the "mutual attraction" of certain men and women, which does not happen just between any two; such attraction can lead to a remarkable "compatibility in sexual rhythm, which often operates at first sight without either of the individuals being aware of it."[2] It is absurd to try to see this rhythm as a matter of two minds in unconscious connection, as if the bodies just happen to fall into place. Nor is such rhythm reducible to what a baby feels with its mother — the adult bodies make a real difference.

Reich's theory of the orgasm might be put to work in literature whenever sexual quality is being evoked. In the following excerpt from the acclaimed novel by Ursula K. LeGuin, *The Dispossessed*, the hero, Shevek, has just come back to his wife (or "partner," as LeGuin would say), after a four-year separation:

> They went back to Domicile Eight, Room 3, and there their long desire was fulfilled. They did not even light the lamp; they both liked making love in darkness. The first time they both came as Shevek came into her, the second time they struggled and cried out in a rage of joy, prolonging their climax as if delaying the moment of death, the third time they were both half asleep, and circled about the center of infinite pleasure, about each other's being, like planets

circling blindly, quietly, in the flood of sunlight, about the common center of gravity, swinging, circling endlessly.[3]

I admire LeGuin's decision to try to write about this sexual experience. That is not the norm in science fiction, which is often arbitrary in what it does with the sexual body, when it does not aspire to be above it altogether. From a Reichian perspective, however, the claim to having desire "fulfilled" here is suspect. The first orgasm is very fast, but its qualities are not described. The second one involves mutuality, all right, but one of trying to inject a delay into the sexual rhythm, and it is mixed with the old and unwise fantasy that equates orgasm with death. We could also ask what sort of coming together has "rage" in it, given the oxymoron of a "rage of joy"? As for the third part of the experience, from a Reichian point of view it is not an orgasm at all. It is more like a mutual standoff, based on the popular fantasy — which goes well beyond any fact of the human body — of "infinite pleasure." "Circling endlessly" may sound lovely, but it cannot be the completion of the human act of love. On the other hand, all that part of the description concerning the "common center of gravity" may be an oblique suggestion of a potential for the interweaving of two energy systems, the woman's and the man's, in one continuous act.

3. The connection between adult sexuality and chronic energy blockage, or "armoring," with the character structure that anyone lives out within society.

Armor, one of Reich's most famous discoveries, is a kind of rigidifying of the body and of the mind; he discussed both "muscular armoring" — which goes on in muscles, the respiratory system, and visceral responses — and "character armor," the ingrained way in which one reacts to life as if one were a certain "type" of person. Where other theories tend to idealize the fact of "character structure," and can see no difference between it and the very fact of human identity, Reich found that most character (and most identity) is a way of warding off life rather than living it. It is not the disturbing or crippling symptom that makes someone unhealthy, it is the character structure itself. The character gives rise to the symptom.

Armoring is also an expression of the mind/body relationship, because muscular and character armor are actually a single process in each person, but viewed from two different angles, that of the body and that of the mind. In his early work, Reich found that all his patients had disturbances not only of the orgasm; they all had unnatural breathing patterns and rigid bellies as well. They *also* believed in compulsory marriage and could not imagine that work was a creative necessity.[4] But these correlations were deeply rooted in society itself:

4. The complete dependence of "normal," authoritarian society — including both our own society of property relations and the society of what Reich pointedly called "Red Fascism" — on the "armored" character.

5. The social issue of the child's and the adolescent's bodily reality: the problem, in other words, of creating a family context in which the child will not have to undergo armoring.

6. The place of bodily energy within overall vital energy in the cosmos, an energy that Reich eventually concluded could not be understood as "libido," nor as "electrophysiological," but which required a special name, "orgone," whereby Reich admitted and in fact claimed that life-energy does not fit the generally accepted mechanistic paradigm of standard science.

7. The further hypothesis that we all "know" there is something wrong with armoring; that is, we have a "longing," though it is usually undefined, for our natural patterns of bodily energy and a deep desire for being able to live our lives in accordance with them. Reich believed that human nature is a part of nature, and that this is a meaningful, guiding, relationship.

8. The theory that earlier society, prior to the rise of patriarchy some six thousand years ago, had a much better social realization of the nature–human nature relationship. Although there is no "noble savage" as such, there is great value to our understanding that social life was once far more natural and vastly less armored, and that these early social arrangements worked effectively for a huge span of time.[5]

9. The relation of vital energy and armoring to diseases of the modern era, such as cancer.[6]

10. The overall reformulation of what science should be, given that orgone energy exists.[7]

In my reading of psychoanalytic theory, I have encountered the attempt to lift one of Reich's perspectives, namely (3), on armoring, out of its context and to fit it into the politically conservative thought of psychoanalysis. Most practitioners of such sciences as chemistry and physics, and those who construct theories of science, would deny out of hand the validity of Orgone or anything of the sort. There is a growing conviction, nonetheless, among various thinkers (some literary critics, medical practitioners, scientists, therapists) that the theories of Reich — including some that I have not mentioned, such as his "Mass Psychology of Fascism," his theoretical contribution to the women's movement, his criticism of pornography, etc. — all belong in one great unified theory. Reich, in fact, postulated a Common Functioning Principle for all life energy that was intended to apply to all fields. My own position is that there are no solid grounds for rejecting any of the ten perspectives listed above; indeed, there are quite good reasons for taking all of them seriously as descriptions, insights, and theories that are intended to be, and may well be, grounded in fact. In a recent study of Reich's ideas, W. Edward Mann and Edward Hoffman put the issue succinctly: "As it has now become clear, Western civilization is virtually unique in history in its failure to recognize each human being as a subtle energy system in constant relationship to a vast sea of energies in the surrounding cosmos."[8]

Considerable application has been made of Reich's theories in the interpretation of literature. There are, however, wide gaps and great variations in the completeness with which the theories are consulted. In poetry, all poets in the tradition of cosmic vision, those poets who place human life within cosmic energy movements, ranging from the ancient poet Lucretius on up through Walt Whitman and Charles Olson, might be illuminated by an informed Reichian analysis. Frederick Rusch has pioneered in the application of Reich to Whitman,[9] but his good beginning needs to be expanded. Our readings of the multiple traditions of love poetry would be seen in a new way, if their metaphoric language of energy were considered to be based on literal body energies. These lines from the Alba (love-song of dawn), by the medieval poet Heinrich von Morüngen, might be considered from non-Reichian as well as Reichian perspectives:

Alas, shall her body never again
Stream its light through the night for me?[10]

From a non-Reichian perspective, the "light" is in the eye of the beholder, or it is moonlight invested with value by that mind. For a reader informed by Reichian concepts, the light is also a seen and felt charge of energy connected with the orgasmic cycle in love, and its movement is important: this is a body that might once more "stream its light," not just glow. In fact, *streaming* was Reich's word for the perception anyone has of the sweet flow of sexual energy during gratification; here the lover who speaks the lines can imagine this streaming in his own body as well as in the lover's. The fact that the energy is moving "through the night" is meaningful in Reichian terms, since it must be part of a larger atmosphere, whereas a non-Reichian reader might simply reduce the time location of "night" to a convention of this kind of poetry. Reich enables us to better ask: What lies behind such conventions, in human life?

A different type of poem that has been read with Reichian insight is Baudelaire's "Elevation," from his *Flowers of Evil*. Baudelaire evokes the experience of soaring high above the earth, into the atmosphere itself, but unlike much science fiction, the experience is an uncannily bodily one, and it contains a criticism of the energy-damaged realms of ordinary social existence,

> . . . where cares and boredom hold dominion,
> Which charge our fogged existence with their spleen.

Roger Dadoun has shown how these lines and the entire poem can make sense in terms of orgone energy, without reducing it to a clinical transcript or scientific report.[11] It remains a poem, but it can be felt with more immediacy, and certainly with a new impact, as a result of Dadoun's reading.

In criticism of the novel, more than a little Reichian work has been done. Paul Goodman began it with a difficult choice, Kafka, in Goodman's book *Kafka's Prayer* (1947).[12] David Boadella and Dennis Hoerner have each given book-length, compelling interpretations of the fiction of D. H. Lawrence, whose world view overlaps Reich's, though it also differs seriously.[13] For Thomas Hardy, Michael Steig has analyzed the perplexing character of Sue Bridehead in *Jude the Obscure* with the concepts of Reich's character analysis, and I have offered a reading of the opening chapters of the same novel in relation to life-energy.[14] Steig has also shown how Saul Bellow's novel *Henderson the Rain King* virtually calls for a Reichian approach, rather than a Freudian one.[15] Bellow, in fact, was in Reichian therapy for a time and was certainly familiar with the ideas at a personal level. Among earlier authors, Hawthorne has been taken up for Reichian discussion by John M. Bell and David B.

Downing. Bell's article is a straightforward Reichian approach to *The Scarlet Letter*, while Downing's book-length work is a contextualistic reading of most of the Hawthorne canon, with special attention to Hawthorne's treatment of the human body.[16] David Kiremidjian has given a Reichian interpretation to the murders in Dostoevsky's *Crime and Punishment*, while Jerome Greenfield has argued for the artistic superiority of Tolstoy, from a Reichian perspective, over Dostoevsky.[17] A consideration of *Don Quixote* as a work of cultural criticism from a Reichian perspective has been one of my own concerns.[18]

A Reichian Interpretation of *Wuthering Heights*

Here I would like to give an idea of how Reichian criticism can be carried out by offering an interpretation of one of the most widely read novels in literature, *Wuthering Heights*. A Reichian approach to Emily Brontë's masterpiece (published in 1847) can enhance and deepen a reader's feeling and understanding in that novel. I will concentrate on the "first generation" of characters — Heathcliff, Edgar Linton, Catherine Earnshaw, and Nelly Dean — because that is where the greatest challenges lie. Perennially discussed and disputed questions of the novel occur in this generation: what was the nature of the extraordinary relationship between Catherine and Heathcliff? Why do we care about it? How do the childhood and adolescent years of their life link up with their encounter after Catherine's marriage to Edgar? What has "Wuthering Heights," the place, to do with their relationship? What were the qualities of the marital life of Catherine and Edgar? Why is Catherine's death such a powerful event in the novel? Inasmuch as there is no orgasmic sexuality (in fact no sexual union as adults) between the two most memorable characters, Catherine and Heathcliff, I will not be able to provide the sort of analysis I gave for the passage describing sexual love in LeGuin's *The Dispossessed*. Nonetheless, a Reichian reading of *Wuthering Heights* will have ample scope. My approach will be to take the characters as if they were people, with real bodies. This way of reading literature is often frowned upon, but I believe that it is the way most people, even teachers of literature, still read novels. I also maintain that it is the best way from the point of view of literary theory.[19]

In chapter 9, the fifteen-year-old Catherine tells Nelly Dean of her decision to marry Edgar Linton, and is overhead by Heathcliff, who leaves at once. If we "pay attention to the body," following the Reichian rule of thumb as I have suggested, one of the most eminent features of Catherine's telling is her "striking one hand on her forehead, and the other on her breast," as she describes with passion her deep intuition that it is wrong for her to have accepted Linton. The "obstacle," as Nelly calls it, lies "Here! and here!," in feelings that Catherine locates in her body.[20] A "semiotic" aproach might tell us (in fact, such an approach would have to maintain) that Catherine strikes her breast because the human breast has become a sign of feeling, and that Catherine has simply learned that particular code of using it. No doubt Catherine grew up in a culture that had its full share of traditional body gestures, but a Reichian approach will insist that we first pay heed to the likelihood that there really is a lot of feeling in the area of the breast, especially during feelings of upset and anguish.

The assumption of Reich is also that the brain is within the body, a part of it. The brain is not the immovable base, within the skull, of some purely mental mind; the brain also has its energy movements, its rhythm of blood supply, and even its minute pulsations.[21] When Catherine strikes her forehead, she is not referring to some taunt of the moral faculty, "conscience," nor to a soul that is distinct from body; instead, as the gesture suggests, she is indicating a palpable disturbance behind the surface of her forehead. She knows there is something very wrong with her decision to marry Edgar, because her body is letting her know, and she is able to listen to what her body is saying. Beyond that, however, she is unable to be very precise; when Nelly needs an explanation, Catherine warns that though she can explain, "I can't do it distinctly, but I'll give you a feeling of how I feel." This is followed by her face growing "sadder and graver," while her "clasped hands trembled." Nelly notices that "Catherine had an unusual gloom in her aspect." At this point, there is no problem of Heathcliff's having left; he has yet to do that. For all Catherine knows, she will be able to carry out her willful plan of marrying Edgar but keeping Heathcliff with her, using her future husband's money to educate and advance him. Yet she already knows, with her body, that her "soul" just won't have this.

Catherine next insists on telling her dream of being flung out of heaven, where she found herself to be woefully unhappy, back "into the middle of the heath on the top of Wuthering Heights; where I woke sobbing for joy. That will do to explain my secret, as well as the other. I've no more business to marry Edgar Linton than I have to be in heaven . . ." Moreover, if Heathcliff had not been degraded by the abusive treatment he had received at the hands of her own brother, "I shouldn't have thought of it" (p. 72). From a Reichian perspective, what is most significant in this expression of Catherine's feeling is the contrast, between waking up, "sobbing for joy," in "the middle of the heath on the top of Wuthering Heights" — and the thought of Linton as her husband-to-be. Linton does not belong among the very deepest feelings that Cathy has. The feelings that she is painfully touching upon are not to be understood as her personal integrity or personal identity, in any of the conventional meanings of those terms; these are feelings that center on the moors and are throughly suffused with her years of romping with Heathcliff out there. Catherine's passionate statements that follow in this scene, where she memorably declares, "I *am* Heathcliff — he's always, always in my mind . . . — as my own being . . ." are made in the context that Catherine has felt; it is a context consisting of Heathcliff, herself, and the moors.

From a Reichian perspective, it is natural to credit this context as a reality. There on the moors were she and Heathcliff, distinctly set off from the civil/sick demands of the household, where her boozy brother was in authority and his Bible-quoting servant Joseph was his agent. Those moors are where the flow of great natural energy is felt. Different as the households of Wuthering Heights and Thrushcross Grange are, they are both in the same context, namely that of nature denied. In a Reichian perspective, what will be denied as she marries and moves to the Grange is not nature "out there," the moors, nor personal integrity, but both of these at once, as the necessarily whole human organism.

The point is a key one. A psychoanalytic approach might deploy its concepts to show that the statement "I *am* Heathcliff" leads to identity confusion, unacknowledged symbiotic union (Catherine's mother and father are dead), and incest fantasy (Heathcliff as the brother-lover). All this has been said, nor is evidence lacking for its support, but something is always left out: the moors, the heath, nature. It *must* be left out, because it simply is not part of a primary category available to psychoanalytic thought.[22] And to leave out the moors is to miss the novel. The moors would have to be explained away as "projection" or as unconscious identification with the mother.

The remainder of the chapter offers an account of emotional disturbance, natural energy discharge in the atmosphere, and the onset of a bodily anchored disease in Catherine. Cathy learns that Heathcliff is missing. She intuits that he really has left after overhearing her say she could not marry him, degrading as such a marriage would be, and she becomes disturbed, virtually out of control. A storm beats down on the Heights, and the "willful girl" stands out in it, "crying outright." The willfulness is a summary interpretation of Nelly's (here, as later in the novel, it is Nelly's defense against Catherine's emotional immediacy). A psychoanalytic reading might have it that Catherine stood in the rain in order to punish herself. This would be about as interesting as it is to maintain that Tess of the d'Urbervilles, in Hardy's novel, is a "masochist." Actually, Catherine might have punished herself in any number of ways, such as striking herself with her fists or with an object. Here she stands out in a storm. A Reichian awareness of a sudden irresistible longing for a sense of reimmersion in the storm as turbulent natural energy — the very opposite of Catherine's commitment to the placidities of her promised union with Edgar — seems more important to understanding her, and to feeling the force of the scene itself.

Catherine's crying is not an artifact of Nelly's interpretive overlay upon the narrative; it is really there, forcefully part of the story, as Nelly well knows. After the storm, Catherine "burst into uncontrollable grief." She becomes inarticulate at the realization that she really has lost contact with Heathcliff. ". . . I shall never forget what a scene she acted," says Nelly, "when we reached her chamber. It terrified me. I thought she was going mad . . ." In other words, this is not an "acted" scene. The delirium and dangerous illness that follow are serious. Moreover, "serious threats of a fit often attended her rages . . ." (p. 78). For a reader with a sense of Reichian values, the storm will not be dismissed as Romantic background, nor as a convenient metaphor of Catherine's disturbance. It is, just as the narrative sequence of the chapter suggests, an integral part of the disturbance. Emily Brontë is showing us a Catherine whose personal existence is also a natural existence; it involves that storm.

The damage of losing Heathcliff is not only a psychological one (object loss, or separation anxiety, as psychoanalytic theory would probably have it), but an illness that anchors itself in the body. The disposition is established here, to have "serious threats of a fit," connected with the expression of rage. These qualities will prove important in the breakdown of Catherine as a grown woman married to Edgar some years later. Through Nelly's moralistic eyes, Catherine simply has been spoiled, that is, encouraged and allowed to indulge her whims and outbursts. This is still probably the first reaction of most readers. Such moralism can never come to grips with the quick transition in the outbursts from seemingly willful to wildly uncontrolled quality. Nelly herself is aware that Cathy "never had power to conceal her passion; it always set her whole complexion in a blaze" (p. 65). In Reichian terms, Catherine has never been forced during childhood to armor herself against her own feelings; her inconsistent upbringing has taken a pattern of parental indifference and freedom to feel any way that her energy level demands, alternating with bouts of sudden, physical punishment; this pattern Reich described on the basis of his own childhood.[23] Being spoiled, in Reichian terms, means in Cathy's case an ability to release all her energy of rage and grief that she feels within her.

Attention to Catherine's and Heathcliff's bodily expression of emotion also corrects the tendency to simplify and thus allegorize the characters. Many times I have read or been told that Catherine and Heathcliff are passionate, indomitable, wild, violent, angry, irresponsible, immature, etc. To be sure, their refusal to give up their raw emotions in order to become good citizens is important, but it is also important to see and feel the range of emotions they have. In the early part of the book, during Lockwood's visit, we are presented with Heathcliff "bursting . . . into an uncontrollable passion of tears" (p. 33). Even the Heathcliff thought of as a devil and a fearless brute speaks like a very helpless man when he learns of Catherine's death. He begs her: "Be with me always — take any form — drive me mad! only *do* not leave me in this abyss, where I cannot find you" (p. 139).

The account of Heathcliff given by his wife, Isabella, who thinks of him as a devil, contains another indication of his purely human emotional vulnerability. The narrative accomplishes this through attention to bodily expression, and thus implies that even a generally uninsightful person like Isabella can have better contact with what really goes on in people's feelings if only she will allow herself to pay attention to the body:

> Heathcliff did not glance my way, and I gazed up and contemplated his features almost as confidently as if they had been turned to stone. His forehead, that I once thought so manly, and that I now think so diabolical, was shaded with a heavy cloud; his basilisk eyes were nearly quenched by sleeplessness, and weeping, perhaps, for the lashes were

wet then; his lips devoid of their ferocious sneer, and sealed in an expression of unspeakable sadness. Had it been another, I would have covered my face in the presence of such grief. (p. 148)

Isabella's account powerfully implies that we fully credit "the presence of such grief" in Heathcliff. For Isabella, it is sufficient to think of Heathcliff "now" — actually not very long after the grief has appeared — as diabolical, but the "unspeakable sadness" remains for the reader, as it remains for the continuing bodily felt emotions of Heathcliff. It goes much deeper than his hatred.

Catherine similarly is not all rage and grief, nor does all her tenderness move toward the "mild" Edgar as opposed to the "wild" Heathcliff. After her longest illness, she leaves her room, on a March day, and looks at "a handful of golden crocuses" that Edgar had left for her. "These are the earliest flowers at the Heights! . . . They remind me of soft thaw winds, and warm sunshine, and nearly melted snow" (p. 114). The qualities of softness, warmth, and melting connote pleasurable and tender surrender to feelings. Such feelings are as much a part of the human core as the more dramatic ones, and are significantly linked with Wuthering Heights, not with Edgar's world. In fact, Edgar, for the only time in the novel, intuits that Catherine does not belong with him but needs the free energy forces out of doors: ". . . last spring at this time, I was longing to have you under this roof; now I wish you were a mile or two up those hills; the air blows so sweetly, I feel it would cure you."

Just after Catherine's death her body is "suffused" by sunlight, giving it and the whole room "a mellow, tender, glow" (p. 137). Although Nelly soon slips into her favorite fantasy of "perfect peace" and "infinite calm," implying a thorough denial of energy movement and feeling, the "mellow, tender glow" is definitely evoked. It owes nothing to Edgar, who lies down next to his dead wife, because, as Nelly says, "*his* was the hush of exhausted anguish . . ." For a psychoanalytic reader, both the tender glow and the infinite calm are "projections" of Nelly's, but according to Reichian energy considerations, Catherine has attained a "release" that makes her body belong, for the moment, with the softness and warmth and genuine gratification that she had experienced long ago, beyond familial control, on the moors with Heathcliff.

Such gratification between the boy and the girl may not have been sexual, but it would be in keeping with a Reichian approach to assume that their union included their own bodies, in whatever sexual dimensions are natural to children, rather than to adopt a Victorian stereotype of the child and endow Catherine and Heathcliff with pure, that is, sexless, contact. To assume that some degree of sex play must have gone on is consistent with the report that they slept for some time in the same bed, and with the poignant location of their out-of-doors contact on the heath. Non-Reichian approaches might incline the reader to assume that either no sex was involved in their contact, or that if there was any, it was merely the exploration of sexual bodies that children frequently make when they have the chance. The sense of Catherine and Heathcliff that would be gained through either of these assumptions would be difficult to connect with the impression of two powerful presences living within the untamed energy movements of the heath.

E. M. Forster, David Cecil, Wayne Burns, and other critics have seen the love of Catherine and Heathcliff as something greater than, or other than, merely human love.[24] From a Reichian approach, Catherine and Heathcliff as children and as adults were alive within the natural energy movements of the heath, where their sexuality was a part of that nature. They look larger than life only because life as we have it in our own society splits us off from our roots in vital energy. The strong sense of identification many readers have with Catherine, Heathcliff, or both, is almost inexplicable, if we take these lovers as larger than life; it would become mystical, in other words. For Reich, to be mystical is to commit the cognitive error complementary to being mechanistic; for while vital, orgone energy is not understandable within the assumptions of standard science (the science of today or the science of Brontë's time), it is not outside of natural life, either. By crediting the possibility that there is such an energy, the reader may become better able to recognize his own longing for a life commensurate with it, and to see in Catherine and Heathcliff a male and a female who are in fact seeking such a life. As children, they had had a great taste of it; this makes the prospect of its loss all the more poignant.

From Reich's position, all of us have some intimations of the natural. These longings cannot be explained away in an infinite regression of textual levels, in the manner of Derrida or other skeptical philosophy.[25] (The thousands of people who value being in national parks because they can experience being "out in nature," are wiser than the philosophy that denies there is any "nature," except as a metaphor that reeks of nostalgia). Experiencing *Wuthering Heights* is partly a matter of connecting these intimations with the struggle of Catherine and Heathcliff.

A non-Reichian approach to sexuality will be led to conclude that Catherine and Linton, since they get married and obviously do have sexual relations, are the actual sexual lovers, and that the bond between Catherine and Heathcliff as adults must be other than sexual.[26] Reich's theory that the *quality* of sexual embrace is what is important, not its occurrence, allows for a finer differentiation. Reich would have us ask: What was it really like between Edgar and Cathy? Brontë's Victorian text is not necessarily silent on the issue. A first consideration is: What was Cathy's energy state like when she married Edgar? We know that three years had gone by since the great scene of the storm, discussed above. Those were three years of being without Heathcliff, a loss that meant bodily illness at the outset, and the development of a predisposition toward having "fits." If we assume, through Romantic typecasting, that Catherine was a "passionate" woman, we will miss the Reichian insight that by the time she married Edgar, she probably had moved very far from the passion she once felt. Edgar never married the fully vital woman. Looking back at her time spent in marriage with Edgar, she tells Nelly of an unseen "agony" that Nelly would not have been aware of. This agony, I take it, refers to the overall texture of her life as the mistress of Thrushcross Grange, but it is also a statement about the quality of her and Edgar's sexual life together.

Ellen's own report that they were "in possession of deep and growing happiness" (p. 81), must be taken into account, but it suggests that happiness is a thing one comes to own, rather than a function of genuine gratification. Ellen's estimate seems based on the pleasant, rather unvarying energy level in the household, which was broken some of the time when Catherine had "seasons of gloom and silence," or "depression of spirits." At those times Edgar left her alone. But how many "seasons" could there have been in a time span that lasted, by Nelly's own account, "half a year"? This is Brontëan irony. All in all, Ellen's testimony proves the opposite of what it was intended to show: the marital life of the Lintons that she saw as very happy was usually characterized by a suspension of energy shifts, connoting a level of sexual activity too mild to cause any change in mood. The deeper disturbance in Catherine, dating from the traumatic departure of Heathcliff, remains as if in a separate compartment from the marriage.

We get some further notion of the quality of sexual life between

Catherine and Edgar during their fierce verbal exchanges after the collapse of their "deep and growing happiness." "Your cold blood," Catherine accuses, "cannot be worked into a fever; your veins are full of ice-water, but mine are boiling, and the sight of such chillness makes them dance." Edgar regards this as a ploy, and refuses to allow himself to be alarmed, accusing in his turn: "I have found that you can be as stoical as any one, when you please" (pp. 100–101). These accusations emerge as the hidden agenda in a confrontation over the issue of whether Catherine will continue to allow Heathcliff to visit the house. They are meant to hurt, and no doubt they do; what they may imply is a long-standing sexual dissatisfaction with each other. I have suggested that Catherine probably entered the marriage already in a state of energy "stasis" over her three years of missing Heathcliff; and Edgar, who is said to have a general lack of "spirit" by even his admirer Nelly (p. 62), might have taken to bed a wife who was "stoical" rather than responsive.

During the great crisis of Catherine's illness, her frustration centers on both Edgar's and Nelly's obtuseness in understanding what she is all about as a passionate, bodily woman. Nelly's belief is that Catherine is to blame for her illness by causing the symptoms to occur, and that therefore Catherine is not sick. The problem is partly that both Nelly and Edgar deny their intuitive understanding of the energy of the human body; they concentrate instead on Catherine's willpower, and assume that her conscious direction of her body can turn illness on and off. Nelly hears very well when Catherine confides that she wants to frighten her husband, and that she wishes it were true that she were in danger of being seriously ill. But she does not pay attention to the preamble to this statement, which strongly suggests that Catherine already is in danger:

> "I'm nearly distracted, Nelly!" she exclaimed, throwing herself on the sofa. "A thousand smith's hammers are beating in my head! Tell Isabella to shun me — . . . should she or anyone else aggravate my anger at present, I shall get wild." (P. 100)

Catherine's long speech ends with instructions to "remind" Edgar of her "passionate temper, verging, when kindled, on frenzy." These instructions are clear enough, and as Nelly notices, are "delivered with perfect sincerity," but Nelly decides to ignore them, on the grounds that since Catherine "could plan the turning of her fits of passion to account, beforehand," she could very well also "manage to control herself tolerably even while under their influence" (p. 101).

As a result, Catherine's intuitive knowledge of what her constitution can and cannot tolerate is immediately violated, and Edgar enters to aggravate her anger indeed, with his ultimatum concerning Heathcliff. In what Nelly calls a "senseless" rage, Catherine grinds her teeth violently, is unable to get her breath, and stretches out stiffly, in "the aspect of death" — but Nelly intuitively understands that this is *not* just an act, even as she tells Edgar, "There is nothing in the world the matter." Nelly acknowledges, "I could not help being afraid in my heart." Catherine at this point gets up, and Nelly can only think that this movement, too, is proof that she had been but acting her distress. But if Catherine were incensed at Nelly for giving the game away, she would no doubt attack Nelly, as she had on other occasions. Nelly expects such an attack; instead, Catherine "only glared about her for an instant and then rushed from the room" (p. 102). Later, when her condition has become more serious, she tells Nelly this: "I couldn't explain to Edgar how certain I felt of having a fit, or going raving mad, if he persisted in teasing me! I had no command of tongue, or brain, and he did not guess my agony, perhaps; it barely left me sense to try to escape from him and his voice" (p. 107). It is as if the quality of Edgar's voice (not his ideas, or his specific ultimatum about Heathcliff) could directly touch and hurt Catherine, in the vital processes that make her body stay alive.

Catherine has a premonition of a fit coming on, a sense of warning from the body that is normal in many disturbances, and she tries to convey that feeling as well as instructions for preventing the attack. But having all that pressure in her brain, where "a thousand smith's hammers are beating," counts for naught. The sequence reveals a perceptual bar between the unarmored body, Catherine, and the armored Nelly and Edgar. They simply do not feel the reality of what they see, and thus might as well not see it. If we read with Reichian awareness, we will recognize a common problem. Reich concluded that the perceptual gap between the armored and the unarmored is a constantly recurring obstacle in human relations (and in natural science). The armored person fails to credit the energy shifts that are basic in emotional life; to do so would be to credit these shifts in one's own body, and that can be extremely threatening. What the armored reader perceives is not energy *movement* — Catherine's distress — but a sequence of events that fits into a conceptual *structure*: is Catherine in earnest, or is she playacting? Reich finally saw no way out of this dilemma except through new child-rearing patterns that honor the reality of the body's energy from the start. No, Catherine "couldn't explain to Edgar" what she felt in her body. That may be one reason she tries to get the highly armored Nelly to speak for her: Nelly speaks Edgar's body language.

This does not mean that the reader should use Reichian ideas to dismiss the indications that Catherine is indeed wishing, if not willing, her illness in some way. Part of the experience implied in these difficult, intense scenes is to go through the conflicting cognitive sets that suggest both deep organic disturbance that is beyond control, and consciously sought illness. It should be noted, however, that each of Catherine's threats to damage herself have different contexts and qualities. When she first speaks of breaking her own heart in order to break the heart of the two men, she follows the statement by labeling it as "a deed to be reserved for a forlorn hope," and certainly not one to put into action when, as she recognizes, Edgar has not yet "provoked her" to extremity (p. 101). Once Edgar does so provoke her, she soon rushes to her room and fails to accept food for nearly three days. The quality of her feelings during those days, described at some length and in some of the most memorable prose of the novel, consisted of feeling genuinely distraught and disturbed. It involved a process of recovering, and having a large access of feeling into, memories of her earlier life at Wuthering Heights.

It is unwise to conclude that she is basically determined to starve herself, based on this hunger strike and the one mention to Nelly that she will "starve at once" (or "leave the country"), as soon as she learns how Edgar "feels." She does not act on either of these alternatives. Her claims to be "dying" have grounds other than willful self-destruction. The two months of illness that follow, called a "brain fever," are not voluntary on her part. Her death itself occurs while pregnant, and while in the fragile condition that follows her deep illness. It also occurs in the specific context of a final confrontation with Heathcliff. Catherine's last words spoken, or rather shrieked, in the novel, are once more about her death, but this time there is no suggestion of willfulness: "Heathcliff, I shall die! I shall die!" (p. 136). The matter of life or death is now beyond her control.

Catherine's illness, partial recovery, and death, form a complicated sequence of great vividness. The underlying need, however, is clear enough: she needed so badly to get back in touch with the deep feelings that had gone underground in her after her earlier traumatic separation from Heathcliff, that she took illness as the pathway to make this contact. The "brain fever" is an organic and unplanned result of an effort to open herself most vulnerably to these vital feelings; it is the only way she can overcome her own armoring. In fact, from a Reichian perspective, we must say that Catherine has become considerably armored by the time Heathcliff returns from his years away from her, and that he, too, is subject to armoring. Catherine's body could not have escaped the consequences of her decision to marry Edgar. Heathcliff's separation from her would have threatened his own existence so much that he survived only by practicing, and later willfully fixing himself upon, the hatred he had learned in his time of being abused and brutalized as a child. Had he not been capable of such extreme armoring, the "unspeakable sadness" of Catherine's loss would have killed him. At Catherine's grave, he is distraught until he is able to feel that she is alive in the body, at which point he reports in a notably Reichian language that "a sudden sense of relief flowed from my heart through every limb" (p. 230). Apparently, however, he was unable to feel that closeness during most of the long years after her death until his own demise.

At the point of Heathcliff's return from his wanderings, when he finds that Catherine has married Edgar, he is, as Nelly remarks, "altered!", and her immediate guess that he might have been in the military suggests a body that has become rather rigid (p. 82). Emily Brontë gives much attention to the state of Heathcliff's body, in fact. She suggests an inordinate capacity for holding stock-still, as in Nelly's discovery that he has been standing outside so fixedly and long that birds building their nest fly right next to him, as if he were a tree (p. 138). Even as a child, he had taught himself not to express pain when he had no way of keeping himself from being hurt by his "betters" in the household. Hit in the chest by an iron weight thrown by Hindley, Heathcliff "staggered up . . . breathless and white," and when Hindley knocked him down again, Nelly says she was surprised "to witness how cooly the child gathered himself up and went on with his intention . . . and then sitting down on a bundle of hay to overcome the qualm which the violent blow occasioned . . ." (p. 41). Unlike Catherine, Heathcliff has known how to armor himself, even though he did not need or want to do so when he was with her. When he comes back into her life as an adult, however, he is much less able or willing to allow his feelings their spontaneity.

70

Reichian Criticism

A Reichian interpretation of the adult development of the two major characters might be that they each have not only lost direct contact with each other, but that they have lost much of their ability to experience the flow of energy and the openness toward feelings that they once had together on the moors. Catherine's first plan, to install Heathcliff as a household friend who would bring back her happiness, represents a magical hope that she could restore this contact without confronting the adult sexuality that is now central to their bodily life. That plan fails, largely because Heathcliff spitefully takes his adult sexuality and uses it to make a marriage with Isabella, Edgar's sister. He does this after a suggestion from Catherine herself.

I cannot avoid the implication that Catherine's perverse suggestion is a consequence of her refusal to face her own sexual feelings. As Reich hypothesized, perverse sexual fantasies are a function of disturbances of adult sexual life. There could hardly be a more perverse fantasy than Catherine's linkage of Heathcliff, whom she knows is interested only in her, to the one woman in the world who will make Edgar cancel the agreement to have Heathcliff in the house. In effect, Catherine is admitting that her plan of having herself, Heathcliff, and Edgar all live together in harmony is not really gratifying. Without her suggestion, Heathcliff would have taken no notice of Isabella.

Catherine's illness, a problematic mixture of the willful and the involuntary, is finally not merely a magical hope for the restoration of her vital connections with Heathcliff and the moor. No doubt one strand of her motivation was to try to force the two men to bring about a magical compromise solution to the adult dilemma that all three were in. But throughout the scenes of illness, we are being shown that it is Catherine who is giving the most. From a Reichian perspective, the deeper reason for her getting sick is to allow her conscious plan and all other armoring to lapse, in the intuitive hope that she would be able to get back to her natural self. Only by opening herself, by dissolving her armor, could she hope to have a real change.

But there is a risk in any self-dissolution so total. Tremendous energy has to be expended to release the blockage. There also should be a context of care within which to undertake such a release. Such a context involves an intuitive understanding of what is happening on the part of those who care. I am suggesting, in other words, that in her own way Catherine is attempting to do therapy, body therapy, on herself. And to a great extent, she succeeds: she analyzes her situation better

71

than she had ever been able to do previously. But she is unable to come
back out of the illness.

She recounts to Nelly that she "recovered sufficiently to see and
hear," after the initial near break into madness, and what "kept recurring and recurring" in her thought after that was a vision of herself
enclosed in the "great oak-panelled bed at home." The bodily energy
dimensions of her memory are notable:

> my heart ached with some great grief, which, just waking, I
> could not recollect. I pondered, and worried myself to dis-
> cover what it could be; and, most strangely, the whole last
> seven years of my life drew a blank! I did not recall that they
> had been at all. I was a child; my father had just died, and
> my misery arose from the separation that Hindley had
> ordered between Heathcliff and me. I was laid alone for the
> first time, and rousing from a dismal doze after a night of
> weeping . . . then memory burst in — my late anguish was
> swallowed in a paroxysm of despair. (p. 107)

These words of Catherine indicate that her discovery is indeed a sur-
prise to herself. The years since separation from Heathcliff had been
emotionally "a blank," an energy stoppage in mind and in body. The
memory that "burst in" could come only from a deeper layer of her experience. It could be aroused only by the prolonged assault on her own
armor that she has made in the form of weakening herself through not
eating, then in recognizing the ache in her heart and accepting her need
to understand it — and by crying all night. Further, the discovery of
how much of her life has been lost makes her previous "anguish" mild
by comparison; she is convulsed in "a paroxysm of despair," by which I
understand that she actually moved in a convulsive manner. At any
rate, she did not just think these things in her head.

Her analysis continues at this point to find clearly that had she been
allowed to stay at the Heights and continue her early life, and not been
cast out "from what had been my world," she would still have been
whole. Significantly she defines her wholeness as being outside of
society's character structure demands:

> Oh, I'm burning! I wish I were out of doors — I wish I were
> a girl again, half savage, and hardy, and free; and laughing
> at injuries, not maddening under them! Why am I so

changed? Why does my blood rush into a hell of tumult at a few words? I'm sure I should be myself were I once among the heather on those hills. (p. 107)

The connection between insight and bodily energy also is continued in this part of Catherine's declaration. Her "burning" leads to the wish to be outside, and the "hell of tumult" that she feels now in her blood — which would have been rushing through her body, moving differently after her seven years of stagnation — is a feeling that resembles the discoveries of many patients in Reichian therapy who are astonished and often terrified at the strength of the feelings that are released when the armor is suddenly felt to be gone.

If we allow that Catherine and Heathcliff have both become what they did not want to become, namely armored man and woman, and that in Catherine's body there has even been organic damage done by her separation, and that they both have implacable memories of what it was like not to be what they are as adults, then we will avoid several common misreadings such as regarding them as inhumanly strong, or taking Cathy as a pure rebel who dies because she has said that she would. It also disposes of the simplistic suggestion that if they had been truly interested in each other, they would simply have run off together. They cannot run off with the heath (although they might sneak away as conventional "lovers"), nor can they just ignore what they have become in their own bodily life and just "get together."

We will also avoid the mystification of regarding their love as somehow too good for this earth. Catherine analyzes quite well the conditions that led to her misery, during her self-therapy. The key event was her enforced separation from Heathcliff, with whom she had been playing and sleeping at about age twelve; this analysis[27] complements the one I have drawn of their traumatic break, when Heathcliff departs and a great storm occurs. Reich maintained that it was absurd to claim that real human happiness cannot be attained in principle. People are going to continue to need happiness and to seek it, and if what it takes to have it is unimpeded sexual expression as a child and as an adult, based on self-regulation rather than society's imposition of its norms, then we can make the social changes necessary to make this fulfillment possible.

What Reich called "The Sexual Revolution" has begun those very changes. Specifically, it would be well within human capability to leave Heathcliff and Catherine together at age twelve. It is possible also to take adult sexuality out of the realm of property relations. Catherine, after all, was caught in the midst of a struggle for property that required her to marry properly — and that means that Heathcliff would have to be gotten rid of. I do not mean to suggest that it would be easy to make such changes. As Reich well knew, they would ultimately require vast changes in social structure. Making that evident, however, is one of the strengths of the Reichian perspective. For almost any other approach, talking about changing the ways of child-rearing and allowing for the self-regulation of sexuality by adolescents would be brazen didacticism, but from a Reichian approach these longings are as integral to the aesthetic experience as anything can be.

In the final meeting with Heathcliff perhaps the major contribution of a Reichian approach is to validate the sense of the human body in that scene. The human body in non-Reichian terms is identified largely with its stable appearance, its *body image*; but such stability may mask the natural, relatively mild pulsation of breathing (which we tend to overlook), or, in other instances, it may connote the armored self. (One of my favorite administrators always sits rigidly at the conference table where decisions are made, and turns his head to and fro in a mechanical, lighthouse-beam fashion, while talking: a mockery of natural movement). The Reichian sense of the body as continual energy movement, with the capacity for major shifts of energy, implies quite another body. In 1933 Reich treated a man whose armoring took the form of being literally stiff-necked. It was an unusually difficult resistance to overcome, and when it finally was, there came three days of alarming bodily oscillations: "The color of his face kept changing," Reich reports, "from white to yellow or blue: the skin was mottled and of various tints; he had severe pains in the neck and the occiput, the heartbeat was rapid; he had diarrhea, felt worn out, and seemed to have lost hold. I was disturbed. True, I had often seen similar symptoms, but never that violent."[28]

Prior to my own awareness of Reichian theory, I tended to glide over, or to tacitly dismiss as melodramatic prose, such descriptions as Catherine's "Why does my blood rush into a tumult of hell at a few words?" In her final illness, her meeting with Heathcliff makes her once more totally sensitive and responsive in her own body: "every movement" Heathcliff makes, as she gazes at him, "woke a new sentiment in her" (p. 134). Soon the emotional action reaches frightening dimensions. The reader might ask whether he is capable of empathy with Heathcliff, whose eyes "burned with anguish" (p. 132), and if the description of Catherine's heartbeat, visible and audible all the way across the room to Nelly, is feasible: "the violent, unequal throbbing of her heart . . . beat visibly and audibly under this excess of agitation" (p. 133).

Most literary criticism of the scene concentrates solely on what the characters say to each other. But if we follow the energy shifts of the live bodies, that emphasis bears correction, and the whole scene will be felt differently. At Heathcliff's entrance, there are no words; he and Catherine embrace "for some five minutes . . ." Then, when they begin their last quarrel, Catherine not only holds Heathcliff forcibly by his hair, she gives vent to a longing to be united with him unto death: "I wish I could hold you . . . till we were both dead!" As the scene goes on, Catherine almost has this wish come true: Heathcliff takes her in another embrace, one "from which I thought my mistress," Nelly says, "would never be released alive" (p. 134).

Heathcliff's greatest failure to understand Catherine is in this scene. He knows at once that she is about to die, and not only insists on discussing the responsibility for her death with her, but he lays this entirely upon her, for giving in to "the poor fancy you felt for Linton" (p. 135). For a reader of the novel who knows something of Catherine's illness, the death she is threatened with is not directly a result of her earlier decision to marry Edgar. It has much more to do with her illness as a result of longing to return to herself, Heathcliff, and the moors. Heathcliff's energy is split in two different directions in this scene; in Reichian terms he oscillates between responding from the "core" of unarmored energy within him and from the "periphery" in which he is quite armored. Heathcliff even comes close to duplicating the armored vision of Edgar by accusing Cathy of dying on purpose, calling her a murderer of herself. In an entirely other mode, he does not say much at all, he just feels anguish and holds Catherine. Catherine's armor is really gone, but I want to suggest that something is happening to his armor as well: it is failing him. He is reacting, at times, from a level so deep that it can only be called the "core," in Reichian terms.

Nelly, who goes so far as to wish Catherine dead at the very height of this scene, can only recall the vivid bodily details by straining her narrative capacity. As she sees it, Heathcliff, holding Catherine in one of the scene's major embraces, "gnashed at me"; he "foamed like a mad dog, and gathered her to him with greedy jealousy" (p. 134). Could there have been saliva dripping from Heathcliff's mouth? Possibly so, and if so, it is one of the details that might make the "true romance" reader give up. Let us hope so! From a Reichian perspective, we are still dealing here with Nelly's memory of something she cannot allow herself to understand, namely the emotional life in direct expression between man and woman. To her, it can look only like the action of a mad dog. But if we read around Nelly as well as through her, we can feel this description as a way of registering Heathcliff's loss of armored self-control, and his giving in to the grief, rage, and despair he has been feeling deep within his body for years. When he is approached by Nelly at just the time that he is most vulnerable, his energy in an interweave with Catherine's and not under his own domination, of couse he wants to keep Nelly away: she does not belong in their world.

The taunts hurled in this scene between Catherine and Heathcliff seem to have a connection with his feeling of breaking down and trying to resist the dissolution of his armor; Catherine sees that his agony over her fatal condition is exactly what is causing Heathcliff's distress, and reacts in such a way as to make him feel the agony and thus to break down all the way, so that finally he is wide open, unarmored, in their last embrace. Just after Heathcliff's entrance into this scene, Ellen "plainly saw that he could hardly bear, for downright agony, to look her in the face!" A moment later, however, Heathcliff stares at her "so earnestly that I thought the very intensity of his gaze would bring tears to his eyes; but they burned with anguish, they did not melt." A Reichian might comment that this is exactly what happens to eyes when tears are held back so deliberately: the eyes "burned with anguish."

Catherine at this juncture leans back, and, "returning his look with a suddenly clouded brow," begins to berate him unmercifully. It is as if she senses that Heathcliff *ought* to weep. His plea for her to not "torture" him any further is followed by a savage accusation of his own, driving her to a dangerous "paroxysm" of bodily response. She then becomes tender and begs him to get close to her again: "Won't you come here again? Do!" (p. 133). Heathcliff comes near, but will "not let her see his face, which was livid with emotion." When Catherine changes position in order to see his face, "he would not permit it," and walks away again. This she will not tolerate: "in accents of grave disappointment," she lashes out again at him, verbally, ending the speech specifically with "I *wonder* he won't be near me." A direct appeal, "Do come to me, Heathcliff," makes him look "absolutely desperate."

Heathcliff senses that if he does come near her, he will feel all her pain and his own. "His eyes wide, and wet at last, flashed fiercely on her; his breast heaved convulsively." In another instant their embrace is restored, apparently spontaneously: "How they met I hardly saw . . ." (Soon Nelly is seeing him as a mad dog.) Even then, while "covering her with frantic caresses," Heathcliff still is split: he accuses her of cruelty to him. After a time, however, both are silent in their embrace, and both are crying (p. 135). Nelly, who has herself noted that Heathcliff had already wept earlier in the scene, can still not quite report straightforwardly that Heathcliff's tears exist, but even she admits that they probably do.

Earlier in the chapter, before all the words were spoken, there was a sound to be heard: "The full mellow flow of the beck in the valley . . ." (p. 131). Nelly remarks that later in the summer this sound would be inaudible; it would be "drowned" in the "murmur of the summer foliage." On this day there are no murmurs. The "beck," a dialect term that denotes a swiftly running stream with steep banks, seems appropriate for the clear stream of feeling, finally, between Catherine and Heathcliff. Once again, individual energy, the energy of the couple, and that of nature, are all of a piece.

Understood in the way I have been suggesting, the scene's violent accusations take on a different function than they do in conventional thought. Too many readers and critics have allowed themselves to pull back from the scene, appalled that two people would fight verbally when one of them is plainly about to die. When someone you love is going to die, you are "supposed" to be all-forgiving, all-supportive, in awe, and give them a loving send-off. For Catherine and Heathcliff such peace is not to be faked. They fight over their resentments because they feel them, in order to actively dissolve the energy blockages and thus come together in actuality. The result is a death scene possibly unique in literature, where *both* parties release anger and arrive at a bodily expression of love.

The accusations Heathcliff and Catherine exchange in this last meeting are complex in their own right; they are well worth the attention that readers have given them. It has been futile, however, through the years of *Wuthering Heights* criticism, to have analyzed these verbal exchanges in isolation from the body interaction. It is also possible that the bodily action in the scene finally has more to "say" than do the spoken words. In the bodily action, the lovers are not bent on contending with each other, but on holding each other, and on doing so without the intervening armor of civilized character structure to impede their contact. Much has been written on what it is that Heathcliff and Catherine really want; here in their last meeting they are unforgettably showing what they want, through their body language. Somehow, they are trying to get together, body to body: the energy movement of a man and the energy movement of woman, meeting. They want this as the center of their lives. But to want that meeting implies a great deal more about how life would have to be led and how society would have to be changed. The body dynamics of the scene show that it is not easy for them to accept this desire. The fact that they finally do is all the more impressive.

The advantage of a Reichian approach is that it provides a way to consider both the powerful alliance of the two lovers, and the intimations of a radically different social existence that seem to be implied. Such intimations underlie the action to the very end of the scene; the couple finally having got into their silent embrace, after great struggle, are at once forced to break it. The husband — for whom Catherine has made it clear she has no further connection — enters the room, and Heathcliff, in order to assure that Catherine receives emergency medical care, places her bodily into Linton's arms. The "rights" of the husband are exposed here as irrelevant and impertinent. Surely all this has been felt by many readers without benefit of a Reichian reading, but at least such a reading leads toward, rather than away from, the major center of energy in the novel, Catherine and Heathcliff.[29]

I do not wish to suggest that Catherine and Heathcliff are alone in the novel, nor that I have discussed them fully. My goal has not been to provide a complete interpretation, nor to suggest that if we bring enough Reich to the novel all problems will disappear. But a Reichian approach can open up new, central interpretations, and it can sensitize us to qualities having to do with the human body and its energy patterns. If we are willing to try to allow the interpretations and the sensitivity to work, we must go back and read the book, experiencing it anew. That is the real test of a Reichian approach, as it is of any other.

Approaching Literature
Through the Social Psychology
of Erich Fromm

by Frederik L. Rusch

In a 1961 overview of utopian literature, Erich Fromm, discussing "negative utopias," posed a key question that he believed had philosophical, anthropological, psychological, and maybe religious implications: "Can human nature be changed in such a way that man will forget his longing for freedom, for dignity, for integrity, for love — that is to say, can man forget that he is human?"[1] The eclecticism suggested in this question is typical of the thinking of Erich Fromm. He was curious about all aspects of human experience, and his writing, which went far beyond a strict psychoanalytical approach, demonstrated this. These broad interests led anthropologist Margaret Mead to say of Fromm's *Escape from Freedom* that "it bridges the gap between economics and psychology and shows how no theory which invokes only man's way of earning a living or man's human nature alone is sufficient."[2] Mead was correct. With influence from social historians like Marx and Tawney, Fromm's emphasis in psychoanalysis tended to be more sociological than biological. He chose to see "psychic forces as a process of constant interaction between man's needs and the social and historical reality in which he participates." Furthermore, he wrote, "I believe that Marxism needs such a psychological theory and that psychoanalysis needs to incorporate genuine Marxist theory. Such a synthesis will fertilize both fields."[3] For these reasons, Fromm is often considered a neo-Freudian or "social-psychologist."[4]

Fromm's sociological bent led him to diagnose society rather than the individual. As a boy of fourteen, living in Germany, he was impressed with the anti-British hysteria of the German people at the beginning of World War I, and he wondered what caused such a mass pathology. This early fascination with the irrationality of social behavior moved him later, when he was practicing orthodox Freudian analysis, to question psychoanalytical theory and look for other clues to human behavior.[5] However, Fromm did not wish to be called a neo-Freudian because he felt that the label too closely linked him with the work of Karen Horney and Harry Stack Sullivan. He thought that he was closer to Freud than were Horney and Sullivan. He said that in his work he wanted "to translate Freud into philosophical and sociological categories which seem to me to correspond more with recent philosophical and sociological thought patterns."[6]

Nevertheless, despite his feeling of closeness to Freud, Fromm did disagree with some of Freud's ideas. His major departure from Freud was his belief that it is an oversimplification to see man's problems only in whether or not his instinctual drives and needs are satisfied. In *Escape from Freedom*, he wrote, "Although there are certain needs, such as hunger, thirst, sex, which are common to man, those drives which make the *differences* in men's characters, like love and hatred, the lust for power and the yearning for submission, the enjoyment of sensuous pleasure and the fear of it, are all products of the social process. . . . Society has not only a suppressing function — although it has that too — but it has also a creative function. Man's nature, his passions, and anxieties are a cultural product. . . ."[7] Social forces are stronger than biological forces in determining human behavior. Consequently, for instance, in discussing the Oedipus complex, Fromm emphasizes the social aspects of parental pressure rather than the sexual attachments that Freud emphasized (*Freedom*, 200–201).

Toward the end of *Escape from Freedom*, Fromm summarizes his differences with Freud quite succinctly: In the first place,

> we look upon nature as essentially historically conditioned, although we do not minimize the significance of biological factors and do not believe that the question can be put correctly in terms of cultural *versus* biological factors. In the second place, Freud's essential principle is to look upon man as an entity, a closed system, endowed by nature with

certain physiologically conditioned drives, and to interpret the development of his character as a reaction to satisfactions and frustrations of these drives; whereas, in our opinion, the fundamental approach to human personality is the understanding of man's relation to the world, to others, to nature, and to himself. We believe that man is primarily a social being, and not, as Freud assumes, primarily self-sufficient and only secondarily in need of others in order to satisfy his instinctual needs. (pp. 317-18)

However, while Fromm saw society as a definite influence on the individual, he strongly rejected the concepts of what he calls the "environmentalist," whose "view of the social sciences is essentially relativistic; according to it, man is a blank sheet of paper on which the culture writes its text. He is molded by his society for better or worse. . . ." On the contrary, Fromm believed "that man has an immanent goal, that man's biological constitution is the source of norms for living. He has the possibility for full development and growth, *provided the external conditions that are given are conducive to this aim.*"[8] It is with this view that Fromm saw himself allied with Karl Marx and socialism: "Marx proposed a concept of 'human nature in general' as distinct from 'human nature as modified in each historical epoch.' . . . For him certain social conditions, such as capitalism, produce a 'crippled' man. Socialism, as he conceived it, will be conducive to the full self-realization of man" (*Destructiveness*, 259n).

The essence of Fromm's thought can be summarized as follows: Man does have needs, or instincts, but, unlike animals, it is man's culture that allows these needs to be satisfied. Man is extremely undeveloped at birth, and thus the culture into which he is born teaches him a great deal. Furthermore, cultures vary greatly throughout the world. The way that a human being relates to his culture will determine his behavior, and the way an individual relates to his outside world is not constantly the same. Thus, it is an oversimplification to say that the problems of human behavior lie only in the necessities of biological needs. Since man is acutely aware that he is separate from nature — made up of more than the sum of his biological needs and their satisfactions — he must turn to his society for meaning. "Even if all his physiological needs were satisfied, he would experience his state of aloneness and individuation as a prison from which he had to break out in order to retain his sanity. . . . The necessity to unite with other living beings, to be related to them, is an imperative need on which the fulfillment of man's sanity depends."[9] To return to the question posed by Fromm at the outset of this paper: an effective — or sane — society will provide an environment in which the needs of freedom, dignity, integrity, and love will be fulfilled. Indeed, these needs can be realized only through society. However, if these needs are not satisfied in the majority of its inhabitants, the society is deemed sick, or pathological.[10]

Perhaps because of his broad concerns about human behavior, Fromm often cited works of philosophy, poetry, and fiction as illustrious of his psychological/sociological theories. An example of his interest in a wide area of literature is a book he edited with Ramón Xirau, *The Nature of Man*. This book contains seventy-two selections, ranging from excerpts from the Upanishads through Rousseau, Emerson, Sartre, and David Riesman, the purpose of which is to make the reader "sensitive to the problem of the nature of man, to give him food for his own thought."[11] Fromm saw reading as "a conversation between the author and the reader"; a good novel can be read "with inner participation, productively. . . ."[12] It is with this spirit that we approach literature in terms of the ideas and analyses of Erich Fromm.

In looking at fiction, drama, and poetry from the Frommian point of view, the critic understands literature to be social portrayal as well as character portrayal or personal statement. Society and character are inextricably joined. The Frommian approach opens up the study of literary work, giving a social context to its characters, which suggests why those characters behave as they do. The Frommian approach recognizes human beings for what they are — basically gregarious individuals who are interdependent upon each other, in need of each other, and thus, to a certain degree, products of their social environments, although those environments may be inimical to their mental well-being. That is, as stated earlier, the individual's needs and drives have a social component and are not purely biological. The Frommian approach to literature assumes that a writer is — at least by implication — analyzing society and its setting as well as character.

No claims are made for the universality of such an approach to literature. As a psychologist, the society that Fromm was most keenly interested in was his own, Twentieth-century Western. Because of this, a Frommian approach to literature may be best applied to work of the twentieth century in the West. For this reason, the works of T. S. Eliot, F. Scott Fitzgerald, and Arthur Miller have been chosen here.

In T. S. Eliot's "The Love Song of J. Alfred Prufrock," Prufrock is talking to himself, expressing a fantasy or daydream. In his monologue, Prufrock, as noted by Grover Smith, "is addressing, as if looking into a mirror, his whole public personality."[13] Throughout the poem, Prufrock is extremely self-conscious, believing that the people in his imaginary drawing room will examine him as a specimen insect, "sprawling on a pin, / . . . pinned and wriggling on the wall. . . ."[14] Of course, self-consciousness — being conscious of one's self — is not necessarily neurotic. Indeed, it is part of being a human being. It is only when self-consciousness, which has always led man to feel a separation from nature, becomes obsessive that we have a problem. Prufrock is certainly obsessed with his self-consciousness, convinced that everyone notices his balding head, his clothes (his prudent frocks), his thin arms and legs (p. 4).

On one level, however, Prufrock is merely expressing the pain that all human beings must feel. Although his problem is extreme, he is quite representative of the human race:

> Self-awareness, reason, and imagination have disrupted the "harmony" that characterizes animal existence. Their emergence has made man into an anomaly, the freak of the universe. He is part of nature, subject to her physical laws and unable to change them, yet he transcends nature. He is set apart while being a part; he is homeless, yet chained to the home he shares with all creatures. . . . Being aware of himself, he realizes his powerlessness and the limitations of his existence. He is never free from the dichotomy of his existence: he cannot rid himself of his mind, even if he would want to; he cannot rid himself of his body as long as he is alive — and his body makes him want to be alive. (*Destructiveness*, 225)

This is the predicament of the human being. His self-awareness has made him feel separate from nature. This causes pain and sorrow. What, then, is the solution to the predicament? Fromm believed that mankind filled the void of alienation from nature with the creation of a culture, a society: "Man's existential, and hence unavoidable disequilibrium can be relatively stable when he has found, with the support of his culture, a more or less adequate way of coping with his existential problems" (*Destructiveness*, 225). But, unfortunately for Prufrock, his culture and society do not allow him to overcome his existential

predicament. The fact is, he is bored by his modern, urban society.
In image after image, Prufrock's mind projects boredom:

> For I have known them all already, known them all: —
> Have known the evenings, mornings, afternoons,
> I have measured out my life with coffee spoons. . . .
>
> . . . .
>
> And I have known the eyes already, known them all —. . .
> Then how should I begin
> To spit out all the butt-ends of my days and ways?
>
> . . . .
>
> And I have known the arms already, known them
> all —. . . .   (p. 5)

Prufrock is completely unstimulated by his social environment, to the
point of near death. The evening in which he proposes to himself to
make a social visit is "etherised upon a table" (p. 3). The fog, as a cat,
falls asleep; it is "tired . . . or it malingers, / Stretched on the floor . . ."
(pp. 5, 6).

Prufrock, living in a city of "half-deserted streets, / . . . one-night
cheap hotels / And sawdust restaurants with oyster-shells" (p. 3), gets
no comfort, no nurturing from his environment. He is, in the words of
Erich Fromm, a "modern mass man . . . isolated and lonely" (*Destructiveness*, 107). He lives in a destructive environment. Instead of providing communion with fellow human beings, it alienates him through
boredom. Such boredom leads to "a state of chronic depression" that
can cause the pathology of "insufficient inner productivity" in the individual (*Destructiveness*, 243). Such a lack of productivity is voiced by
Prufrock when he confesses that he is neither Hamlet nor John the Bap-
tist (pp. 7, 6).

An interesting tension in "The Love Song of J. Alfred Prufrock" is
caused by the reader's knowledge that Prufrock understands his own
predicament quite well.[15] Although he calls himself a fool (p. 7), he has
wisdom about himself and his predicament. This, however, only reinforces his depression and frustration. In his daydream, he is able to
reveal truths about himself that, while they lead to self-understanding,
apparently cannot alleviate his problems in his waking life. The poem
suggests no positive movement out of the predicament. Prufrock is like
a patient cited by Fromm, who under hypnosis envisioned "a black bar-

ren place with many masks," and when asked what the vision meant said "that everything was dull, dull, dull; that the masks represent the different roles he takes to fool people into thinking he is feeling well" (*Destructiveness*, 246). Likewise, Prufrock understands that "There will be time, there will be time / To prepare a face to meet the faces that you meet . . ." (p. 4). But despite his understanding of the nature of his existence, he cannot attain a more productive life.

It was Fromm's belief that with boredom "the decisive conditions are to be found in the overall environmental situation. . . . It is highly probable that even cases of severe depression-boredom would be less frequent and less intense . . . in a society where a mood of hope and love of life predominated. But in recent decades the opposite is increasingly the case, and thus a fertile soil for the development of individual depressive states is provided" (*Destructiveness*, 251). There is no "mood of hope and love of life" in Prufrock's society. Prufrock is a lonely man, as lonely as "the lonely men in shirt-sleeves, leaning out of windows" (p. 5) of his fantasy. His only solution is to return to the animal state that his race was in before evolving into human beings.

Animals are one with nature, not alienated from their environments. They *are* nature, unselfconscious. Prufrock would return to a preconscious existence in the extreme: "I should have been a pair of ragged claws / Scuttling across the floors of silent seas" (p. 5). Claws *without a head* surely would not be alienated, bored, or depressed. They would seek and would need no psychological nurturing from their environment. And in the end Prufrock's fantasy of becoming claws is definitely more positive for him than his life as a human being. He completes his monologue with depressing irony, to say the least: it is with human voices waking us, bringing us back to human society, that we drown (p. 7).

In *Escape from Freedom*, Fromm sees the rise of Protestantism and the growth of capitalism in the West as two great forces leading to a grave social malady. Protestantism's emphasis on the individual was reinforced by the growth of capitalism, which allowed a new economic freedom and social mobility. However, in freeing the individual from dependence on the Catholic Church, Protestantism destroyed the comfort and communion offered by the Catholic structure. According to Fromm, "freedom *from* the traditional bonds of medieval society, though giving the individual a new feeling of independence, at the same time made him feel alone and isolated, filled him with doubt and anxiety, and drove him into new submission and into a compulsive and irrational activity" (*Freedom*, 123).

F. Scott Fitzgerald also tells of the burden of freedom, in *The Crack-Up*, when he describes himself "as a little boy left alone in a big house, who knew that now he could do anything he wanted to do, but found that there was nothing that he wanted to do."[16] But Fromm and Fitzgerald are describing a peculiar twentieth-century dilemma: a newfound freedom leads not to happiness, but to the insecurity of a lonely, noncommunal, nonsupportive, but highly competitive existence. The pursuit of happiness leads to unhappiness. Or, as Erich Fromm sees it,

> what Protestantism had started to do in freeing man spiritually, capitalism continued to do mentally, socially, and politically. . . . The individual was no longer bound by a fixed social system, based on tradition and with a comparatively small margin for personal advancement beyond the traditional limits. He was allowed and expected to succeed in personal economic gains as far as his diligence, intelligence, courage, thrift, or luck would lead him. His was the chance of success, his was the risk to lose and be one of those killed or wounded in the fierce economic battle in which one fought against everybody else. (*Freedom*, 126–27)

The independence and competition of capitalism cause a situation in which "economic activity, success, material gains, become ends in themselves" (*Freedom*, 130). Objects and wealth have become more important than people, who are seen as competitors to be beaten or destroyed, and "the concrete relationship of one individual to another has lost its direct and human character and has assumed a spirit of manipulation and instrumentality. In all social and personal relations the laws of the market are the rule" (*Freedom*, 138–39). Goods and products have become the supreme things in life. One's competitor is not a flesh-and-blood human being, but only a hindrance to personal success. This glorification of objects leads to "necrophilous" people who "love mechanical gadgets more than living beings." Furthermore, the necrophilous person, while not loving life, glories in a dead past.[17]

Fromm's concept of the necrophilous person provides us with insight into the characters and society of F. Scott Fitzgerald's *The Great Gatsby*. In this novel, Tom and Daisy Buchanan and Jay Gatsby are portrayed as the products of the most successful capitalist system in history: they are the end of the American Dream. They are products of a sick society.[18] Tom Buchanan is the clearest example of a necrophilous personality in the novel. Fromm describes the necrophilous person as one who is overly sentimental about the past, and a lover of force, control, and order — order that is antilife because it counteracts the spontaneity and disorder of thriving life and nature (*Heart of Man*, 40-41). Nick Carraway, the narrator of *The Great Gatsby*, is constantly pointing out necrophilous characteristics in Tom's personality and behavior. Nick sees Tom as "one of those men who reach such an acute limited excellence at twenty-one that everything afterward savors of anticlimax."[19] Tom is dead because he is looking for the dead past; he is "forever seeking, a little wistfully, for the dramatic turbulence of some irrecoverable football game" (p. 6). That Tom is yearning for a football game is also significant: football is a game of brute force and control. Tom is a man who must always be in control, and he sometimes gains that control through violence.

Fromm uses Adolf Hitler as the prototype of the necrophilous person, and although Tom is not quite Hitler, given political and military power he might be a Hitler.[20] Nick describes him as a sort of storm trooper with a body of "enormous power . . . [in] glistening boots" (p. 7). Nick imagines Tom as the type of man who suggests to others that he is "stronger and more of a man" than anybody else (p. 7). Fromm says that necrophilous people "approach life mechanically, as if all living persons were things," because they have been brought up in the marketplace, which values good and profits above people (*Heart of Man*, 41). In fact, Tom usually treats people as if they were things. For instance, at one point Fitzgerald shows him compelling Nick "from the room as though he were moving a checker to another square" (p. 12). Later, Tom literally forces Nick from a car (p. 24). Tom is constantly acting the brute, completely disregarding the life and freedom of other human beings. Typical of his behavior is the scene in Myrtle Wilson's apartment where Tom suddenly terminates his argument with Myrtle, his mistress, by breaking Myrtle's nose with "a short deft movement" (p. 37). Appropriately, Fitzgerald's description of this violent act suggests the precision of a very efficient machine.

Tom's mania for order is also expressed in his ideas about science and civilization. Life threatens him. He sees civilization as disintegrating because the colored races are becoming more powerful than the white, and he sees himself as the last hope for control over the colored hoards before the world is overcome by chaos. He has read books on the subject of the colored threat, and he emphasizes that the books are very scientific. The books have everything worked out, and so "it's up to us, who are the dominant race, to watch out or these other races will have control of things" (p. 13). Science, then, is just another means of control to Tom, because, in Fromm's words, the necrophilous person "is interested in people as objects, in their common properties, in the statistical rules of mass behavior, not in living individuals" (*Heart of Man*, 57). Tom's is a science without a heart. Fromm called such science a "deterioration of reason" because it is reason used not for understanding but for manipulating. This science is merely mechanical, not creative.[21]

Fromm suggests that the necrophilous person's love of things mechanical is dramatically illustrated in modern man's worship of speed and the automobile: "Consider the indifference to life which is manifested in our rate of automobile accidents. . . . The affinity between the necrophilous contempt for life and the admiration for speed and all that is mechanical has become apparent only in the last decades" (*Heart of Man*, 59). Similarly, in his notebooks, Fitzgerald wrote of the absurd compulsion for speed:

> "I'm in a hurry."
> "I'm in a hurry — I'm in a hurry."
> "What are you in a hurry about?"
> "I can't explain — I'm in a hurry." (*Crack-Up*, 99)

Further on, he simply notes: "Three hundred a day die in auto accidents in the U.S.A." (p. 99). Man in a car becomes part of a destructive machine; he is no longer human. In the short story "The Ice Palace," Fitzgerald shows Clark Darrow driving his car, "sitting bolt upright at the wheel [wearing] a pained, strained expression as though he considered himself a spare part, and rather likely to break."[22] Man becomes a part of, or slave to, the violence of the machine.

In Fitzgerald, the automobile is a grotesque and fascinating symbol of death — the modern death in the modern society. In his notebooks Fitzgerald wrote: "The Sport Roadster: When I was a boy I dreamed that I sat always at the wheel of a magnificent Stutz — in those days the Stutz was the stamp of the romantic life — a Stutz as low as a snake and as red as an Indiana barn." In the same notation, Fitzgerald wrote that once in his youth he sat in the family car "with that sort of half-sneer on my face which I had noted was peculiar to drivers of racing cars" (*Crack-Up*, 226). Further on in his notebooks, we find this isolated scene: "They had been run into by a school bus, which lay, burning from the mouth, half on its side against a tall bank of the road, with little girls screaming as they stumbled out the back" (*Crack-Up*, 229). The bus is pictured as a dragon with fire coming from its mouth, and again death and the motor vehicle are joined.

Fitzgerald's final entry in this section of the notebooks is: "Hearing Hitler's speech while going down Sunset Boulevard in a car" (p. 229). This is a telling string of images: from automobiles, to death, to California, to Hitler, we see the progression of necrophilous existence. Fitzgerald sensed what Fromm saw as a prominent trait in many people of our modern society. According to Fromm, "the highly necrophilous person can often be clearly recognized by his appearance and his gestures. He is cold, his skin looks dead, and often he has an expression on his face as though he were smelling a bad odor. (This expression could be clearly seen in Hitler's face)" (*Heart of Man*, 42). Similarly, Fitzgerald puts an unpleasant expression on his face while he sits in a car in his youth; much later, as an adult, he thinks of Hitler while driving in the ersatz world of Southern California.

It is, of course, Gatsby's car that kills Myrtle Wilson while Daisy is driving, and Gatsby's description of Daisy as she hits Myrtle suggests that Daisy is indeed completely in the power of the machine she is driving: "I tried to make her stop, but she couldn't, so I pulled on the emergency brake. Then she fell over into my lap and I drove on" (p. 145). Furthermore, Nick's hyperbolic description of Gatsby's car pictures a machine mighty, dazzling, and terrifying: "It was a cream color, bright with nickel, swollen here and there in its monstrous length with triumphant hat-boxes and supper-boxes and tool-boxes, and terraced with a labyrinth of wind-shields that mirrored a dozen suns" (p. 64). Gatsby's car is swollen as if diseased, is monstrous and somehow supernatural, multiplying the mighty sun twelvefold.

The violent death of Myrtle Wilson is the most striking scene in *The Great Gatsby*. It occurs on an unbelievably hot day soon after the hopelessness of Gatsby's love for Daisy has been revealed in the plush setting of the Plaza Hotel in New York City. From the hotel, we travel at great speed to the valley of ashes and George Wilson's barren garage.

Fitzgerald has created a perfect image of a sick society. The comfort and elegance of the Plaza Hotel cannot bring love. Indeed, the society that produces the Plaza is a wasteland not fit for human existence. It is the valley of ashes, "a fantastic farm where ashes grow like wheat into ridges and hills and grotesque gardens; where ashes take the forms of houses and chimneys and rising smoke and finally, with a transcendent effort, of men who move dimly and already crumbling through the powdery air" (p. 23). This surrealistic picture presents a symbolic image of a dead environment no more nurturing than Prufrock's city. Here wheat, the universal symbol of wholesome food and growth, is ashes, and men in ironic transcendence are crumbling.

Here, also, George Wilson cries to God, but stares into the empty eyes of Doctor T. J. Eckleburg. These eyes "look out of no face, but, instead, from a pair of enormous yellow spectacles which pass over a nonexistent nose. Evidently some wild wag of an oculist set them there to fatten his practice in the borough of Queens, and then sank down himself into eternal blindness" (p. 23). It is to this empty image, created to make money, that George Wilson looks for solace after his wife has been killed by Daisy's reckless speed as she is driving Gatsby's fantastic car. There is no nurturing here. There is only Myrtle Wilson's left breast "swinging loose like a flap, and . . . no need to listen for the heart beneath. The mouth was wide open and ripped at the corners, as though she had choked a little in giving up the tremendous vitality she had stored so long" (p. 138). In imagery suggestive of Picasso's *Guernica*, but predating it by more than a decade, Fitzgerald paints a striking picture of a destroyed and destroying society.

Gatsby's car has torn off Myrtle's breast and stopped her heart, and Tom and Daisy are simply an extension of the brute, nonhuman automobile; their reaction to Myrtle's death is completely without feeling. They, themselves, have become machines because "they were careless people . . . — they smashed up things and creatures and then retreated back into their money or their vast carelessness, or whatever it was that kept them together, and let other people clean up the mess they made" (pp. 180–81). Machines have no consciences.

However, although her personality is clearly necrophilous, perhaps Daisy is less of an automaton than Tom. Voicing her necrophilous feelings directly, she seems to be more conscious of her problem than Tom is. She sees no value to life. Finding herself in a big house with nothing to do, she cannot bear the burden of freedom. Her wealth has allowed her to go everywhere and do everything, but she sees all of it as terrible and desperately hopeless: " 'What'll we do with ourselves this afternoon?' cried Daisy, 'and the day after that, and the next thirty years?' " (p. 118). Tomorrow, and tomorrow, and tomorrow creeps in this petty pace from day to day. As bored with her society as Prufrock, it is only the superstructure of her wealth that gives Daisy the appearance of being alive. On meeting Nick at the beginning of the novel, she says, "I'm p-paralyzed with happiness" (p. 9). In truth, she is not happy, but she *is* paralyzed. She is paralyzed emotionally, paralyzed with boredom. Daisy's oxymoronic declaration of happy paralysis is evidence of her necrophilous personality. Fromm suggests that expressions such as "it kills me," "thrilled to death," and "dying to" are characteristic of a civilization that gets pleasure and excitement from death (*Heart of Man*, 59).

The character of the hero of *The Great Gatsby* is more complex than either Daisy's or Tom's. In one sense, Gatsby is the victim of Tom and Daisy's necrophilous behavior, the victim of the "foul dust [that] floated in the wake of his dreams" (p. 2). And, while Tom the storm trooper wields power, and Daisy finds little to live for, Gatsby loves, and is motivated by love. But it is the nature of his love that causes problems.

In *The Art of Loving*, Erich Fromm discusses the developing patterns of love and marriage in the twentieth century. He notes that traditionally in the West marriages were arranged by the parents of the betrothed, and so the object of love was not as important (since the partners had little choice of mates) as the function of love. But "in the last few generations the concept of romantic love has become almost universal in the Western world" so that the loved person is idealized, and the act of loving is de-emphasized.[23] With the shift in emphasis away from the *function* of loving to the *object* loved, our contemporary consumer mentality — the mentality of the marketplace — becomes an important factor in love because love is thought of as something that can be purchased. "Two persons thus fall in love when they feel they have found the best object available on the market, considering the limitations of their own exchange values" (*Loving*, 3).

This is Gatsby's problem: he has created in his mind Daisy as an object of love. He then sets out to buy Daisy by becoming wealthier than Tom Buchanan. Everything he does is to that end. His identity is realized only in terms of his love for Daisy. Fromm calls this kind of situation "a form of pseudo-love . . . often experienced (and more often described in moving pictures and novels) as the 'great love' [or] *idolatrous love*. If a person has not reached the level where he has a sense of identity, or I-ness, rooted in the productive unfolding of his own powers, he tends to 'idolize' the loved person" (*Loving*, 83). Creative and true love cannot exist without a real sense of identity. *"Love is union with somebody, or something, outside of oneself, under the condition of retaining the separateness and integrity of one's own self. . . .* The experience of love does away with the necessity of illusions" (*Sane Society*, 37).

But Gatsby's very illusions have created his love object. He has created his Daisy. It is significant that Fitzgerald describes Gatsby's illusions of Daisy in terms of a flower: flowers are beautiful but unsubstantial. Fitzgerald's description of Gatsby's first kiss with Daisy suggests the delicate fantasy: "Then he kissed her. At his lips' touch she blossomed for him like a flower and the incarnation was complete" (p. 112). Gatsby bases his whole adult life on this flower of fantasy, a fantasy sprung from only one month of active love (p. 150).

Loving a fantasy is not really loving, and the incapacity for love is often related to adult narcissism (*Sane Society*, 40). It is not hard to see Gatsby as a narcissist. After all, anybody who "sprang from his Platonic conception of himself" (p. 99) must, almost by definition, be narcissistic. Fromm wrote that "for the narcissistically involved person, there is only one reality, that of his own thought processes, feelings and needs. The world outside is not experienced or perceived *objectively*, i.e., as existing in its own terms, conditions and needs" (*Sane Society*, 40).

In *The Heart of Man*, Fromm describes "a narcissistic man who falls in love with a woman who does not respond. The narcissistic person will be prone not to believe that the woman does not love him. He will reason: 'It is impossible that she does not love me when I love her so much'" (p. 68). This is an accurate description of Gatsby. In the crucial Plaza Hotel scene, Gatsby just cannot understand why Daisy will not throw off Tom completely and say that she loves, and has always loved, only him. Gatsby can see Daisy only in terms of himself, only in terms of his created fantasy of Daisy the flower. He cannot see Daisy as a separate individual who has a life separate from his own. Gatsby demands that Daisy declare she has never loved Tom, and Daisy replies:

"Oh, you want too much! . . . I love you now — isn't that enough? I can't help what's past." She began to sob helplessly. "I did love him [Tom] once — but I loved you too."
Gatsby's eyes opened and closed.
"You love me *too*?" he repeated.
"Even that's a lie," said Tom savagely. "She didn't know you were alive. Why — there're things between Daisy and me that you'll never know, things that neither of us can ever forget."
The words seemed to bite physically into Gatsby. (p. 133)

The words bite physically into Gatsby because they destroy his fantasy, and by destroying his fantasy, they destroy his life, his Platonic conception of himself: he "had broken up like glass against Tom's hard malice, and the long secret extravaganza was played out" (p. 148).

And so it is inevitable that Gatsby die. He is, in fact, spiritually dead before George Wilson, who mistakes Gatsby for the killer of his wife, shoots him. And, as Nick Carraway suggests, Gatsby probably realizes he is as good as dead after he is rejected by Daisy. On the day after the plaza Hotel scene and the killing of Myrtle Wilson, Gatsby waits for a never-to-materialize telephone call from Daisy, and Nick speculates "that Gatsby himself didn't believe it would come, and perhaps he no longer cared. If that was true he must have felt that he had lost the old warm world, paid a high price for living too long with a single dream" (p. 162). And so Gatsby goes for a swim in his pool, and the gardener tells him that the autumn leaves will soon start falling (p. 153). Death is in the air. While swimming, Gatsby is shot by George Wilson. Gatsby's real world was never warm, never nurturing, only obsessed with things and his fantasy love for Daisy. When the fantasy is shattered, he has little reason to live.

Of course, Gatsby, like Tom and Daisy, is tainted with death. He suffers from the necrophilous tendency of living in the past. His lost football game is his month of love with Daisy, long ago. He actually wants to stop time and move back to the past. When Nick tells him that he cannot repeat the past, Gatsby unrealistically replies, "Why of course you can!" (p. 111).

With two instances, Fitzgerald skillfully emphasizes the ideal of freezing time. On first entering the Buchanan house, Nick describes a guest, Jordan Baker, as "extended full length at her end of the divan, completely motionless, and with her chin raised a little, as if she were balancing something on it which was quite likely to fall" (p. 8). Jordan is seen statically, as a statue, isolated from the inevitable movement of time. Later, at one of Gatsby's parties, where Nick describes a movie director and his star actress, time is stopped: "They were still under the white-plum tree and their faces were touching except for a pale, thin ray of moonlight between. It occurred to me that he had been very slowly bending toward her all evening to attain this proximity" (p. 108). All evening, this couple at Gatsby's party are frozen in a static pose suggestive of Gatsby's kiss of Daisy, five years before, now frozen in Gatsby's mind. And that the couple at his party are movie people reemphasizes the fabrication that is Gatsby's life.

Earlier Fitzgerald uses a clock to suggest Gatsby's attempt to stop time. When he meets Daisy after the five-year separation, Gatsby knocks a "defunct" clock off the mantelpiece. A defunct clock is a clock that has stopped. A defunct life is a life that has stopped. Gatsby does not let the defunct clock fall. He catches it and sets it back on the mantelpiece (p. 87). The symbolic action is obvious. But time cannot be caught. Life is dynamic.

For Gatsby, Daisy, like time, is an object to be caught, or purchased. Fromm wrote: "When love is experienced in the mode of having it implies confining, imprisoning, or controlling the object one 'loves.' It is strangling, deadening, suffocating, killing, not life-giving."[24] With his wish to return to the past in his love for Daisy, Gatsby is denying that life is dynamic, always changing. He is denying life, itself. "Living structures can be only if they become; they can exist only if they change."[25] Gatsby's inability to change causes his spiritual death. He is fooled by the seeming permanence of the material goods that his great wealth allows him to purchase with ease. He is fooled by a society that constantly tells him that the purchase of objects will bring him fulfillment. Such a promise is as empty as the eyes of T.J. Eckleburg.

In turning to Arthur Miller's *Death of a Salesman*, we focus on a character whose role in a capitalist society is just as important as Gatsby's: while Gatsby is the consumer, Willy Loman, the hero of the play, is the pusher, so to speak. In Frommian terms, Willy exhibits a character that is clearly a product of a "marketing orientation." The marketing orientation is a phenomenon of the modern age. According to Fromm, in past ages marketing had a social aspect. At small, local markets, people would come together to barter their goods and meet with other people. Most producers knew their customers and their customer's needs. The whole process of exchange was quite personal and congenial. However,

> the modern market is no longer a meeting place but a mechanism characterized by abstract and impersonal demand. One produces for this market, not for a known circle of customers; its verdict is based on laws of supply and demand; and it determines whether the commodity can be sold and at what price. No matter what the *use value* of a pair of shoes may be, for instance, if the supply is greater than the demand, some shoes will be sentenced to economic death; they might as well not have been produced at all. The market day is the "day of judgment" as far as the *exchange value* of commodities is concerned.[26]

It is this "day of judgment" that Willy Loman must face every day as he climbs into his old car and attempts to peddle his stockings to various stores in New England. Willy's sense of his own value is derived almost entirely from his success or lack of success as a salesman. Willy himself is not much more than a mere commodity to be sold. Of this transference of marketable value from the product to the person, Fromm writes, "The market concept of value, the emphasis on exchange value rather than on use value, has led to a similar concept of value with regard to people and particularly to oneself. The character orientation which is rooted in the experience of oneself as a commodity and of one's value as exchange value I call the marketing orientation" (*Man for Himself*, 76).

Willy as a salesman is, of course, an excellent example of the marketing character orientation. However, the marketing orientation is quiet pervasive in modern society, and it is not just salesmen who fall victim to it: "In our time the marketing orientation has been growing rapidly, together with the development of a new market that is a phenomenon of the past decades—the 'personality market.' Clerks and salesmen, business executives and doctors, lawyers and artists all appear on this market. . . . All are dependent for their material success on a personal acceptance by those who need their services or who employ them" (*Man for Himself*, 76). For Willy, to be well liked is paramount.

95

For him, it is only logical to expect someday to have a business bigger than Uncle Charley's, "because Charley is not — liked. He's liked, but he's not — well liked."[27] Similarly, Willy is convinced that his older son, Biff, will be a success because "he's got spirit, personality" (p. 40).

But it is all show, all sham. Willy is living in a fantasy created by the hype of the new American marketplace. He says that he is vital to the New England market, but his boss wants to fire him. He is so convinced that his worth depends on how much he sells that he falsifies his sales figures to his wife, Linda. Indicative of how he and Linda value the fantasy of the marketplace hype more than reality is Linda's reason for buying a particular make of refrigerator: the manufacturer has "the biggest ads of any of them!" (p. 36). The reality is that the fan belt is broken on the brand new machine. Like some modern-day Polonious, Willy spews forth two-penny wisdom to his family: the United States is "the greatest country in the world" (p. 16); "Chevrolet . . . is the greatest car ever built" (p. 34); "start big and you'll end big" (p. 64).

Much of the time Willy sounds like a recording machine that has been fed mindless clichés by some patriotic corporate executive. Consequently, he is often inconsistent in his advice. For instance, when Biff is planning to see Bill Oliver, a man Biff had once briefly worked for, to ask for financial help in getting started in business, Willy, the experienced salesman, tells Biff how to conduct himself in the interview: "Walk in very serious. You are not applying for a boy's job. Money is to pass. Be quiet, fine, and serious. Everybody likes a kidder, but nobody lends him money" (p. 64). However, only seconds later, Willy contradicts himself with this bit of wisdom: "Walk in with a big laugh. Don't look worried. Start off with a couple of your good stories to lighten things up. It's not what you say, it's how you say it — because personality always wins the day" (p. 65).

Personality wins the day: "Success depends largely on how well a person sells himself on the market, how well he gets his personality across, how nice a 'package' he is; whether he is 'cheerful,' 'sound,' 'aggressive,' 'reliable,' 'ambitious'; furthermore what his family background is, what clubs he belongs to, and whether he knows the right people" (*Man for Himself*, 77). But in reality neither Willy nor Biff knows the right people. Bill Oliver does not even remember Biff, and on the same day that Biff sees Oliver, Willy is fired because he is not selling enough. His boss, Howard, tells Willy, "It's a business, kid, and everybody's gotta pull his own weight" (p. 80). It is business as usual, and Willy is out of his job. It is judgment day. Willy protests to Howard: "I put thirty-four years into this firm. . . . You can't eat the orange and throw the peel away — man is not a piece of fruit!" (p. 82). But Willy is wrong. Howard is unconcerned and unmoved. In this final interview with Willy, he pays more attention to his new wire recorder, the latest thing in gadgetry, than to Willy. Howard, exhibiting necrophilous characteristics, is more interested in a machine than a human being.

The irony is that Willy has always packaged himself as a commodity, but, of course, when he is treated like a useless commodity — one no longer in demand — he suffers as a human being. While caught up in the marketing orientation, Willy can more or less convince himself that he is a success. But this leads him to confuse himself with the stockings he is selling. "Since success depends largely on how one sells one's personality, one experiences oneself as a commodity or rather simultaneously as the seller *and* the commodity to be sold" (*Man for Himself*, 78). This may be fine when one is selling well, but when one is not successful, the bottom falls out of one's life. Without success on the road as a salesman, Willy has no support for his life.

To the very end, Willy sees himself as a commodity. His final sale is his life: he kills himself so that his family can collect on his insurance policy. It is a fitting end to a character almost solely determined by the marketing orientation. With the act of suicide, Willy proves, for once, his success as a salesman.

However, although he is dominated by the marketing orientation, Willy Loman is more than a salesman. Despite his brainwashing from the competition of the marketplace, Willy is also struggling to be a father and a husband, with needs beyond just being well liked. In fact, by placing Willy in a family, Miller has provided the essential dimension to his play that will allow his audience to empathize with Willy and be moved by his tragedy.

As noted earlier in this chapter, Fromm views the Oedipus myth as illustrative not of sexual needs, but of social needs within the family. Fromm emphasizes that his approach is different from Freud's, "one in which not sexual desires but one of the fundamental aspects of interpersonal relationships, the attitude toward authority, is held to be the central theme of the myth."[28] Furthermore, in the complete Oedipus cycle of Sophocles, "the myth can be understood as a symbol not of the incestuous love between mother and son but of the rebellion of the son against the authority of the father in the patriarchal family; that the marriage of Oedipus and Jocasta is only a secondary element, only one of the symbols of the victory of the son, who takes his father's place and with it all his privileges" (*Forgotten Language*, 202).

In his interpretation of the Oedipus cycle, Fromm, typically, places the family in the larger context of society as a whole. Drawing upon J. J. Bachofen's analysis of Greek mythology, Fromm describes history as the movement away from an original matriarchal society to the emergence of a new patriarchal society in which the male dominates both within the family and within the society. However, "the figure of Oedipus was always connected with the cult of the earth-goddesses, the representatives of matriarchal religion" (*Forgotten Language*, 211). Thus, Oedipus and his daughter Antigone represent the older, matriarchal society while Creon represents the newer, patriarchal society. The matriarchal principle embodies "love, unity, and peace."[29] The patriarchal society embodies the power of "the state, man-made laws, and obedience to them" (*Forgotten Language*, 213). Fromm sees Sophocles' trilogy "as an attack against the victorious patriarchal order by the representatives of the defeated matriarchal system" (*Forgotten Language*, 210).

Using the Frommian interpretation of the Oedipus myth, we view Willy as a character of split allegiances, similar to many tragic figures in literature. On one hand, Willy represents the patriarchal order. He often lashes out at his family in an authoritarian manner. He thinks he has complete control over his two sons, at times completely ignoring his wife as a member of the family. Of course, his profession is representative of the new, patriarchal order, which, in modern history, grew stronger with the Protestant Reformation and capitalism (*Forgotten Language*, 229n). On the other hand, Willy represents the older, matriarchal order, in his desperate desire for love and unity in his family. At the end of the play, like King Lear, when Willy realizes that Biff, who he thought hated him, has always loved him, Willy is overwhelmed by love, exclaiming, "Always loved me. Isn't that a remarkable thing?" (p. 135). Furthermore, the pull of the matriarchal element in Willy is clearly symbolized by his desire to grow a garden in his backyard. The nurturing aspect of matriarchy is traditionally symbolized in growing things, and Willy, finding himself boxed in by the huge apartment buildings of an industrial society — a patriarchal society — would counteract that presence with a garden. But, because of the tall buildings, there is no longer enough sun for his vegetables.[30]

It is Biff, however, who more completely represents the matriarchal society. He rebels against the pressures of his father's marketing character and the industrial Northeast by roaming the West, his mind filled with vague ideas of having a ranch. And, although Biff seems an ineffectual and impotent character when up against the forces of the patriarchal order, it is he who finally confronts Willy with the truth that the family is not the go-getter, successful, well-liked family of Willy's marketing fantasies. He says of his father, "He had the wrong dreams. All, all wrong" (p. 138). And, although Willy cannot really overcome his destructive patriarchal role, making his final sale through suicide, Biff at least has come to a better understanding of the family's predicament and of himself. At the end of the play, Happy, Biff's younger brother, who is obsessed with his macho role of woman chaser, sounds like the patriarchal side of his father: "I'm not licked that easily. I'm staying right in this city, and I'm gonna beat this racket! *He looks at Biff, his chin set.* The Loman Brothers!" But Biff answers, "I know who I am, kid" (p. 138). Free at last from Willy's marketing claptrap, Biff knows who he is. Earlier, he has said that his father "never knew who he was" (p. 138), suggesting the matriarchal-patriarchal split in Willy. But Biff has learned from his experiences and the death of his father. Somewhere he will grow a garden.

Willy is both victim and purveyor of an insane society while Biff is finally the voice of a sane society. But Prufrock drowns when he hears human voices. Nobody comes to either Jay Gatsby's or Willy Loman's funeral. All three characters, Prufrock, Gatsby, and Willy Loman, have fantasy existences. Society and culture no longer nurture these people and provide for their needs. Without such nurturing, humankind is not fulfilled.

Jacques Lacan, Literary Theory, and *The Maids* of Jean Genet

---

by Ellie Ragland-Sullivan

M y explication of the French psychoanalyst Jacques Lacan (1901–81) will attempt to bring into clearer focus some of his major concepts: his mirror-stage in its relation to narcissism and aggressiveness; the division of the human subject into conscious and unconscious parts; the other (maternal and societal language and Desire) as the source of identity; the Oedipal structure as the cornerstone of one's social personality, as well as of both neurosis and psychosis; the structural-linguistic and symbolic nature of the unconscious, which makes of human beings representational animals. Finally, I shall add some ideas as to Lacan's potential value for literary studies, along with some applications of Lacanian theory to specific texts.

In the beginning of his career Lacan was particularly influenced by phenomenology. His dissertation explored the "human significance" of psychosis and attributed the paranoid psychoses to phenomena of personality and to a dialectical movement of the psyche, as against deterministic genetic and environmental factors. If it were not for his special attention to psychotic language and to narcissism here, one could read this 1932 text as a prefiguration of R. D. Laing's existential-phenomenological psychoanalysis. By 1936, however, Lacan had enunciated his basic concept of the mirror-stage, which he came to describe in 1949 as formative of the function of the 'I'. A heightened understanding of the process of mimesis by animal ethologists pushed Lacan to extend the concepts set out in Freud's articles — "On Narcissism: An Introduction" and "On Mourning and Melancholia" — of 1914 and 1916 respectively.

The human animal is born prematurely by comparison with other animals, without motor control or any inherent means of processing the world it perceives. Its helplessness and lack of a fixed center place a gap or void (*béance* or *fente*) at the center of being. In the first six months of life — the pre-specular period — this perceptual gap between perceived images and bodily sensations is gradually filled in by symbols of the outside world. The most important of these are constituted for the "instincts" themselves and serve as part-objects of Desire or primary symbols. These images or fragments—the breast/sucking, excrement, the urinary flow, the gaze (*regard*), the voice or phonemic chain, the nothing — are prototypes or matrices of imagistic meaning, as well as of a primordial bank of representational knowledge. During this period infants merge with elemental images, actually *becoming* them in fantasy. Lacan denoted this merging phenomenon by Frege's mathematical #0.

Between six and eighteen months of age — the mirror-stage proper — an infant comes to perceive the (m)Other as an extension of itself in the same way that its own limbs and organs are. By identifying with its own body image as a unity in a mirror, and the (m)Other as metaphorical mirror, an infant passes cognitively from #0 to #1. During this period the effects of the (m)Other's language (*parole*), in conjunction with visual *perceptum*, leave traces of meaning within perception, meaning that is repressed once the infant begins to speak. The result is that the elemental sense of any "self" is taken on from an-Other's discourse and Desire. Both perception and identity are from that time on set in a dialectical line of fiction and alienation.

The evolution through pre-mirror, mirror-stage, and post-mirror stage processes of identification is accompanied by the growth of Desire. The first objects of Desire are perceived as fragments, but in the mirror-stage these are linked libidinally to the (m)Other, whose recognition ensures an infant of its own continuity. Lacanian Desire, correlated with libido and "drive," is thus the fundamental desire for the recognition that preserves unity. Lacan placed Desire in a Hegelian line of a lack or absence that seeks to overcome itself. Desire, both *of* the Other and *for* recognition from the Other, remains as the unconscious force behind human striving and motivation. Essentially, Desire derives from the "impulse" to refind the primordial (m)Other, or at least the illusion of a psychic unity or wholeness that characterized mirror-stage *jouissance*. In adult life Desire is put into motion within human interactions (others substitute for the original Other), and is "observable" as well in the other objects people choose for fulfillment (*objet a*). We can see that Lacan has dispensed with Freud's biomechanistic instincts, and similarly with his evolutionary instinctual stages (oral, anal, genital) that are supposed to govern psychic maturation. Instead, Lacan attributed human drive to the alleged split he hypothesized as occurring between the "natural" subject of identificatory fusion, and the post-mirror stage cultural subject of speech.

The effects of the images and sounds that engrave symbolic meanings on the first layers of perception make biology a second cause in the structuring of personality. Lacan's deconstruction of ego psychology with its instinctual base returns control of the human psyche to the unconscious, and replaces the id by an "intelligent" unconscious subject with its own logic, language, and intentionality. Lacan called this subject the *moi* and located it in dreams, narcissism and aggressiveness, identification dialectics, and in all that is disruptive and mysterious in the supposed unity of the conscious subject. Whereas Freud's largely autonomous ego was contiguous with the perception-consciousness system, Lacan equated perception with the unconscious, the visual, and the verbal. Moreover, Lacan subverted the ego of classical psychology by making the *moi* the subject of perception, identity, and intentionality. Lacan thereby greatly limited the scope and powers of consciousness (which he called a *scotoma*), as well as those of the conscious subject. But it would be incorrect to see the Lacanian (after Freud) split (*Spaltung*) in the subject as a clear split between consciousness and the unconscious. The *moi* imposes itself in consciousness, but is unaware of its own manner of construction and its roots in an objectlike relationship to a repressed Other.

Lacan called the speaking subject the *je*. Initially formed as a means of mastering separation from the (m)Other, the *je* comes to represent the *moi* and to deny it as well. When an eighteen-month-old infant begins to use language coherently, s/he has the capacity to perceive self/other boundaries because s/he can name them. Thus, when the father (or mother's brother or any other third term, such as the group in certain societies) is seen to intervene in the infant/(m)Other symbiosis by bidding for the (m)Other's recognition (*regard*), the infant associates this unwelcome reality with prohibition, compromise, and separation. The beginnings of law are to be found in this psychic moment of the infant's passing cognitively from Frege's #1 to #2. It takes three entities to teach the infant that the two of the (m)Other/infant dyad were not one. Lacan described the pain of this division as Castration, and its agent as the Phallus. The Phallus stands for various symbolic equivalents such as the first "pure" signifier, a set of information, a metaphor, but does not refer to the penis.

The *effect* of this drama on the infant's perception is that of taboo, which is generally internalized in the Law of the Name-of-the-father. But it is not the biological father who is at issue here. Certain tribes do not even associate copulation and fatherhood. Instead, it is the principle opposite to the (m)Other that is involved. Societally speaking, patriarchy has always embodied public prestige, and exists on the obverse of the personal, private value of women. The simultaneous entry of speech and separation into the infant's paradise of symbiotic unity imposes a second division within the subject. Divided first between the *moi* and the Other, the subject is now additionally divided between the Other and the *je*, between the "natural" and the cultural.

In Lacan's epistemology the Oedipal structure is the result of an inherently meaningless drama of birth and development, whose impact, nonetheless, gives rise to the arbitrary gender myths that underlie cultural institutions. Paradoxically, the Oedipal "no" both gives rise to secondary repression (*Unterdrückung*) — repression of the (m)Other's discourse and Desire — and permits the growth of psychic freedom. Within Lacan's purview, a psychotic is a person who has never assimilated the Law of prohibition, and thus can lose the "self" (*moi*) concept that tenuously keeps him or her separate from the Other. The phallic signifier stands at the juncture between the *moi* and the *je*, and can be equated with the Lacanian superego, thereby pushing Freud's Oedipal stage backward by about three years. The subsequent answer to Oedipus's identity question — his "Who am I?" — is to be sought by answering Lacan's rephrased: "What am I here in my parents' discourse?".

The structural scaffoldings by which Lacan described normalcy, neurosis, and psychosis can be traced to mirror-stage and Oedipal effects in the first five years of life. All three structures involve a balance (or imbalance) among the Imaginary (identifications), the Symbolic (language and cultural codes), and the Real (things and experiences). Personality itself is a Symptom (the fourth order Lacan added in 1975) of the correlation among the other orders. Although neurosis and psychosis can be studied "structurally" in light of formalized "laws," the particular messages and Desires that compose them are unique, and known only to a given individual. Generally speaking, however, neurosis involves difficulty in counting — Lacanian mathematics borrowed from Frege — to three; that is, difficulty in accepting the arbitrary gender dicta imposed upon one by a specific (m)Other, family, and culture. Psychosis, on the other hand, is seen as the condition of never having accepted the Law of the Name-of-the-father, a process Lacan called foreclosure (*Verwerfung*).

This metaphorical law works triadically like language to break up the illusory symbiosis (Frege's #1) of the infant/(m)Other mirror-stage dyad. Thus, language not only inscribes traces and phonemic impressions (attached to images) in the first eighteen months of life, it also has the functional capacity to help an infant master separation — Castration — from its (m)Other. Words are at first attached to objects (as in Freud's account of the *Fort! Da!* game with the bobbin reel) and parallel the play of presence/absence required by the separation trauma. As words gradually take on abstract and symbolic value, they themselves serve as the "transitional objects" that give a child the tools by which to feel her/himself complete.

In his celebrated formula "The unconscious is structured *like* a language," Lacan, therefore, means several things. On one hand, the unconscious comes into existence only because individuals speak, and thereby repress — or defer — the experiential state of identificatory fusions that constitute preconsciousness. This primordial bank of representations, libidinally attached to sensual and narcissistic identification with the (m)Other, prohibits the future possibility of generating a metalanguage that is adequate to describe itself. The effects of language and images have structured perception from the start of life, giving rise to the subsequent ambiguity around words: are they images or signs? The imagistic language that "speaks" in dreams provides an answer to Freud's pregnant question: How can the unconscious think? It "thinks" by the verbal associations and assonances that attach themselves to imagistic networks of relational meaning.

More specifically, Lacan means that the unconscious is structured *like* a language insofar as the psychic laws of condensation and displacement work analogously to the principal laws of language, which Roman

Jakobson designated as metaphor and metonymy. Taking Freud's *Der Witz und seine Beziehung zum Unbewussten* as a manifesto for his language theory of the unconscious, Lacan's own discourse imitates *Witz* by circumventing the rules and norms of everyday discourse. Lacan never stopped trying to demonstrate that there is no human subject (generally called the ego) beyond speech, although there is speech (*parole*) beyond the subject, which presents itself to one who is analytically astute as a hieroglyphic to be deciphered in its dynamic connection to the repressed Other. Such decoding can be accomplished by interpreting psychic material in light of the functions of metaphor and metonymy. Metaphor creates meaning by substituting one element for another, or by combining two similar elements. The new creation "means," however, only in reference to something else. The matter of reference to something else brings us to metonymy as that which refers to an unstated (absent) idea or object. In Lacanian psychoanalysis, metaphor can be used to comb through language — the analysand's or the text's — to find substitutions and combinations that lead metonymically right back to the first six months of life. This primordial representational bank of meaning is ungraspable, however, unsayable. The more interesting point is that Lacan shows meaning itself as arising out of concrete experience, out of corporal effects, and in reference to a prematuration at birth that later links love, anxiety, knowledge, and truth.

If the mind is but the material of its language, then the relationship of truth and knowledge to language is no longer the philosophical one of static essences, or even of subjective components that one falsely assumes can be "put to one side." The Imaginary "self" text — in which images, words, and perception are wed — operates retroactively on consciousness to insert primary-process "logic" into supposedly objective, pure, rational, secondary language. Thus, the Imaginary brings the unconscious into language as repeated sounds, words, or unanticipated substitutions — fragments of an archaic "self" text — as well as an intentional pressure for recognition that conveys either narcissism or aggressiveness. In a Lacanian epistemology, therefore, language, a phenomenon Lacan denoted by using Saussure's term *parole*, always means more than it appears to "say." Thus, Lacan viewed the "act" of speaking as dynamic, referring in its implicit duality to the discourse of an-Other, which only substitutes for an intrasubjective discourse with one's own unconscious *dite maternelle*. The fact that humans form societies and speak with each other is not due merely to economic demands, biological bonding, or any other "necessity." Human beings project themselves because only in this way do they achieve a sense of themselves. The tragedy of the human condition, then, lies in the "fact" that the visible subject of intentionality, perception, volition, representation, and meaning is unconscious of its source in narcissistic fixations and the *Desire of an-Other*.

The *moi* is the source of individuality that plays in consciousness, although it does not generally reflect upon its own roots. Created narcissistically in the mirror-stage captivation by an-Other's messages and Desire, the *moi* is actually an object that only imagines itself to be a subject. Language offers the perfect means by which the *moi* can ignore its fictional, artificial, bric-a-brac nature, a situation Lacan called *méconnaissance*. The speaking subject — the *je* — becomes an agent of denial, a promoter of ideals of the ego over realities. By capitalizing upon the distinctions between "saying" and "being," Lacan built a new epistemology upon this familiar phenomenon. Lacan's *je* is separate from the *moi*, although they work in tandem. We begin to see that Lacan's theory complicates any standard picture of subject-object relations.

The "true" subject of being is the *moi*, which, paradoxically, is alien and fictional. Throughout life the *moi* is dialectically engaged in a discourse with its own Other — unconscious topology — in a multileveled effort to "know" the Other and to escape it. The *moi* tries, on one hand, to reaffirm mirror-stage *jouissance* or a sense of wholeness through seeking samenesses in identificatory relations. In this context the *moi* is the source of human grandiosity, rigidity, dogmatism, belief, and certainty, for its function is to paper over the structural insufficiency caused by prematuration, and which created a primordial gap between body and perception that Lacan named metaphorical "death." The speaking *je* emits the "empty word" of social clichés and conventional opinions. When the conscious speaking subject is led to see its own *moi* at a distance, the person has evolved a "full word." To take one's own *moi* as only one object among the many in one's relationships is a state that Lacan equated with relative "cure" or "symptom relief."

Lacan's familiar Schéma L depicts the dialectical quadrature of the human subject, and mocks the general idea that in discourse and relationship autonomous egos "relate" in a transparent fashion. Several things emerge from this diagram:

Jacques Lacan

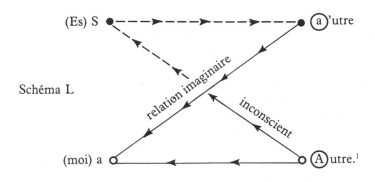

Schéma L

Below the bar of the je/Other interactions is the constantly evolving, dynamically retroactive tension between *moi* and Other, which, although unconscious, inserts its fixations and effects into conscious life. The *moi*'s narcissistic passion to validate ("know") itself is reflected circularly in *o*ther relationships. Since the Other is not knowable in any substantive or conscious sense of transparency, the *moi* dramatizes the "drive" toward an impossible fusion. The realities that mark the structure of human identity are narcissism, aggressiveness, guilt, paranoia, depression, alternating with momentary fulfillments and elations. While the *moi* brings the Imaginary order of homogeneous identificatory mergers into play, the link between *je* and Other is that of the Symbolic order that allows humans to formalize their Imaginary perceptions and lived (Real) experiences via substitutive language. Although the Imaginary always tries to subvert the Symbolic order of norms, the Symbolic gives structure and meaning to the Imaginary.

With this theory Lacan rejected the idea that there are substantive aspects to the unconscious. Gone are Jung's primordial archetypes, Freud's static thing representations divided off from language, Hegel's deep-well of memory, Piaget's sensorimotor, logical (genetic) structures. In place of ontology Lacan showed the unconscious to be a Desiring/lacking space in the here and now, made up of potential that would be activated — and thus realized — only within Real, and therefore variable, situations. Lacan's unconscious is only "observable" trans-subjectively, then: in unravelings of the *moi* that surface as anxiety, unexpected affect, repetitious themes, words, or sounds; in the universal phenomenon of transference that activates the unconscious meaning system; in the subjectivity that *is* reality for each individual.

The Lacanian picture of perception is circular. Man defines himself linguistically from within a subjective system of relations and references, which he, in turn, considers "natural," objective and true. Instead, Lacan showed the Imaginary as a residual meaning system born out of a conjunction of the Real and the Symbolic. In merry-go-round fashion the Symbolic tries to account for the Real and for the Imaginary by language (and many linguists equate the linguistic with the Real). The Real, in truth, can never be directly apprehended, and as such stands outside the Imaginary and Symbolic, although it is the "first cause" of each. The Real accounts for the never-ending quest to reduce that which *is* to something sayable or repeatable. Although any act of consciousness requires a coordination of these three orders, the most "visible" and accessible order is the linguistic Symbolic.

When language merely conveys information, Lacan called it *Langue* (borrowing Saussure's idea of the system of language). But when identity dialectics are engaged, Lacan saw *parole* (Saussure's idea of a personal use of language) as attaching itself to language. Here discourse itself is as "overdetermined" as dreams, slips of the pen, and so on. Reformulating Fernand de Saussure's concept of the linguistic sign in which the signified (concept) governs the use of the signifier (sound or form), Lacan erased the distinction between sound and concept. He showed sounds as building into words, and gradually into ideas. The separation to be made is, instead, between language and the unconscious. Thus, Lacan called the system of language itself a system of signifiers. With a signifying chain made up of a free-flow of meaning, Lacan replaced Freud's idea of a free-flow of energy.

But language does not equal the Real, because its effects, traces, and fictions create a repressed—unconscious—meaning system, which Lacan denoted as a system of signifieds. Structured by the plethora of signifiers of a person's unique history, as well as by those of cultural language and myth, signifieds — few in number — are nonetheless weak and elusive, although they give value and contextual meaning to the otherwise neutral words of language. Signifiers cross the bar between consciousness and the unconscious to become signifieds, and then return metaphorically transformed into consciousness. In mixing and overlapping, signifiers and signifieds render all discourse inherently lacunary and subjective. Occasionally, signifiers and signifieds meet in a fixed moment — an anchoring point — that just as rapidly disappears. The analyst listens for these moments, which reveal the effect of an Imaginary text upon the Symbolic one.

Jacques Lacan

How, finally, can Lacan's theories be of any value to literary criticism? Generally speaking, Lacan has problemized the relationship of humans to words so as to radically alter the connection between them. Man is the *matière* of language, the relationship of the *parole* resonating in him beyond anything conceived by a psychology of ideas. Going beyond Jakobson's binary oppostions, Chomsky's deep and surface structures, Saussure's linearity *(tout se tient)*, Derrida's endless deferments, Lacan has made language constitutive of reality, rather than a screen between mind and reality, or subordinate to reality. As long as there are gaps in the signifying chain, references to references, plural possibilities, ambiguities, there is an implicit metonymy in language — and no system or method will close, resolve, or deconstruct it. If there is no final separation between conscious and unconscious subjects, or between intellect and affect, or fantasy and reality, then no use of language is ultimately objectifiable. If the perceiving subject is made up of symbols and representations — both visual and acoustic — then unconscious effects will permeate the language of literature, the literary critic, and the author, as well as the reader.

Lacan's linking of being to speaking (meaning and "self") by the substitutive nature of metaphor, in conjunction with the referential-displacement character of metonymy (both being and meaning are grounded in an absent Other discourse), requires a rethinking of poetic language. The "laws" of poetry are certainly not those of linguistics — not even the "objective" ones proposed by Jakobson — but those of primary process in its representational link to secondary-process language. Literary genres would have to be rethought as well, in light of Lacan's depiction of the human subject as a multilinear constellation of images, words, structures, and effects. Fiction becomes the written form of *moi* experience, and in that sense it is both true and Real. Comedy and tragedy become specific treatments of the Real impact of Desire and Law on the human subject. Comedy denies the human pain that tragedy dramatizes, thus throwing into the arena of debate the question of what "drama" really is. A Lacanian literary theoretics would also lead to a reconsideration of memesis insofar as Lacan largely erased final distinctions between art and life.

A Lacanian theoretics of literary studies would also herald the death of formalist structuralism in the sense that structuralism divorces interpretation from the "I" of the author and of the reader, thereby aiming at closure and stopping up the holes that Lacan insisted on valorizing. Although Lacan has been called a structuralist, his structuralism is not that of linguists or semioticians who seek to "explain" literature as a variety of univocal codes, patterns, conventions, and performative maneuvers that create meaning. Lacan's thought points to the "more than language" within a literary text that gives it its force and compelling power over readers. The reason people use language at all — and read texts and interpret them or even write them—rests on an unconscious space in being, which makes its repressed presence felt both in language and Desire. Lacan's belief in the "openness" of language points to the proliferation of structuralist, semiotic, cognitive definitions of meaning as paradoxical proof against the closure they seek. Lacan's structuralism inheres, instead, in his move away from ontolgy and toward associations of signifiers and signifieds that join conscious and unconscious systems in disconnected, enigmatic networks of association and relation. Moreover, "meaning" itself is problematic because in Lacanian thought it can by equated with "truth" only in an unconscious system of meaning. All substantive concepts are merely efforts to cope through language, system, ideology, and myth with the elemental effects that created and divided the human subject during the first eighteen months of life.

Finally, Lacan's thought points toward a new theory of interpretation itself: the very act of using language is already an interpretation (a metaphorics). The Other is interpreted by author, reader, or critic. There is, then, no metalanguage that is privileged in reference to a literary text, nor any finally objective interpretation. Literature thus viewed would be a place where the potential of polysemous signifiers is stretched to the limit; where "key" words and character interactions are enigmatic, dynamic representations of aspects of an author's psyche. The very existence of literature is an invitation to interpretation, for any text lays bare the mysteriousness of the human subject (to) itself. A Lacanian theoretics of literary interpretation would not consider gaps and blanks within a text as passive, thereby giving tacit assent to their being hermeneutically ignored. Reading theoreticians with a phenomenological bias would be compelled to take the unconscious into account, for they would unwittingly be the recipients of its opaque messages and parasitical Desires. Reading theoreticians oriented toward cognitive theory or the psychology of perception would be required to rethink the dynamic role of language in the structure of the human subject. Lacan's view of the *moi* — a person's identity or individuality — as an enigmatic, but surface, linguistic phenomenon that uses language to disguise itself, and often is in conflict with its own alien Desires, could join psychology-of-perception theoreticians who see the reader as primary in making meaning (Holland, Bleich), to phenomenologically oriented critics (Iser, Ricoeur). The latter find reader response too variable and subjective to yield up any real insight into a text's meaning, and, consequently, look instead at how a text works. From a Lacanian viewpoint, subjective *moi* meaning is interpretable via signifieds and repetitions in relation to Other effects.

More than simply "applying" psychoanalytic concepts to literary texts, Lacan's thought unveils the existence of literature as itself problematic. Literary texts implicitly pose the question: To what does a text really refer? Critics have sought answers in all the substantive offerings of the ages — history, society, autobiography, language, identity, myth, and so on — without ever really explaining the power of literature, or the "drive" to read/interpret. In my estimation, Lacan's epistemology implicitly looks toward literature as the best proof of his own theory of a divided subject that seeks to "know" its diachronic unconscious "truth" by synchronically using language. Unconscious Desire is both a libidinal force and a substance. It "drives" people to write, read, and criticize, and at the same time is the hidden linguistic/imagistic source of meaning and perception. Therefore, a Lacanian perspective on a literary text must utilize his thought, but will not be a "psychoanalysis" of the text. Such analysis can occur only within a clinical setting where the medium of treatment and cure is spoken language. A critic must work with words frozen at one moment in the author's life, and reworked perhaps again and again. All the same, a Lacanian criticism is possible in light of the paradoxical theory that *any* use of language is itself a resistance to unconscious "truth," at the same time that a person uses language to seek that very "truth."

The point to be stressed is that unconscious "truth" appears in signifieds that elaborate Desire (the Other's lack) and Law (the impact of the Oedipal structure on being). But signifieds are not transparent or static. They do, however, play upon and in language, and are as enigmatic to the writer as to a critic or reader. The question of an author's intentionality does not come into play in any conscious or substantive way, then. But intentionality is itself comprehensible if viewed as an unconscious response to Castration (Oedipal structure). In this context, intention will always point to structural underpinnings that elaborate themselves around issues of power, freedom, necessity, and social prestige. In like manner, Desire will always play itself out in individual yearnings for love, recognition, fulfillment, and "self" wholeness.

An excellent literary example of a "drama" in which mirror-stage and Oedipal structures are themselves the "subject" of the play is *The Maids* (1947) by Jean Genet.[2] The secondary meaning in the play — the language used to describe feelings — merely elaborates a primary "drama" of effect and impact: the fusionary process of taking on identity, and the psychic pain that follows if the social order of conventions, language and laws does not intervene in the symbiosis between *moi* and the Other. The reading of *The Maids* that I offer is not, then, an attempt to psychoanalyse Genet himself, but a suggestion that any revelation of meaning from the Other — the author's or the reader's — will be at best an attitude toward love, sexual identity, and power. The myriad stories that proliferate from the essential unconscious structures of Desire and Law make up the history of fiction and drama. (Lyric poetry, in my estimation, harkens back to a pre-Castration nostalgia, while other types of poetry — epic not included — play with the interface among image, tone, rhythm, and sound in creating a meaning or evoking a mood.) But narrative parallels the *moi*'s effort to "write" its life story in a daily Imaginary confrontation with Real events, Symbolic order obstacles, and an alien, but internalized, Other's Desire. The *moi* must continually reconstitute itself in the Real, via its own reflection (recognition) in the eyes of others. Each piece of fiction one reads allegorizes this Real-life *moi* effort. Drama, on the other hand, is more consistently concerned with the implications of Desire and Law — on a cast of characters or a social context — than is narrative. While the two genres overlap in terms of plot, fiction, character, stylistic device, and so on, fictional narrative is more closely associated with *moi* narcissism, and drama more closely affiliated with Other effects.

My reading of Genet will be an intersubjective dialogue between the diachronic messages of his unconscious Desire dialectically engaged with his *moi* narcissism, and mediated in concrete language; and the same psychic structure behind my "listening to him." My written interpretation elevates me from the category of reader to that of "critic in print." Although Genet's interpretation of his Other, and my interpretation of his interpretation, are both written texts, the only similarity is one of Imaginary "truth-value." Both author and interpreter "make meaning" in terms of the "truths" in their own Others. They find an affinity with each other because the structural axes underlying "interpretation" are the major "stuff" of life experience for every person. The reason one interpretation differs from another—and the author's own interpretation of his text is at this level just another interpretation — resides in the specificity of the *moi*. The "key signifiers" in the Other may be the same for all people (regardless of age or culture) — birth, love, procreation, death — but Real experiences, Symbolic order conventions, and Imaginary interpretations of the Real and Symbolic ensure a uniqueness to the signifieds that cluster around any *moi*. Writing, reading, and interpreting, then, are kaleidoscopic experiences in which sameness and difference interact to produce a kind of *vertige*.

Genet's play seems a well-made object, a completed thing. But since it is made of language, readers can always open the seams to pour their own Imaginary interpretations of Desire and Law into an essentially inert system of language. Yet, interpreters are not writers — but merely voyeurs — because they lack the capacity to use language metaphorically; i.e., unconventionally. We read, then, not just to find patterns of unity — a mirror-stage effect — but to seek/deny the meaning of our own lives in the domain of literature, literature being the effect whose first cause is the speaking, thinking unconscious itself. Jean-Paul Sartre said that Jean Genet wrote plays because he *did not know* the answers to the mysteries of identity and reality. The play *The Maids* was inspired by an actual crime committed by the Papin sisters, a crime that also intrigued Jacques Lacan as well as the film director Claude Chabrol.[3]

Christine and Léa Papin, sisters aged twenty-eight and twenty-one years old, had been model servants for years in the home of a respected bourgeois family in the French village of Le Mans. One evening in 1933 the maids accidentally caused an electrical breakdown in the house's lighting system. The mistress was atypically angry at the mechanical inconvenience. Suddenly, without warning or prior planning, the sisters attacked and murdered both the mother and her daughter by using available kitchen utensils. Afterward, they washed the utensils, bathed themselves and went to bed together. Upon their arrest they could give no motive for the crime. After five months of being isolated from each other in jail, each sister manifested the symptoms of paranoid psychosis. To Lacan, this strange phenomenon suggested that psychosis is itself based on problems of narcissistic identification. He described the Papin sisters as persecuted by the unattainable ego ideal — who they would like to be — of their mistress and her daughter. That the sisters became psychotic only after months of separation was evidence, for Lacan, that neither sister had a sufficiently individuated sense of "self" (*moi*) to resist psychic retraction into the alien "graveyard" of the Other, itself a paranoid principle behind any "ego" structure.[4]

I do not believe that Genet intended to use fantasy or language (*parole*) to reveal the psychic structure of narcissism in his play. But, unwittingly, in his depiction of a mirror-stage relationship between two sisters, he dramatized the Lacanian theory of the process by which identity is structured. Moreover, he intuitively went beyond Lacan's 1936 explanation of the reasons for the unanticipated crime and subsequent psychosis of the Papin sisters. I read *The Maids* to mean that the lack of Phallic separation — the nonsymbolization of the father's Name — motivates the maids' ritual drama and predetermines the play's conclusion in a suicide/murder. In other words, each sister's dilemma is how to gain a sense of individual selfhood beyond the mingling of their fantasies of each other and of their mistress. In playing out this *moi* drama of frustrated narcissism, the sisters take a position toward the Law (the father's Symbolic name). I would argue that *The Maids* dramatizes the two universal structures of any psyche: mirror-stage identificatory fusions, and Oedipal differentiations. At this level of "meaning," *The Maids* is about the Real of any psychic scaffolding, about the structures that operate the human quest for identity as elaborated in Desiring (certain people or things), and in one's attitude toward the artificially imposed requisites of Law.

The maids are sisters named Solange and Claire. In a sustained dialogue, whose quality is monologuelike, the sisters reveal the jealousy, anger, boredom, frustration, and despair of their lives. They portray their world as diametrically opposed to Madame's world of beautiful clothes, parties, and romance. If Madame were the sole target of the maids' hatred, then the play would remain a sociopolitical study of the master/slave dialectic, and Sartre's interpretation of the play would be correct. The maids would symbolize merely the absurdity and nothingness of lives conceived and lived in *mauvaise foi*.[5] Lacan's early emphasis on the pain of narcissistic symbiosis would take us far enough to produce a viable theory for why the play ends in murder and suicide. But Lacan's later theories regarding the cause of psychosis make much greater sense of the psychic depths of Genet's play. An insufficient psychic separation from the (m)Other's Desire, caused by identification with her at the expense of assimilating the paternal principle of separation, locates the roots of identity in mirror-stage and Oedipal effects. Psychosis becomes equatable with lack of "self" boundaries. I would argue that the dramatic power of Genet's play derives from the unconscious structures that resonate behind the play's language and movement. The ritual fantasies of the maids could be interpreted as increasingly desperate efforts to save themselves from psychic suffocation. The route to escape is by mirror-stage Imaginary identification (projection of self) with Madame. Such identificatory fusion has two purposes: to escape the image of "self" worthlessness that they mirror in each others's eyes, and to identify with the Symbolic order of difference and otherness represented by Madame.

The doubling of the maids provided Genet with a stylistic means of moving forward his own subjective material, as well as a way to build a story around the idea of difference between self and other. In a Lacanian context, this distance becomes a way to measure Desire/lack. Characters are no longer static entities (representations of real people or fictive), no longer psychological conventions, but are the *o*thers toward whom a dialogue moves in the projection of Desire/lack; narcissistic messages that are implicit questions.[6] Literary language itself becomes an example of Lacanian *parole* (as are dreams). All interactions (real or fantasized) and all words (spoken or implied) become metonymies that point to the meaning of the play as an implicit enigma whose key lies in the Other. But since the only link the literary critic has between conscious and unconscious domains is language, a Lacanian interpretation can only imply a meaning, not "apply" one.

The interpretive meaning will not, however, be without a theoretical support. Lacan's formalization of the Imaginary order and development of its logic, in fact, offers literary critics a way to study literary language within the "logic" of *its* own domain. For literature, although it uses conventions, codes, and laws, is neither linguistics nor information. Literature, instead, is about the Imaginary effort to cope with misunderstandings, misrecognitions, thwarted strivings, abased prestige, unfulfilled love, the stench of power, the pain of failure. Literature is about fiction and fantasy, but these are not finally separable from the Real effects of life. Described through the unconventional power of rhetorical tropes and recognizable linguistic conventions as well, and illustrative of one author's Imaginary "self" text, both literary text and interpretation operate from the same three perceptual bases (Real, Symbolic, and Imaginary). While Imaginary readings may proliferate to infinity (at least regarding some textual details), Symbolic order conventions will delimit interpretations and texts both linguistically and historically. But the point of psychic join between the author and the interpreter is the Real domain of psychic "truth." Although psychic meaning is both imagistic and verbal, this representational material has a Real *effect* in being. Literature, then, is about the Real of psychic experience, even though that experience is itself a history of fiction, illusion, and confusion.

In *The Maids* the sisters repeat a fantasy ritual in which one plays the role of maid to Madam, while the other plays at being Madame. They reverse roles. The play within a play has taken on a more urgent aspect in Genet's rendering of the final ritualistic game. This time the maids must cope with a new element. They had blackmailed Madame's lover, who had actually been jailed. In the middle of their maid/ Madame game — played every time Madame is absent — the telephone rings to disclose that Monsieur has been released from jail. He is innocent. The sisters realize that their guilt will soon be discovered. How can they escape punishment? The enigma of the play lies not only in its ending, but also in the unresolved mystery of why the maids would have blackmailed their mistress's lover. Most of the play portrays the maids' efforts to find a solution to their imminent exposure.

I would argue that the real (fictional) dilemma is revelatory of a Real psychic dilemma. What is missing in the play is a means to transcend the mirror dilemma of sameness and self-hatred. While the obvious "interpretation" for many critics has been that the maids imitate Madame, who is socially more worthy than they, a careful scrutiny of the text shows that almost all references to Madame attribute her value to her sexual ability to attract males. Madame's cosmetics, perfume, and clothes become the props that support Claire's and Solange's fantasies of trapping a male of their own. But the play is not so simple. The male principle is implied again and again, the signifiers of the text finally yielding up a signified: the male is sexually desired and hated. (This can be verified from Genet's journals as a personal obsession of his.) It is not Madame's lover himself the maids covet, but the idea of grieving for his loss, the fantasy of following him from prison to prison (p. 39). The lackeys who visit their attic bedroom at night are pretend lackeys, the maids' only lovers themselves (p. 40). Whereas their own hands "befoul the sink" (p. 41), the imaginary devil who carries them away at nights has fragrant arms (p. 42). But paradoxically, the "male" with fragrant arms is a mythical male, a fallen angel.

Throughout their ritual play the sisters fantasize seduction and impregnation by the milkman. They fantasize as well about the police, detective magazines, and the glamour of crime. As the play nears its conclusion, the psychic bind of the sisters intensifies. That the final solution to their deadlock is a suicide/imprisonment makes better sense within a Lacanian context than in terms of the usual interpretive "explanations" that cite jealousy of Madame, retaliation against the master class, a stylistic device for ending the play. At the end of the play Claire drinks the poisoned tea and dies while Solange prepares to be arrested. But jail appears to her as a place of escape and salvation.

In a brilliant paradox, Genet gave the couple victory through death and imprisonment. As Claire/Madame dies — an ego ideal sacrificed — Solange is freed from the claustrophobic symbiosis that was "killing" the sisters. Paradoxically, life was for them a "death," while only an actual death opens the door to the sense of freedom one equates with "livingness." That one sister would die and the other live suggests a rebirth of one aspect of Genet's psychic sense of self, and the death of another part. The sister who goes joyously to prison has transcended the pain of an inadequacy in sense of "self" by identifying with a new self; the law or (in Lacanian terms) the Phallus. Madame and Monsieur as incarnations of woman and society have been rejected in favor of a new ego ideal: prison institutionalizes (thus accepts) rejection of social norms and simultaneously acts as a patriarchal mother. The ending, more than the play, illuminates the essential meaning of the drama. Trapped in the Imaginary realm of specular fascination with the Other, the maids dramatize the nature of mirror-stage structuring of identity in the eyes of the other, as well as the necessity of (Oedipal) differentiation for any attainment of psychic freedom.[7]

Most interpretations of *The Maids* have discussed the drama as a split between fantasy and reality. In Lacanian terms, "reality" refers to any person's Imaginary interpretation of the world, a unique intertext between the Real of the world and the referentiality of language. But because Imaginary meaning is diachronic, dependent on an unconscious dialectic, and subject to the impact of Real and Symbolic forces, Imaginary meaning is unstable. The fantasy-ritual articulation of Genet's Imaginary "self" text articulates his own intrasubjective dilemma: a writing out of his *moi* text in reference to an absent "letter" that insists in the Other. What the play "reveals" is in part the fact that something always remains concealed. The enigma of the play is the enigma of a psychic topology within being whose effects are visible, but whose logic is ungraspable. Lacan used the law of metaphor to decode unconscious effects in conscious language: what is substituted for what? To what do the substitutes refer in the metonymic chain of Desire?

Hamlet peered into the abyss in the hope of learning what his (m)Other's Desire was for him, beyond his father's Name. What was he to be, or not to be . . . ? Shakespeare's Richard III also looked to his (m)Other for the gaze of love and recognition that would appease his Desire (lacks, insufficiencies), a positive gaze withheld from before his birth. If he could not be the object of his (m)Other's love, he would become the incarnation of social power, the symbol of the father's Name. The deaths of people along Richard's way serve only to emphasize the depth of the psychic struggle *en jeu*.

The *Casa de Bernarda Alba* (García Lorca, 1936) shows, on the contrary, the failure of the Phallic principle to penetrate the claustrophobic world of the all-female prison. The play begins and ends in death and silence. As Sandra Gilbert and Susan Gubar showed in *The Madwoman in the Attic: The Woman Writer and the Nineteenth-Century Literary Imagination* (1979), nineteenth-century England was full of madwomen in attics whose fictional function was to separate true lovers.[8] In Lacanian terms, symmetrical unity or harmony in love is impossible since the true partner of each lover remains their own Other: an out-of-reach principle of loss, absence, and palpable mystery. In literature any progress toward meaning as "truth" will be some illumination of the meaning of Desire in the Other, a meaning that will always be a coefficient of a certain posture taken in relation to the Phallus.

A Lacanian literary theoretics would be as vast as the enterprise of literature itself, for literature is the verbal allegory of the structure of the human psyche, rather than the reverse. But any study of literature in light of Lacan's epistemology would require that one embrace Lacan's multileveled concepts in their psychoanalytic, anthropological, philosophical, linguistic, metaphysical complexity. Lacan's concepts depend upon one another in order to make any final sense. One cannot reduce a Lacanian literary criticism to the "application" of models, or even to the use of mathemes (such as $\overline{\varnothing}$, $\math$, A, a). For a Lacanian literary criticism would require that one reconceptualize the relationship of the human subject to language, the links between mind and identity, the role of perception in "self" representation, the multileveled functioning of metaphorical laws, the implicit Imaginary-order related source of intentionality behind discourse, and so on. The basis of such a literary criticism would be a "new" poetics that has rethought age-old questions on the source and nature of language and logic. A new genre theory would emerge, eliminating the static separation of writer or reader and text. An appreciation of literature would emerge that would reveal — not the wisdom or insight of an author, or the brilliance of an interpreter, but — literature as the privileged Symbolic order unveiling of the inherently ambiguous and enigmatic nature of the human subject.

Reading One's Self and Others: Holland's Approach to Interpretive Behavior

by David J. Kann

N orman N. Holland's approach to interpretive behavior has been a
source of controversy. Frederic Crews has called it a "unique
going out of business sale." Other critics and scholars have been
threatened by the implications of these ideas and their continuing
refinements. If we take these ideas and extend them slightly, the nature
of interpretive behavior becomes something quite different from what
had been thought by the preponderance of the critical establishment.
The work — be it literature, one of the visual arts, film, or some as-yet-
undiscovered medium — exists at least half in the eye of the beholder.
This approach strips the critic of his cherished robes of critical objec-
tivity, leaving him, like the emperor and the rest of us, standing naked
before the throngs. Yet with all the controversy, the bases and the
development of these ideas are relatively simple.

Holland breaks with the Cartesian view of perception upon which,
until recently, modern science and modern literary criticism was based.
This view assumes the ability of the individual to perceive objectively.
Upon this rock was founded the new criticism. The break with romantic, impressionistic criticism depended upon the assumption that the
reader can view a work apart from its sources and his or her responses.
It follows that the individual can then recognize and eliminate all those
elements of perception that pollute the pure objective vision. That is,
the world-out-there can be seen for what it is, while the world-in-here,

with its mysterious, prismatic, somatic and emotional colors, can be disposed of in much the same way Scrooge does away with Marley's ghost — a whim of the digestion. Those of us who have read Dickens's work know that the apparition inconveniently insisted on its own reality. So, too, does our internal environment.

The attempt to separate the objective from the subjective perception or even of maintaining meaning for those terms is a delusion. For example, my attempts to disown the subjective parts of my perceptions depend upon my ability to perceive those subjective elements dispassionately and clearly. But in order to perceive my subjectivity objectively, I must eliminate all subjective elements from my perception of my subjectivity, and so I must objectively examine my perception of my perception in order to assure myself that that secondary perception is really objective; but to accomplish that task, the tertiary examination must be dispassionate and objective, and so forth. Having written that last sentence as deliberately as I possibly can, I am struck by how meaning seems to seep away from "objective" and "subjective." The nature of the infinite regress is such that distinctions turn upon each other, calling their opposites into question. And so occurs the frustration of trying to objectively assess the subjectivity of my perceptions.

Holland's approach begins with the inextricability of the inner and outer worlds as a given and attempts to define, allocate, and describe the interactions of the components of perception and judgment. It ends with the idea that interpretive behavior is a transaction between the interpreter and the interpreted and an act of perception. From Holland's standpoint, perception is a function of identity, and the resources of perception are contained in the environment.

Interpretation is perception and perception is behavior. Behavior is an outgrowth of the individual's identity. Thus, the place to begin is the identity of the individual, its nature and its sources.

One of the linchpins of Holland's approach is Heinz Lichtenstein's article "Identity and Sexuality: A Study of Their Interrelationship in Man."[1] The central element of Lichtenstein's thesis is that identity has its sources in the first moments of life. Once established, it continues to express itself consistently in behavior. In the earliest unit formed by the mother and the infant, the latter is utterly dependent. It is from this dependence that identity grows. To use Lichtenstein's metaphor, the mother constitutes a total surrounding organism, and within the organism, the infant is an organ. Thus, the infant is both one with the surroundings constituted by the mother and a part within the whole, subject to the needs or demands of the whole. Just as an organ serves a purpose for the organism, so does the infant serve a purpose for the mother. In short, the mother makes use of the infant. The infant responds to these demands. The individual, then, first expresses his or her identity in terms of what he or she is for someone else. To be sure, the mother satisfies the infant's needs, but the forms those needs take are created by the mother as well.

This still point from which identity and thus behavior radiates is called the Primary Identity. It is essentially unreachable, standing as it does prior to behavior. It is not a noun, really. It is closer to an adverb, present in its modification of every action the individual takes. A musical metaphor will serve. In the theme and variation form, the central theme is established at the opening of the piece and then expresses itself in various transformations In much the same way, the individual in all his or her actions, rings changes upon a central theme. Thus, identity can be perceived in behavior. An individual's actions, taken all in all, will reveal a central structuring principle.

Like any other action, interpretation is behavior. Indeed, as reading, going to a film, or looking at a work of art are behaviors that are essentially passive taking-in, they may have a particularly important place in terms of their relation to infantile behavior. As with any behavior, reading takes place in an environment. That environment is the text. It is here that the nature of the environment and the use that is made of it become important. Each person makes use of the environment in a way structured by his or her identity. This is to say that from among all the thousands of perceptions impinging upon any individual at any moment, he selects a certain number of them, depending on the task he is engaged in and his feelings about — or responses to — it, and arranges them in a way characteristic of that perception and probably of no other. This we call perception. Such individual structuring has been shown to be present in behavior as automatic as the way a person scans a picture seen for the first time.[2] How much more true, then, of the more complex act of engaging ourselves with environment of a work of literature and making sense of that engagement.

We transform the resources for perception offered us by the environment in ways consonant with our identities. But since identity also consists of drives and fantasies that may or may not be gratifying and that may, at the same time, be considered mad or bad by each of us or by the culture through which we move, identity must also consist of habitual ways of defending. The identity theme that structures the way in which we select and order material offered by the environment includes as well the necessity of eliminating or shape-shifting those elements in our selection that elicit threatening responses, fantasies, or drives.

Thus, the process of selection and structuring that constitutes perception includes also the resources of the defense mechanisms that further shape perception until we find it congenial with our identities. In the examination of defense as behavior and thus a function of identity, lies the second primary element of Holland's theory of interpretation.

Much of Holland's thought in this area begins with Robert Wälder's article "The Principle of Multiple Function: Observations on Over-Determination." Wälder sets out to determine what problems the ego must solve to maintain itself. He proposes eight problems that divide into two classes. There are those problems that are thrust upon the ego. These arise from the external environment, the internal demands to act stemming from the id and the superego, and from the compulsion to repeat. The second class of problems arise from within the ego itself. These are the pressures to hold its own in the external environment, the need to respond to the demands of the id and superego, and the compulsion to repeat. Wälder proposes that no solution arising from the ego is possible unless it satisfies all the loci of demand. Thus, the process is dynamic. Each decision reorders all the parts, creating new demands, changing the texture of the internal environment, forcing new solutions. The ego acts again, and the new ordering creates new pressures. In short, the choices an identity makes to maintain itself may be seen as a constantly circulating feedback loop — a system.

Each system is different. Everybody has a mode of solving these problems characteristic of his or her self. The individual chooses a defense, or set of defenses, that itself gratifies the drive or fantasy it defends against while satisfying other demands as well. Ideally, every choice is a point of convergence. It is a nexus of simultaneous denial and satisfaction, thus serving a multiple function. It builds a structure of being and behaving in the world that is the individual's alone and unlike any other.

Wälder's idea reinforces Lichtenstein's concept of the identity theme. Each of us has a primary identity, indefinable in itself, but accessible as an identity theme in all our actions. Each action is the result of engagement with the environment and engages us further with that environment, both internal and external, and each action is a choice founded on previous experiences of these environments. These previous experiences are a series of perceptions, each one the result of a process of selection and structuring and defense that is a function of the primary identity manifesting itself. Each choice redefines the environment, necessitating a new perception, relationship, and selection. Each choice and perception and choice is specific to each person.

When the term "environment" is applied specifically to the arts, the ideas presented thus far take on a more particular form. The environment exists neither external to, nor entirely within, the observer, but as a field between and including the two. While the perceiver may impose a characteristic structure upon his sensations, he is limited by what the environment offers. Thus, perception and the meaning each person creates from it is a function of the identity of the perceiver and of the environment. In the arts and criticism of the arts, the implications of this view are, to say the least, striking. Authority no longer resides in the work. While the particular piece, be it a sculpture, a film, or a work of literature, may exercise control in that it is finite in what it offers the perceiver, it is also shaped by the perceiver in ways that reinforce and are a function of his or her identity.

Holland's attention is centered primarily, though not entirely, on reading. The basic statement of how reading happens can be found in *The Dynamics of Literary Response*. To be sure, his later works extend his ideas further and place more emphasis on the reader as well as giving clinical evidence to support his contentions, but for me much of the fundamental material can be found in *Dynamics*.

Holland first directs our attention to what happens when we read. When we are wrapped up in a work, we cease to pay attention to what is outside of it. Absorbed in a book, we make a regressive move to a prior stage of development in which we do not differentiate ourselves from the environment.[3] Since we are not called upon to act, we take the work in.

At this point the question might well arise as to what is satisfying about this behavior, given the apparently defenseless taking in of material coupled with the disturbing nature of a good deal of literature for many people, and the practical certainty that any work is bound to be threatening for somebody. In answer to this question, Holland links the typical defense mechanisms with the elements to show that within the work and within the reader ways of managing fantasy material arise. Defining form as the way of ordering parts so as to control the reader's awareness at any moment, Holland shows how a work can shape wishful/fearful fantasies into themes that are satisfying to the ego and to the demands placed upon the ego. Thus, the content of a work, corresponding to an unconscious wish, is shaped by the formal elements of the work, corresponding to certain defenses, to give pleasure through control of those wishes while simultaneously gratifying them.

Language also works defensively by displacing the reader's attention to the utterance and away from the fantasy the utterance contains. Here Holland draws a distinction between popular writing and literary writing. The language of popular writing is relatively straightforward. Thus, the embedded fantasy comes through more or less directly. A good example is the Harlequin series of romances. These books contain rather safe, romantic, and rather gratifying fantasies for a number of people. They make no demands upon the reader, nor are they meant to. They are simple, safe wish fulfillment. Thus, the language is simple, demanding no attention on the reader's part.

More literary writing presents the reader with a more difficult utterance, forcing his or her attention to the language itself. Significantly, the reader tends to feel that the effort involved in reading a difficult utterance is worthwhile when the material it contains is important to him or her. Further, making sound is a muscular act. When the sounds — the utterance — present difficulty and the embedded fantasy strongly affects the reader, he or she is given the opportunity to act out muscular ways of dealing with the fantasy material. In effect, the reader can displace to somatic behavior energy aroused by the fantasy. The displacement to language allows still other verbal devices to manage fantasy content. For example, rhyme and repetition give the reader a sense of completion and mastery, a point Poe made implicitly in "The Philosophy of Composition." For example, the limerick traditionally deals with explicit and often perverse sexual material, but because its rhyme and meter is so explicit, conventional, and strong as to be an important part of the poem, it can do so with impunity, and the reader can laugh at the behavior described, although he or she might not countenance a direct, plain prose description of that same behavior.

The meaning of a work creates elements of defense as well. Meaning, with its reference to larger abstractions, displaces the reader's attention from the level of fantasy and toward the intellectually oriented, referential nature of the work, making it acceptable. In addition, those works that are cryptic on the surface engage the reader in the process of intellection and displace the preponderance of his or her attention to thought. The continually reiterated question of what is going on and what it all means leads to a moment-to-moment intellectual assessment of the work. This essentially adult analytic behavior allows the reader to master threatening drives or fantasies. For example, the famous purple paper scene in Antonioni's *Blow-Up* gratifies a number of childish desires such as voyeuristic gazing, as well as some more adult responses — watching two nubile teen-aged girls pull each other's clothes off. Embedded as this scene is in an unquestionably cryptic work, it becomes an acceptable part of the puzzle.

At the level of characters within the work, the same processes apply. Holland states that characters in literature do not reflect human nature and that to attempt to psychoanalyze a character as if he or she were human leads nowhere. Rather, the characters are shaped by the fictional world in which they exist. Yet readers do identify with characters. As the reader controls and shapes the words in a text, a character emerges that is created by the environment created by those words. If the reader finds his or her defenses in a character, then the character is, indeed, real to the reader. In effect, given the resources of the text-as-environment, the reader creates the character out of his or her drives and defenses.

The Dynamics of Literary Response is Holland's earliest complete statement of his fundamental theory of response. But while, in this work, all the important issues are taken up, much of the authority and control of the reader's responses remains in the text. The model is further developed, and the reader's role expanded, in *Poems in Persons* and *5 Readers Reading,* as well as numerous articles.

Style re-creates style. Given a single scene in a text or a single poem, different readers create extraordinarily variable readings. Holland shows this in five readers' responses to and descriptions of a single scene in Faulkner's "A Rose for Emily." Through eliciting free associations to this scene, to the story as a whole, and other stories, recording those utterances, and transcribing them, Holland kept a record of those varying readings. What emerged for Holland was a clear sense of each subject's identity theme, for while the readings varied from subject to subject, and while individual subjects responded differently to different works, there was a consistency of response for each subject in terms of his or her way of dealing with fantasy material. After formulating an identity theme for each subject, Holland checked his hypotheses against independently administered and interpreted Rohrschach tests, Thematic Apperception Tests, and the COPE questionnaire for each subject. He found that the tests and the material elicited during the interviews dealing with literature differed only rarely.

Style creates style. Readers read in different ways because their identities differ. These differences can be understood in terms of each reader's identity theme. Each reader has his own characteristic way of taking in the environment and of adapting the materials it presents to his own needs while adapting to its finite nature. From this standpoint the idea of a "correct" reading of a text seems irrelevant. With the authority for a reading spread equally between the reader and the text, the work of literature — or any work of art — becomes plastic, enmeshed in the dynamic process of one individual's perception, with his or her characteristic patterns of fantasy and defense, re-creating his or her self and the environment from moment to moment. The critic — and all readers are in effect critics, i.e., discerners — is freed from the tyranny of the demand to be objective and the burdensome inheritance of the seventeenth century.

In addition, psychoanalytic criticism becomes much less reductive. The traditional Freudian symbolism remains, but it has more of the spirit Freud gave it. It stands as a set of abstractions — archetypes, if you will — that take life and form only when they are engaged with an individual's identity and behavior. Until they live in an individual's world, these archetypes are only points of departure. When they are used by the individual, they are his or hers and belong to nobody else. The individual may be understood by his use of these archetypes, but they do not constitute an objective truth. Every reader's language is his own, and so are the symbols he uses.

To use an acronym that is Holland's, we read DEFTly. We avoid the anxiety elicited by unacceptable fantasies and their attendant responses by DEfending against them, re-creating our defenses through the material offered by the text and the way it is formally and linguistically structured, finding analogues for our own defensive behavior in the characters. If the defensive style of the reader and that of the text reinforce each other, then reading the text is a pleasurable activity. When the Fantasies that are elicited are pleasurable but need to be DEfended against strongly, or when they arouse conflict, the reader

Transforms the work, adding, deleting, throwing certain elements into the background, highlighting others, until he or she feels the conflict has been mastered.

Works that do not have a strong component of pleasure for the reader are those that elicit fantasies against which the reader's defenses are inadequate or that do not provide material the reader can use to shape those fantasies in a gratifying way. No transformation is an adequate one in this case. Another possibility is a work that presents a fantasy that is both pleasurable and threatening, and thus must be strongly defended against. Frustration at the loss of gratification results in a negative reaction.

If the reader can find nothing in the work that will allow him to re-create his defenses, then that reader will engage defenses that are not implicit in the work. In short, he will defend against the whole work with either negative affect or affectlessness.

In all of these models there is no clear line of demarcation between the reader and the work. Instead, the two exist together in a sort of field of continuous feedback and revision. There is an ongoing transaction between the two, merging the identity of the reader and the matter of the text as well as its manner. From this standpoint it makes little or no sense to speak of The Text, except as an arrangement of ink upon paper. There are readers and there are texts. Unity does not consist of a single, objective truth about a text. It is re-created over and over by each reader as he or she reads. In Holland's words:

> . . . the only way one can ever discover unity in texts or identity in selves is by creating them from one's own inner style, for we are all caught up in the general principle that identity creates and recreates itself as each of us discovers and achieves that world in his own mind. . . . *Interpretation recreates identity.* The only sensible thing for critics to do is to accept that fact and write and talk accordingly. Let's face up to the emancipating truth. The seventeenth century is over.[4]

Holland's ideas should be shown in process. Of course, Holland himself applies them to numerous texts in his books and articles. An interesting application of his approach might be to apply it to a text he has not dealt with, but that is familiar to practically everybody. With this in mind, I have chosen "Rip Van Winkle," and I have dealt with it in my version of the Hollandaise manner.

"Rip Van Winkle" begins with an act of concealment. How am I to understand the opening epigraph?

> By Woden, God of Saxons
> From whence comes Wensday, that is Wodensday,
> Truth is a thing that ever I will keep
> Unto thylke day in which I creep into
> My speulchre —[5]

I may see it as either an assurance that the story that follows is true, or it may be a statement by the author that he will keep the truth to himself until the day he dies. These possibilities appear to be mutually exclusive. However, if I try to hold them simultaneously in mind, they speak to me of dreams and the nature of dreaming.

On the surface the plot of the tale could not be less dreamlike. It appears to describe a straight chronological line. In addition, the grammar and style of the tale appear to be highly ordered, replete with parallelism and periodic sentences. But against this apparent surface order I must balance my feelings of frustration as I reach the tale's conclusion. It is as if the illusion of order masks a more essential disorder. This dissonance led me to begin thinking in terms of the order I am invited to see as a defense, seducing me into suspending my judgment.

With my suspicions aroused, I returned to the tale and I found further dissonances. Most striking to me is the sequence of affect. The point of view of the narrator, and thus the point of view I am invited to participate in, is far from consistent. It swings from sympathy with Rip to gothic terror, to satiric detachment, to skepticism as to the truth of the story. This sequence doubles back on itself, is contradictory. In many ways it appears to have purely associative rather than logical order. The movement from domestic comedy to horror to irony is difficult for me to accept.

The horror turns on the cliché that we need to be wary when we are granted what we wish. Having escaped the household dictatorship of Dame Van Winkle, Rip sleeps for twenty years. He returns to find all traces of his identity obliterated. In effect, he has died. Immediately following, there is a recognition scene. Following that scene, I am told that everything that happened might not have happened after all. Rip may have regained his coordinates in the world, but by this time I have lost my sense of stability in the story.

My confusion has to do with the issue of truth. While I am willing to accept the truth of what happens to Rip — after all, I've been through

129

the event with him — Rip's compatriots in the town are somewhat less credulous. Soon, however, their skepticism is resolved. At that point, though, I am invited to doubt Rip's story when the narrator tells me that initially he cannot keep his facts straight.

If I accept the narrator's invitation to doubt Rip, I cannot help but doubt my own perceptions up to this point, for there has been no evidence that what has happened did not happen. In effect, I have been put in a double bind. Up to the end of the story I have taken all the events seriously, suspending my disbelief. The radical shift at the end invites me either to doubt myself or to doubt the author. The effect upon me is my attempt to distance myself from the tale, if only to assess what has happened. I begin to suspect a defensive maneuver on Irving's part.

Noticing this, I find my attention returning to the introduction to the tale. The narrator or recorder of the tale, Diederich Knickerbocker, is at first said to write with scrupulous accuracy. Thus, I must assume that the tale itself is true and truly recorded. Then I am told that Mr. Knickerbocker's efforts are trivial at best. *Then* I am told that Knickerbocker was probably not trustworthy, obsessed by his hobbyhorsical ways, possibly senile. Here the same process of giving and witholding that I noted in the story occurs even before the narration begins.

All the above — the shifts in tone; the associative structure or form of affect; the ambiguity as to the matter of truth, especially in the epigraph — leads me to consider the mechanism of dreaming as the closest analogue to the process of Irving's tale. It follows, then, that the riddle of "Rip Van Winkle" might be solved by sorting the contradictory elements out along the lines of a wish, a defense against the wish — especially the denial of that wish.

Rip's actions and attendant desires engage me at an important level of fantasy. He wants nothing more than to become an infant again. He pursues only pleasure and especially the immediate return of affection and nurture from the environment. He shows no interest in deferred gratification, the profit motive. He has no sense of responsibility except to his immediate desires. In distinction, Dame Van Winkle stands at the negative pole in the opposition between wife and mother. Logically, she has good reason to be angry with Rip, but logic does not apply in this case. I am invited to share Rip's perception of his wife, and whenever he takes to the hills, my sympathies go with him.

It is in the midst of one of these flights that the central part of the story occurs. This section is structured along the lines of the initiation ritual. There is the preliminary isolation, the summons by name and ordeal, the ritual, and the communion. In general, these rites mark the transition from childhood to adulthood.

The obvious problem is that Rip's life has been dedicated to avoiding precisely this movement. It seems unlikely that he would willingly participate in such a rite. With this conclusion in mind, and examining this initiation more closely, I find a number of crucial differences from what I know of initiation. To be sure, formally the episode in the Kaatskills is an initiation rite. However, in its content and the nature of its participants it appears to be debased and regressive. All of the stages are made trivial. Rip's isolated meditation is on the consequences of being late for dinner; the ordeal is no more than carrying a keg of gin up the mountain; the ritual is a game of bowling; the communion is a drunken stupor; and significantly, he is summoned by his old name, not a new one.

There is nothing comic here, though. Within the ritual and surrounding it are embedded images of death and decay. Crows fly above. Not a word is exchanged. The members of Hudson's crew seem to me to be like zombies in their behavior. Rip holds communion with this society and slips into a little death. He loses twenty years of his life and he almost loses his self, his identity.

As it is constituted in this tale, it appears to me that the initiation ritual denies generative power and sufficiency. It fills this vacuum with the presence of death. This idea expresses itself in two regressive and threatening fantasies. The first I find in the landscape in which the rite occurs. The narrow gully leading into the sheltered hollow makes the idea of the return to the womb almost inescapable for me. The other, deriving from the actions within this landscape, is the penetration of this hollow while bearing a keg of magical liquid. This childish fantasy with its phallic imagery denies adult genital sufficiency. In addition, the association with death in the fact of the absence of revivifying water, in the dead, dusty dryness of the landscape, in the thunder without rain, is too strong for me to ignore.

Rip's wish is granted, but at a cost. To become a child he must die as an adult. The objects Rip is greeted with upon awakening — his rusted fowling piece, the dead tree, the calling of the crows — all speak of death and the loss of phallic power. The cost is greater still. Upon returning to town, Rip finds his wish granted in ways he never dreamed. To be sure, at his advanced age he can be idle with impunity, but at the price of the loss of his identity and of all the familiar reference points by which he knew his environment, his place within that environment, and himself.

At the greatest point of loss the crisis of identity is resolved. Rip is recognized for who he is, or was. He is ensconced in the bosom of his daughter's family as one of the children.

It is at the point at which my anxiety about Rip's identity begins to build, when Rip first returns to the village, that the dominant tone of the tale becomes political satire. Irving shifts my attention from the horror of Rip's predicament to the disjunction between the actions of the townspeople and what they profess, especially in the presence of their representative, the self-important man. Thus, while Rip's identity is finally restored, it no longer seems quite so important to me. In addition, the possibilities for ironic distance become greater when I am told that Rip cannot tell his story the same way twice.

These shifts invite me to turn my attention from an emotional situation to an intellectual problem, and then to withdraw my belief from the story itself. Again Irving catches me in a double bind. Either I absorb the satirical, judgmental point of view and withdraw my emotional investment from the story, or, in spite of all that happens by the end, I keep my emotional interest in the tale and either feel like a fool or ignore the last third of the text.

As a reader I am presented with a series of invitations to take different attitudes toward what transpires. Overall, I see a pattern of alternating engagement and withdrawal, or of doing and undoing. First I am encouraged to suspend my disbelief and participate in the pastoral fantasy of escape in the fairy mountains. Then I must disengage myself from that fantasy and participate in adultlike comparative, intellectual, judgmental behavior.

Significantly, those shifts in emphasis come at those points when the fantasy of escape seems most satisfying and thus most threatening to adult ego functions, or most threatening in the elements of destruction and death. It is the nature of dreams that the wishes they fulfill are unacceptable or unattainable in waking life, and so they must be compromised or defended against. In this tale the counterwish to Rip's escape — Rip's little death — has its own counterwish in Rip's final affirmation by his community. This essential return to the core wish is in turn defended against by the refocusing of the story upon the satirical treatment of the new republic. And now a further compromise occurs.

Rip is honored by the people who, in the context of the satire, have been shown to be foolish.

Further, if the story contains a regressive fantasy, the description of the ostensible recorder of the story, Knickerbocker, undoes any validity that the fantasy might have by denying Knickerbocker's credibility. If Knickerbocker cannot be taken seriously, neither can the tale. Then the fantasy is an old man's senile, credulous account of a doubtful story he may or may not have heard told by a person who may be something less than reliable.

In "Rip Van Winkle" I find the truth to be both revealed and concealed. The levels at which I can suspend my disbelief and those wherein I must withdraw my trust and displace my attention to an intellectual puzzle circle about and modify each other, denying me a stable point at which to rest. The interplay of logical and associative thinking, of fantasy and irony controlled through the form, language, and tone of the story, both reveals and conceals, confirms and denies, the core fantasy.

Describing Sonnets
by Milton and Keats:
Roy Schafer's Action Language
and the Interpretation of Texts

by Sara van den Berg

Certain poems evoke in the common reader uncommon feelings that no interpretation can entirely explain. Two such poems are Milton's "When I consider how my light is spent" and Keats's "When I have fears that I may cease to be" — very different meditations on the desire to write and the desire to live. Each poem questions whether action — especially the action of writing — can give meaning to life when the prospects for action are clouded. Milton, blind, uninspired, unable to write, can act only when he redefines what action can be. Keats, numbed by thoughts of early death, makes plain the reasons why he fears to die and discovers a new valuing of life and a fuller appreciation of what it means to think and to be.

Each poem is a process of revision: the poet redefines himself, changing his sense of what it means to "stand" in his own time and place, choosing new metaphors and analogues to express his idea of his life. Describing and redescribing himself, each poet discovers the reasons why he has chosen to feel helpless or fearful, and new reasons for acting in new ways. Central to that discovery is the crisis of each poem — those lines that are most puzzling, most confusing, most compelling. A movement from inaction to new action is the content of each sonnet, but because each sonnet is itself an action in words the achievement of its literary form testifies to the poet's affirmation of the act of writing. Each poem enacts its idea of action, and through the responsive act of reading each reader can know — can "prove on the pulse," as Keats would say — what value action can have.

Looked at in this way, the sonnets of Milton and Keats resemble the actions of psychoanalysis, particularly as it has been reformulated by Roy Schafer. A person has an experience, and reports it. The subject matter of psychoanalysis is not the person, and not even the experience, but the report. So also, the subject matter of literary criticism is not the poet but the poet's action — the poem. A critic who attempts to describe a poem using the interpretive methodology Schafer has developed for psychoanalytic narratives must distinguish in the text four separate actions: the action recorded in the poem, the action of recording that is the poem, the act of reading recorded in the interpretation of the poem, and the action that is the interpretation. Such a criticism relies on description or redescription, a theoretically endless series of narratives, each valid.

In describing psychoanalytic concepts, Schafer has demonstrated that a single term — internalization, resistance, anxiety — can be a misleading shorthand for richly varied actions, and that a language of close description may lead to a truer understanding of what an analysand is doing. In describing the actions of analysands, Schafer has turned to the interpretive languages they use: passive disclaimers of action ("Anger overwhelmed me"), metaphors of space and time ("Fear is at the bottom of my resentment"; "I can't fight the clock"), splitting self into different actors ("My impulses flooded my brain and destroyed my better judgment"). The act of psychoanalytic interpretation is revision, reclaiming for the analysand personal integration, personal authority, and the freedom to act in new ways. Both Milton and Keats dramatize such acts of revision. The paralyzing inability to act that marks each poet as these sonnets begin yields to an equilibrium that is quite the opposite of constraint or stasis: Milton can "stand and wait" for whatever comes, Keats can "stand alone" and contemplate what it means to be. Both men recognize in apparent inaction a new and important kind of action.

I

Basic to Roy Schafer's work is his definition of action:

> Action is human behavior that has a point; it is meaningful activity; it is doing things for reasons. . . . For example, to

135

think of something is to do an action; to see or remember something is to do an action; to be silent or otherwise inactive is as much an action as to say something or to walk somewhere. It is one kind of action to say something and another kind to think it and not say it.[1]

Developing a set of interpretive methods and rules — a "language" — to describe human action, Schafer centers on the reasons or purposes of an act, not its deterministic causes or origin. "Psychoanalysis is the study of reasons," he declares, "and of people's problems with reasons."

Schafer's early work set the stage for his theoretical program. His first collection of essays, *Projective Testing and Psychoanalysis* (1967), demonstrates how psychoanalytic concepts can enrich the interpretation of Rorschach tests, and how these tests in turn can monitor psychoanalytic therapy. Using Freud's topographical model of the self (as Conscious and Unconscious), Schafer argues that the single act of responding to a Rorschach inkblot can subsume several actions, distinct and even contradictory. The complex nature of an apparently unitary action is the subject of his first important book, *Aspects of Internalization* (1968). Schafer's explication of this important psychoanalytic concept reveals how one term conflates different kinds of behavior: introjection, identification, incorporation, and learning. The book is a study in object-relations, that is, in how a person (subject) relates to another significant person (object). Using Freud's structural model of the self (as Id, Ego, and Superego), Schafer suggests that each component of the self "internalizes" a significant object (a parent) in quite distinct ways.

Aspects of Internalization both contributes to and implicitly challenges orthodox metapsychology. By pointing out the metaphorical dimensions of the term "internalization," Schafer calls attention to the resultant fuzziness of theoretical discourse. "Internalization," he suggests, is a fantasy for analysands, not an explanation for analysts. Like other fantasies of analysands, such an action — in all its variety — is not a means of interpretation but material to be interpreted. Explanation can be found only through the slow, rigorous process of describing and redescribing the analysand's act of fantasizing, clarifying the reasons why that act is performed.

Schafer outlines his revision of psychoanalytic theory in a collection of major essays, *A New Language for Psychoanalysis* (1976). He rejects

Freud's topographical and structural models of the self because they posit autonomous agents acting within the self. Only a person can act, Schafer insists, and what Freud did in creating these models was to personify modes of action, offering metaphorical apprehensions of behavior, not explanations. Schafer also rejects, on similar grounds, the psychodynamic or "drive-discharge" model of action developed by Freud and accepted by orthodox metapsychology. "For too long," Schafer writes, "we have continued to think, with Freud, of energies, forces, structures, and so forth as *acting on the person* rather than as metaphoric approaches to *actions of a person.*" Although he denies explanatory status to Freud's models of self, he does not reject Freudian psychoanalysis. What he emulates is Freud the clinician, who sought to understand human action in all its complexity. Like Freud, Schafer seeks a language that can describe not "actions and reasons" but "action for reasons."

The first essays in Schafer's book trace the antecedents of the action language, or interpretive method, he advocates: in the clinical papers of Freud, in Wittgenstein's philosophy of language, and in Gilbert Ryle's model of mind. Schafer admits that his emphasis on action seems to echo behaviorist psychology, but argues that behaviorism is grounded in a determinism alien to action language. More pertinent is the existentialism of Jean-Paul Sartre, which is also based on the priority of action. The fundamental tenet of this philosophy — that existence precedes essence, suggests that "self" is the goal of action, not its origin or judge. We do not authenticate our actions by measuring them against our "true self," but work toward becoming a self (or series of selves) through progressive acts of choice. What is available to us as experience to be interpreted is this progression of actions.

Schafer wants to interpret not only the actions of the analysand but also the interaction of analysand and analyst. To describe that interaction, Schafer (almost alone among psychoanalytic theoreticians) has turned for a model to the work of a literary critic. In "The Psychoanalytic Vision of Reality," he describes four modes of action present in all psychoanalytic work, adopting the terminology of Northrop Frye's *Anatomy of Criticism.* However, Schafer subverts the taxonomy he cites. Whereas Frye classifies texts as comic, romantic, tragic, or ironic, Schafer classifies one text — the psychoanalytic interaction — as at once partaking of all four modes. Psychoanalytic work is comic: optimistic, convinced of rebirth and new beginnings, work rewarded with a happy ending. Psychoanalysis is also romantic: life is a perilous quest, its reward exaltation of the hero. This mode is visionary, although in the course of analysis "dragons change, the modes of combat change, and the concepts of heroism and victory change." Not only life but also analysis is a heroic quest, the analysand aided and opposed by the analyst, who is at once monster and guide, villain and comrade. Psychoanalysis is tragic: the work probes the dilemmas, paradoxes, ambiguities, and uncertainties that pervade human life. Every victory is a defeat, every gain a loss. However great the struggle, the result is uncertain, rebirth always illusory. To understand oneself is not only to reconcile oneself to the world, but also to separate from it. In a powerful analytic experience, the analysand attains tragic stature: no longer the suffering victim, the analysand can courageously and painfully choose, taking responsibility for that choice.

Finally, psychoanalytic work is ironic. Recognizing the simultaneous presence of the noble and the demonic, achievement and waste, complete being and complete annihilation that engage tragic vision, the ironist remains detached, disengaged, unconvinced of their scale and absoluteness. Moderating any inclination toward simple or absolute judgments, irony "safeguards good judgment and effective action." The ironic vision also safeguards the participants' awareness that psychoanalytic work is necessarily and importantly artificial, fictive as well as true. Describing these four modes of psychoanalysis, Schafer insists that all four are essential to the work. Rejecting any narrow account of psychoanalysis as scientific "fact-finding," he regards it as an art of interpretation rooted in the humanities, those disciplines doomed to contemplate questions they can never finally resolve.

If psychoanalysis can be understood only by recognizing its different, simultaneous, often conflicting modes, so also the actions that are the subject matter of psychoanalysis must be richly and variously understood. Theoretically, no action can be completely described; there is always the possibility of new valid interpretations. Schafer rejects metapsychology because as a language it reifies actions, thereby preventing full, clear description of them. Accordingly, he reexamines psychoanalytic concepts and redefines them as actions. The most extensive discussion of a single topic is Schafer's redescription of "emotion" as an action or mode of action. He would speak of loving, not love; of grieving, not grief; of fearing, not fear. Anxiety is better described as acting anxiously; even better, acting anxiously *because*. . . . What the analyst wants to describe is not love, and not the person who loves, but the specific way(s) a person loves and that person's reason(s) for loving. When emotion is redescribed as action, verbs and adverbs replace reifying nouns, and the active voice displaces the passive. No poetic force is lost because of this change: it is at least as strong to say "I love you" as to say "I am filled with love for you." But Schafer is not trying to revise everyday speech. His concern is the probing language of theoretical description, which requires a grammar that serves its needs.

Although Schafer argues that "the person" cannot be interpreted but only the actions of the person, his method is profoundly humanistic, honoring in its most basic assumptions and terminology the person's freedom to choose and potential to act. He rescues psychoanalysis from the familiar charge that its account of human behavior is reductive, mechanistic, and so universal as to deny individual freedom or specificity. If his emphasis on action has made him vulnerable to charges that his method is impersonal, his emphasis on describing "action for reasons" refutes such criticism. "The analyst's real commitment," he writes, "is not to determinism in a universe of mechanical causes, but to intelligibility in a universe of actions with reasons." Denying determinism and affirming determinability, Schafer claims for psychoanalysis a place in the long Western philosophical tradition that posits the freedom and autonomy of the individual person.

He celebrates the freedom and potential for freedom in human action in the inaugural Freud Memorial Lectures at the University of London, published as *Language and Insight* (1979). The most important of these lectures defines psychoanalysis as the process of developing the life histories of the analysand. At the beginning of analysis, the analysand is constrained by a single autobiographical narrative, or self-definition, that mandates certain actions and prevents others. That life history is not "false," but is rife with inconsistencies, paradoxes, discontinuities, and repetitive patterns of behavior — most of them unrecognized by the analysand. Analysis consists of forming new narratives, as analyst and analysand redescribe and revise the analysand's actions.

The only action directly accessible to the analyst is the action of the psychoanalysis itself. In his most recent book, *Narrative Actions in Psychoanalysis* (1981), Schafer describes the nature of psychoanalytic narrative. When we tell ourselves to ourselves, he writes, we place ourselves in space and time. Psychoanalysis challenges that placement, as it challenges every other aspect of our self-defining actions. When we place ourselves in space and time, we may neglect or distort the ways we live in more than one place, more than one moment. The analyst, calling attention to the "timeless" and "placeless" quality of experience, and to the complex relationships between the analytic session and the analysand's life, reminds us that "we act in more than one reality."

The analyst also makes narrative choices in offering interpretations and in shaping a case report. Freud, for example, narrates not only the history of his patients, not only the course of their analyses, but also narrates his own creation of psychoanalysis. In a very early essay, "How Was This Story Told?" (1957; reprinted in *Projective Testing and Psychoanalysis*, 1967), Schafer argues that the interpreter of a patient's narrative about a Rorschach inkblot must "undertake a kind of psychological literary criticism, seeking in the choice of language, imagery, and sequence of development, as well as in the narrative detail, cues about the storyteller's inner experience of his creative effort and his creation." Schafer's recent work extends that argument to the interpretation of the analyst's own narratives.

Schafer's concern for interpretive language has also led him to consider its political or cultural dimensions. Recognizing that such language is both socially formed and personally selected, Schafer has written a thorough critique of Freud's often contradictory statements about women, and revised all the essays reprinted in *A New Language for Psychoanalysis* to remove patriarchal idioms.

From his initial protests against interpretive metaphors and narrative conventions, Schafer has begun to consider metaphor and narrative as choices, as material to be analyzed in the work of analysts as well as analysands. These two problems in particular have led him to draw on the work of interpreters in many disciplines: history (Hayden White), art history (Nelson Goodman, E. H. Gombrich), and literary criticism (T. S. Eliot, Owen Barfield, Barbara Herrnstein Smith). Perhaps because his work testifies to his sense that interpretive actions in different disciplines have in common significant problems, he has been invited to publish essays in journals devoted to theories of interpretation (*New Literary History* and *Critical Inquiry*).[2]

Roy Schafer is not a literary critic, and he does not cite or interpret literary texts. His reformulation of psychoanalytic theory, however, has much to offer to literary critics. It is a relief not to have to master the complex, often inconsistent or unclear terminology of metapsychology. Schafer is a theorist in the tradition of the plain style. He seeks a language adequate to the complexity of human action, but one that does not impose a competing complexity of its own. More important, just as his theoretical reformulations accord with traditional clinical practice, so also literary interpretations modeled on the method he advocates will not seem alien or even novel to literary critics trained in "close reading" and "practical criticism," or to those familiar with Kenneth Burke's "dramatistic" concept of literary texts.

It is necessary, however, to specify just what is "new" about a psychoanalytic literary criticism based on the work of Roy Schafer. Such an interpretation does not seek to "psychoanalyze" an author or a character. A text is not reduced to its psychic function as a fantasy for author and reader, although that aspect of a text may be one concern of the interpreter. Meredith Skura, in *The Literary Use of the Psychoanalytic Process* (1981), has surveyed the range of psychoanalytic literary interpretation, describing the different roles possible for critics in different modes of interpretation. To the interpretation of text as "case history" and "fantasy," she adds an account of the text as dream, to be interpreted with close attention to its form, its way of representing "the (Disguised) Fulfillment of a (Repressed) Wish." To understand the meanings of a text or a dream, we must consider the moments when those meanings converge, collide, and displace one another. She then describes literature as a special version of transference, serving a rhetorical and social function. If psychoanalysis is considered as the study not only of what a person represses or wishes but also of how the person forms relationships, the interpreter can find in the exchanges between analysand and analyst a type of the process of reading. The exchange between author and reader implicit in a text can be described as a "transitional" object or space, an experience outside the real world of daily life that offers the interpreter ways to understand that world as well as to escape it.

Finally, Skura defines literature as an action akin to the psychoanalytic process. In texts and in psychoanalysis, modes of being in the world are slowly disorganized and slowly reorganized, new ideas of self and self-conscious choices emerging through attention to everything that is said — the obvious and the trival, the secret and the unrecognized, the crafted and the uncontrolled, apparent enigmas and consistent patterns. Literary critics who understand texts as actions will readily accept Roy Schafer's methods as the "native tongue" of literary, as well as psychoanalytic, interpretation. Describing a text in these

terms does not preclude attention to the other modes outlined by
Meredith Skura; the method is inclusive, not exclusive. The interpreter's focus, however, will remain on the act, or process, of the text
and on the complementary act, or process, of interpretation. Author and
critic act for reasons; it is the task of interpretation to make those
reasons clear.

II

In the sonnets of Milton and Keats, each poet achieves a new vision
through an act of revision, redescribing the framework in which he can
act. Each poet begins in a state of intense self-concern. This kind of narcissism, as Heinz Kohut argues, can lay the foundation for affirmative
relationships with other people or can lead instead toward even more intense self-absorption and isolation. The self-concern of Milton and
Keats is evinced by their preoccupation with dying — that loss of self
both wished and dreaded. From the blindness, or rather the near-
sightedness, of narcissism, each poet attains a quite different vision that
redeems and reaffirms life. The process can be chronicled in the way
each poet reinterprets himself, choosing new figurative language and
new grammatical or syntactic ways to describe himself. Metaphors of
constraint and a syntax of passivity are replaced by a new mode of free
action that supports and confirms the poet's recognition that he can act
and that his acts have value.

Milton's sonnet first depicts the poet as a frustrated, anguished
man, concerned that his life has been wasted, his ambitions unrealized,
his obligations unfulfilled:

> When I consider how my light is spent
> E'er half my days in this dark world and wide,
> And that one talent which is death to hide
> Lodged with me useless, though my soul more bent
> To serve therewith my maker, and present
> My true account lest he returning chide,
> Does God exact day-labour, light denied,
> I fondly ask; but Patience to prevent
> That murmur, soon replies, God doth not need
> Either man's work or his own gifts, who best

142

Bear his mild yoke, they serve him best, his state
Is kingly. Thousands at his bidding speed
And post o'er land and ocean without rest:
They also serve who only stand and wait.

                              (Sonnet XIX)[3]

Milton splits himself into several aspects of himself, so that his act of introspection seems also an act of disintegration. There is the "I" who reflects on his situation, who stands at the boundary of the poem. There is the "I" who is the dramatic actor in the poem, foolishly and rather frenetically seeking an easy, certain knowledge of what God wants of him. It is a sign of his personal fragmentation that Milton depersonalizes his own abilities, describing (in a biblical pun) his "talent" as something extrinsic to him, "lodged" with him. Another sign is his depiction of the discrepancy between what his "soul" longs to do and what he in fact has done.

Against this fragmentation and fearful alienation from God — whom Milton wants to be close to, as his nomination of God as "my maker" implies — Milton sets "Patience." It is not sufficient to describe the action of this poem as a dialogue between the poet and Patience, treating Patience as a personified moral ideal with a dramatic status equal to the "I" of the poet. Patience is the poet's own patience, that is, his own ability to be patient newly recognized. Milton does not personify an abstract moral quality, but transforms his own person into a mode of action that he names "Patience." He has moved, to use a spatial metaphor, "deeper" into himself; he has discovered how to act in a new mode.

What happens at the end of the sonnet is not a sloughing off of the earlier versions of "I" but a reintegration and revision made possible in this new mode. The last three lines of the poem testify to this reintegration. Those critics who regard Patience as an autonomous figure find it hard to specify just who speaks those lines — Patience or the poet. If Patience is considered as the poet, as his new mode of being, then the problem of assigning the lines to one speaker or other dissolves. There is only one speaker, the poet, who has been transformed through the process of introspection and apparent "disorganization" that is the poem. This way of describing an interior drama is not an anachronistic distortion of Milton's text: Christian allegories from *Everyman* to *A Pilgrim's Progress* depict the individual person encountering personified

143

qualities or attributes of himself. What is new in this poem is the dissolving of the allegorical fiction and the resolving of opposed aspects of self into a newly unified self. In the last lines of the poem, Patience speaks and the poet speaks — for they are one and the same.

It is typical of people in this kind of crisis that their angle of vision is very sharp, permitting very intense insights in a very narrow range. Milton's change from this constricted vision to his new sense of transcendence can be described in terms of the changes in his metaphorical discourse. The key word in the opening line of the sonnet is "spent." Milton feels empty, exhausted, bankrupt. The pressure to perform, to produce, to augment himself is evident. He regards life as a moral test or competition to be measured in economic terms. The reference to his hidden "talent" suggests not only his poetic ability (he had not written poetry in the years prior to this sonnet, but had devoted himself to political prose) but also a punning equation of ability and money. Milton alludes to the biblical parable of the talents (Matt. 24:14–30), in which a lord's servants are each given a certain amount of money (one talent) and are rewarded if they use it to make more money. The servant who fearfully buries the money, who merely keeps it intact, is punished. A parable that can be read as a mandate for courage and self-assertion Milton at this point seems to regard as a paradigm of burdensome obligation. He contrasts his own desire to "serve" his maker with the apparently greater success of other people, and cries out in anguished protest. Every measure of this competition, as he sees it, is quantitative, everything counted: half his days, one talent.

When Milton begins to think in a new mode — that is, when Patience speaks — this frame of reference changes from the quantitative to the qualitative. Patience declares that "God doth not need / Either man's work or his own gifts." The economics of getting and spending, of hoarding and increasing, of labor and reward, of service as obligation, is replaced by another vision, apparent in the word "gifts." This new mode of interpreting service posits not obligation but freedom, not competition among servants but autonomy and equivalence.

Milton seems to reject what one might term a "capitalistic" paradigm of social relationships in favor of an older metaphoric model of God's relationship to man: "His state is kingly." For Milton, however, this statement is not a metaphor. God is the only ruler the antimonarchist Puritan would acknowledge. Milton shifts from an earthbound metaphor to a vision of the heavenly kingdom. Unlike the kings of this world, who need to receive the service and homage of subjects and need as well to exercise royal largesse in order to confirm their kingship, God does not need either the tribute of man's service or his own gifts. His rule is gratuitous, based on freedom from all necessity. His light cannot be spent, nor will it be denied.

Milton's new understanding of his own place in space and time dramatizes this theological and psychological movement from control to freedom, from the closed world of obligation to the open world of gift. As the poem begins, Milton is acutely aware of the precise limits of his time. Whether he is fifty or thirty-five is not as important as his sense of being confined in a certain span of time. His "light is spent," and he must now confront "this dark world and wide." If he knows time so definitely, he does not know the world. It looms before him, puzzling, mysterious, described not in the specific terms of number and order but in the vague, ominous, experiential language of sensation.

The trap of linear time closes on Milton when he is caught in the contradictory terms of impulse and control. When Milton asks if God would exact "day-labour, light denied," Patience "to prevent that murmur soon replies." Milton reverses ordinary sequence: the reply comes after the murmur it is supposed to prevent. If Patience were to "prevent" it, Patience would have to speak first. Milton depicts a spiritual problem using the linear narrative of a speech ("that murmur") and a reply. By describing that speech and reply in language that disrupts the illusion of sequence, he dramatizes his movement away from accepting linear time as a matrix of experience toward a recognition that experience is "timeless."

The first line of the sonnet, "When I consider how my light is spent," had implied something of that timelessness. The syntax indicates that Milton has considered this situation more than once. Later, when Milton declares that Patience "soon" replies, he again implies that the experience he describes has been a recurrent one. This sonnet is not intended to describe a single unique experience, then, but a repetition, a pattern. What keeps the poem from giving the impression of stagnation, of a never-ending repetition of the same crisis and consolation, is the last line: "They also serve who only stand and wait." That act of waiting for something both closes the poem and points beyond it to a potential for new experience, new vision.

If the poem moves from definite temporal constraints to acknowledged and accepted timelessness, from defined to undefined measures of experience, the world is depicted in quite different spatial terms. The poet initially confronts an indeterminate, ominous place — "this dark world and wide." Against that world he stands alone — a little world denied light, his talent "lodged with [him] useless." The dark, confined world of self is vulnerable to forces he cannot control; the poet feels he must do what he cannot do, must be what he cannot be. By the end of the poem, because he acts in a new mode, the threatening world is threatening no longer. The emotionally charged description of "this dark world and wide" yields to the neutral terms of geography, "land and ocean." The poet has world enough and time, because neither the limits of time nor the indeterminacy of space defines the value of his action. In his new vision of human action, those who act patiently and purposively, whether speeding "o'er land and ocean without rest" or standing quietly in one place, make equally good use of their allotted time and space.

I have described Milton's poem as an act of internalization. Milton has moved from being the exterior "I" who acknowledges his situation in the world, to the interior "I" who protests against it, to the "Patience" who provides a new mode of accepting the world. According to this reading of the poem, Patience is Milton's own patience, his "innermost" and therefore "true" self. However, it is also possible to describe Milton's meditation as an act of externalization rather than internalization. Milton has dramatized his meditation on action by splitting himself into different speakers, a disintegration that emphasizes his isolation. The poem does not confirm him in isolation, but because he achieves a reintegrated self of himself he can escape isolation and achieve a vision of himself as a member of the human community. To personify patience, to transform a person (himself) into a significant quality (Patience) has the effect of distancing or transcending interior process. By depicting his personal mode of being through the words of an impersonal, autonomous speaker, Milton creates a bridge between his own feelings of isolation and the common experience of all human beings, the "they" who must also find a way to act and to be. Milton unites himself with the unnamed "thousands" who "post o'er land and ocean without rest," and also with those "who only stand and wait." His own restlessness, evident in the twists and turns, the run-on lines and unpredictable emphases of the sonnet, indicate that Milton has more in common with those who travel than with those who stand and wait; the division of the human community into these groups reasserts

Milton's initial sense of contrast between his prior active life and his current state, but his new vision allows him to see value in both. At its most private and interior moment, the poem insists on the universal principle his experience can illustrate. The point of probing his own way of regaining the ability to act has been not only to provide himself an escape from personal isolation, but also to understand and describe the sacred basis of the human community he chooses to join.

This poem, it is said, begins in frustration and ends in submissiveness — whether abject or affirmative, critics disagree.[4] The problem in this poem is not submission to a just or unjust God, but rather the poet's understanding of the basis of human action, and of the basic freedom that can join humanity with God. Milton discovers that his light cannot be spent, or, at least, that it may come again, in ways he cannot predict. He can affirm uncertainty, because he has reached at least a tentative understanding that action and life are far more than he had allowed them to be. He phrases his new understanding as a submission to God, but what he really has come to understand and accept is himself.

III

Keats offers a very different meditation on life and action in a secular poem that finds no refuge in service to God or membership in the human community:

> When I have fears that I may cease to be
>   Before my pen has glean'd my teeming brain,
> Before high-piled books, in charactery,
>   Hold like rich garners the full ripen'd grain;
> When I behold, upon the night's starr'd face,
>   Hugh cloudy symbols of a high romance,
> And think that I may never live to trace
>   Their shadows, with the magic hand of chance;
> And when I feel, fair creature of an hour,
>   That I shall never look upon thee more,
> Never have relish in the faery power
>   Of unreflecting love; — then on the shore
> Of the wide world I stand alone, and think
>   Till love and fame to nothingness do sink.[5]

Keats does not split himself into different speakers, and he writes of an imagined future loss from the perspective of his present fullness, rather than from the present and future emptiness that the blind Milton feared and resented. Both men fear that they cannot write — Milton because he is blind and discouraged, both his spiritual and physical light spent; Keats because he knows how fragile that light is, how near man is to death at every moment.

What both poets share is a growth from helpless passivity to the wise passiveness of understanding and acceptance. Because they understand, they can finally stand — Milton to wait, Keats to think. Milton illustrated his passivity in the metaphoric mode he chose to narrate his own experience, splitting himself into apparently autonomous actors and denying his own status as actor, finally merging those created figures into his own active self. Keats remains a single speaker throughout his sonnet, but seems in the first line to distance himself from his own actions and feelings, to think of his "fears" as objects, as things that he has. His action in this poem is to redescribe those fears as actions. The sequence of describing what he fears to lose indicates how all of them are related, and the changing mode of describing them testifies to his new understanding and overcoming of his fearful imaginings. The first line states in general, passive language that Keats fears he will "cease to be." He unfolds what that means to him by describing what he will lose, what he will never or no longer be able to do, but finally recognizes in visionary active language that what he will lose is not thinking about something but thinking itself, not having but being.

Like Milton, Keats begins with an initial metaphor that suggests that he feels trapped and confined, and that his way of regarding his life is static, reified, and therefore unsatisfying. In the first quatrain, he fears that he will not live long enough to write the books he envisions, to reap the harvest of his "teeming brain." Locating his imagination in his "brain," Keats seems to distance it from himself, distorting it. The image, however, is too commonplace to be exciting, far removed from the powerful, rich evocation of harvest that Keats will later achieve in "To Autumn." Although Keats certainly does not feel, as Milton does, that his light is spent, readers of these first lines may disagree.

What rescues Keats from cliché is his own rejection of this metaphor: he turns from this static language to a dramatic vision of the sources of his poetry and of his ways of thinking. First, he yearns to contemplate the universal, timeless "cloudy symbols" of high romance.

These ideas are always available to everyone, but no author can capture them directly and entirely. A poet cannot control them, or even define what they are, but can only hope "to trace their shadows with the magic hand of chance." In vaguely philosophical terms, this might be called a Platonic theory of art. Each fiction approximates, or shadows, the truth. In the third quatrain, his tribute to "the faery power of unreflecting love," Keats offers what one might call an Aristotelian view of art. The moment of real experience, not the universal symbolic idea, is his inspiration. To be an artist means to attend to the unique, fleeting moment, the "fair creature of an hour" — which cannot be understood or contemplated, but only felt. That moment of experience is as uncontrollable, unpredictable, and evanescent as the "huge cloudy symbols" of myth.

If it is difficult to define what Keats means by the "cloudy symbols," it is just as hard to describe what he means in this third quatrain. It may be that he is not only describing a source of art and a way of being a poet but also an alternative to art, and an alternative to being a poet — celebrating the "unreflecting love" that does not need to be preserved, validated, or exalted by the poet but only relished by the man.

In the last lines of the sonnet, Keats reflects on the first three quatrains, summing up his fears of what he will lose by once again confining them as nouns — "love" and "fame" — that sink to nothingness in the face of what he most fears to lose, life itself. If the high romantic symbols are more than the vehicle of his own fame, if love is more than an occasion for literature, thinking is more than what one thinks about. Like a second Descartes, Keats finds in thinking the essential act, and what he fears to lose is life itself. "Love and fame" are diminished in the face of being, and "sink to nothingness" not only in comparison but also in conjunction with the fact of death.

Keats had begun his poem by contemplating a future that he feared might not be; he ends by confronting the future that must be, and chooses to cherish the present. The progressive unfolding of his "fears" into several different actions indicates connections between them. From his first metaphoric image of books piled high, he shifts to a metaphoric vision of what he could write about. The vagueness of the second quatrain and the contradictory possible meanings of the third take him beyond considering the objects of thought to the act of thinking for its own sake. Keats discovers in that act the power and fragility of life. All his other fears — that he will not be famous, that he will neither love nor be loved — yield to, and make more intense, the fear that he will die young.

The "geography" of the poet's narrative defines and shapes the experience he related. He begins with the landlocked metaphor of farmland, his brain a teeming field of ideas, his dream a loaded granary. What he envisions are books, his art the result of inspiration and labor. Then, turning his face to "the night's starr'd face," he regards art not as the result of inspiration or diligence, but as the leisurely, dreamlike tracing of "chance." In the last lines of the sonnet, Keats considers himself as a world, life as a vast, mysterious sea: "on the shore / Of this wide world I stand alone, and think / Till love and fame to nothingness do sink." Considered in terms of this spatial metaphor, the poet's condition at the end of the poem seems more ominous, not less.

The metaphor of time is equally important to the definition of the poet's meditation. Life is regarded as a span of time analogous to a day; love and fame "sink" like the sun at dusk. Yet the chronological structure of the narrative is not the simple equivalent of a day. The poet begins with a vision of the end of a day, the long harvest complete. The sense of the poet in a landscape is explicit, the moment of time implicit. In the second quatrain, Keats contemplates the night sky, moving from a vision of poetry as day-labor to a vision of poetry as dream. The third quatrain mutes the spatial terms of the narrative to emphasize the temporal, bringing to intensity a single moment of experience. The "fair creature of an hour" might be seen at any hour, any sudden moment, but will not continue. "The faery power / Of unreflecting love" does not depend on, or even recognize, the sequence or the continuity of time. In some sense set free by this intense recognition of the power of a moment, Keats seems to defy the clock and to move backward in time. The final visionary moment suggests sunset: love and fame "sink" below the horizon as the poet stands alone "on the shore of the wide world." Yet that sunset marks a new dawn as well.

The poet is once more, and even more explicitly than in the opening lines, placed in a landscape. Keats finally chooses a spatial mode of narration to describe a temporal experience. That temporal experience is not only the metaphorical (and therefore alterable) sequence of day to night, but also the logical sequence of thought that organizes the syntax of the poem (When . . . then). The advantage of choosing a spatial mode for the final statement of the poem lies in its stability, and in its relationship to both temporal modes — that is, to the sequence in the poem and to the sequence of the poem. That stabilizing power of the poet's and reader's "mind's eye" is not, however, an easy way of resolving the poet's dilemma, but rather a way of declaring it clearly. From the comforting permanence of the landscape at harvest time, Keats finally places himself on the shore of the sea, facing an awesome vastness no one can ever know.

The last line of the poem sums up in two words, love and fame, the two kinds of experience, the two ways of living, the two goals of art, that are the problem of the poem. In the first stanza, Keats sets the fact of being harvested — of dying — against his wish to harvest ideas, to gain fame as a poet. Against that first easy act of metaphor-making, Keats then sets the "huge cloudy symbols" of an art outside his brain, of ideas he does not create but rather perceives. He is moving away from poetry as an act of will, toward poetry as an act of response. The third quatrain celebrates responsiveness without necessarily needing poetry. From wanting to preserve his own ideas or to serve a subject beyond himself, Keats turns to the joy of "unreflecting love," of simply being with someone. Love is recognized as an experience satisfying and complete within itself; art is irrelevant. I have already suggested, however, that these lines can also be read in quite another way, as a description of one source for poetry, not as an alternative to it. The doubleness of the third quatrain sets up the even greater set of possibilities for meaning in the last lines of the poem.

So far, I have argued that "love and fame" are diminished at the end of the poem. The question seems to be, by what? "The wide world" dwarfs the private desires of any person. Thinking about fame and about love is dwarfed by the act of thinking. But if thinking is being, as Descartes suggests, then death dwarfs life, and all the actions that are life. Keats stands alone on the shore, between his own world of self and the vast sea of life, contemplating the end of his own time, and of all time. "They lied when they told me I was everything," admits King Lear, but he had also spoken something of the truth when he declared, in the last moment of his reign, "Nothing can come of nothing." From the lie of everything, Keats, like Lear, must come to terms with "nothingness."

To cope with that fear of "nothingness," Milton turns to faith in something beyond himself, a God known through the light of inspiration and the text of the Bible. Keats, denied that faith, stands alone. What faith he has is vested in literature — in the works of Plato and

Aristotle, Shakespeare and Milton, and in his own writing as well. Against the image of books yet to be written stands this single sonnet, like the poet, alone. Milton, through the action of his poem, affirms his place in the community of God's servants. Moving away from his initial tragic sense of thwarted desire, Milton seeks and finds an antidote to his "murmur" against his state. Keats, much younger, facing only an imagined loss, moves toward a tragic sense. He remains alone. He imagines losing the "fair creature of an hour," losing the only relationship that matters to him. Confronting loss, confronting what it would mean to write no more books and know no human love, Keats achieves a tragic sense of his own mortality. First envisioning harvest, Keats finally confronts nothingness, moving from a dream of "high romance" to an image of his own fate, from "relish in the faery power / Of unreflecting love" to awe at the power and desirability of reflection, of silent thought, cherishing the time not yet over but certain to end.

IV

I have argued that the acts of revision presented in these two sonnets are redescriptions in the mode advocated by Roy Schafer as the language "native" to interpretation. However, to read these sonnets as actions may seem to diminish their status as art. Schafer has developed "action language" in an effort to describe spontaneous discourse, not the shaped artifice that is a literary text. To read poems as actions seems to argue that poems are a kind of overdetermined "super speech." Any text subsumes many subtexts in the rich surface of its language; that is, its language *means* in many different ways. The act of criticism, then, would seem to require reducing that language to its different ways of meaning, reducing it back to its origin in speech.

Keats, however, is not trying to compose "super speech," and the dialogue presented in Milton's sonnet is almost antithetical to speech. For both poets, utterance is crafted in the service of vision. Both want to go beyond the rhetorical poetry of will — Milton to the inspired voice of faith, Keats to the unwilled poetry of sensation and then beyond that as well. To quote Lear again, in mad affinity: "Oh, sir, you are old. Nature in you stands on the very verge of his confine." To Keats, everyone is old, everyone stands on the verge. His sonnet cannot, finally, go beyond the verge of his confine, but can point the way. Looking inward, he has described his own acts of thought and feeling. He has progressed from the rhetorical public mode of the first quatrain, with its reliance on commonplace, unexamined metaphor, to the puzzling sensations of dream and feeling, expressed through metaphor, to the thoughtful apprehension of the metaphors that have shaped his narrative. Because he has turned inward, he can at last stand alone and look, not only downward to "nothingness" but outward to the beyond he cannot know. Paradoxically, because he can stand alone, because he has looked inward and described his fears as the complex actions they are, he is not alone. His feelings are universal, his solitude common to every person who reads his poem.

The act of reading these poems is the act of achieving and affirming a human community. For Milton, the vision of community is grounded in a religious faith; for Keats, the vision of community makes it possible for him to have a necessary faith in himself. His community of poets and readers is the basis, not the goal, of his poetry. What both men share is their belief in poetry as an act of description, a search for a way to transcribe, and thereby imitate, the complex act of being. Interpretation of their poetry requires an equally rigorous description of their complex act of writing and our complex act of reading.

It would be possible to describe the act of reading as Milton and Keats describe the act of writing. From exhaustion, from the fear that one has said nothing and can say nothing, the interpreter can, with Milton, discover what it means to trust in something beyond the narrow confines of self, what it means to be receptive and open to whatever comes, rather than frenetically rushing after what will always be out of reach or despondently giving up the quest. To interpret, the literary critic, like Keats, hopes to harvest ideas teeming in the brain, only to realize that interpretation, like poetry, is a matter of tracing shadows with the magic hand of chance, wanting to keep for just a while longer the "fair creature of an hour" that is the experience of reading a poem. Finally, like Keats, the critic can only stand alone and think.

To interpret a poem is an action, a personal choice. The order of the interpretation is not the order of the poem. Instead, the poem is taken apart, disorganized, and reorganized into another arrangement of ideas and images. For example, interpretation may begin with what is most difficult to understand — in Milton's sonnet the syntax, in Keats's poem the referential meaning of the "huge cloudy symbols" and the "fair creature of an hour." Contexts may be required: the other work of the poet, or of his contemporaries, or — the possibilities are theoretically endless. Yet a text is presented as a single thing, whole and entire, and in describing them I have chosen to honor their integrity as actions. To understand an interpretation as an action, the critic must seek out or acknowledge the reasons why that particular interpretation is put forth: perhaps to "prove" the critic's worth as a reader, or to prove the worth of a poem, or to prove the bond between poet and critic, critic and reader. A critical reading of a poem, an interpretation, is an act of mediation. As the word "interpret" suggests, the critic stands between the text and its readers, standing on the verge, at once alone and one with the poet and the audience of other readers.

If a critic is to be an uncommon reader, what is required is the recognition that all interpretation is based, first and finally, on the common feelings that no interpretation can entirely explain but that every interpretation must honor. Interpretation, therefore, aspires to invisibility. It will be a sign of the true importance of Schafer's "action language" as an interpretive tool if it is difficult for the reader of this essay to identify what is uniquely attributable to his method. The focus should be on the actions of each poet — the texts.

Third Force Psychology
and the
Study of Literature

by Bernard J. Paris

I have been using Third Force psychology since 1964; and I have found it to work remarkably well with a great deal of Western literature (and Western philosophy and theology, too) from the Bible to the present day.[1] Many authors from a variety of periods and cultures have intuitively grasped and artistically portrayed the same patterns of conflict and behavior that are analyzed in Third Force psychology. The theory permits us to recover their intuitions and to formulate them in conceptual terms. The theory is deceptively simple and unfashionably clear, but it yields insights of great depth and subtlety; and I believe that its usefulness in literary, biographical, and cultural analysis will help it to assume its proper place as a major contribution to human understanding. It has its limitations, of course. Different psychological theories address themselves to different aspects of human experience, as do different works of literature. There are many works about which I can say very little from a Third Force perspective; but there are others with which it is highly congruent.

I have used Third Force psychology in a number of ways. After providing a brief exposition of the theory, I shall illustrate its usefulness in analyzing literary characters, the personality of the author, and reader response.

Bernard J. Paris

Third Force Theory

Third Force psychologists see healthy human development as a process of self-actualization, and unhealthy development as a process of self-alienation. Abraham Maslow provides the fullest picture of healthy growth, and Karen Horney gives us the most detailed account of the processes of self-alienation.[2] Since most literature is about self-alienation, it is Horney's theories that I find most useful for critical analysis. Third Force conceptions of health also have critical value, however; and they serve as a norm in terms of which we can judge constructive and destructive behavior.

What Third Force psychologists have in common is their belief that man is not simply a tension-reducing or a conditioned animal, but that there is present in him a third force, an "evolutionary constructive" force, which urges "him to realize his given potentialities."[3] Each man has "an essential biologically based inner nature" that is "good or neutral rather than bad," and that should be brought out and encouraged rather than suppressed. If this inner nature "is permitted to guide our life, we grow healthy, fruitful, and happy." If it is "denied or suppressed," we get sick. This inner nature "is weak and delicate and subtle and easily overcome by habit, cultural pressure, and wrong attitudes toward it" (*PB*, 3–4).

One of the most interesting Third Force contributions to our understanding of man's essential nature is Abraham Maslow's theory of the hierachy of basic needs. According to this theory, all men have physiological survival needs, needs for safety, for love and belonging, for self-esteem, and for self-actualization. The needs are hierarchical in that they exist in an order of prepotency; the physiological needs are the most powerful, and so on. Maslow includes needs for knowledge and understanding and for beauty among the basic needs, but he does not integrate them into his hierachy. The needs at the upper end of the hierachy are much weaker than the lower needs, but they are no less basic. All of the needs are basic in the sense that they are built into man's nature as a function of his biological structure, and they must be gratified if he is to develop in a healthy way.

Each individual presses by nature for the fulfillment of all of these needs, but at any given time his motivational life will be centered around the fulfillment of one of them. Since a higher need emerges strongly only when the needs below it have been sufficiently met, the individual tends to be occupied with the basic needs in the order of their prepotency. His values, fantasies, and motivations will be focused upon the strongest unmet need. The person living in an environment favorable to growth will move steadily up the hierarchy until he is free to devote most of his energies to self-actualization. This is the full and satisfying use of his capacities in a calling that suits his nature. The hierarchy of basic needs establishes, then, the pattern of psychological evolution. Frustration of the basic needs produces pathology; it arrests the individual's development, alienates him from his real self, and leads him to develop defensive strategies for making up his deficiencies.

The concept of the real self is the foundation of both Maslow's and Horney's systems. Under favorable conditions, says Horney, the individual "will develop . . . the unique alive forces of his real self: the clarity and depth of his own feelings, thoughts, wishes, interests; the ability to tap his own resources, the strength of his will power; the special capacities or gifts he may have; the faculty to express himself, and to relate himself to others with his spontaneous feelings. All this will in time enable him to find his set of values and his aims in life" (*NHG*, 17). Since the real self is not very strong, it is frequently abandoned. The child is a weak and dependent being whose needs for safety, love, and acceptance are so strong that he will sacrifice himself, if necessary, in order to get these things.

The person who is able to develop in accordance with his real self possesses a number of characteristics that distinguish him from the self-alienated person. He is open to the world rather than defensive or embedded. He is more congruent, more transparent, more spontaneous: he is in touch with what he really wants, thinks, and feels; he does not send conflicting signals to others; and he trusts his impulses. He has a healthy self-esteem that does not depend upon constant recognition from others. His values are not generated by his defensive strategies but by his healthy basic needs, and they reflect what all men require in order to achieve self-actualization. His relation to the world is allocentric (other-centered) rather than egocentric. As a result, he is able to perceive the external world more clearly and to love people for what they are rather than for their fulfillment of his needs. He has more "peak experiences" than other people, that is, more natural highs in which he feels internally integrated and one with the world. He has a good tolerance for change, uncertainty, and difference because he is confident of himself and is not easily threatened. If his real self is imperiled, however, he will fight to preserve it.[4]

The person whose basic needs are relatively well gratified remains in touch with his real thoughts, feelings, and wishes and develops in a self-actualizing way. Frustration of the basic needs produces a number of defensive strategies, all of which cut us off from ourselves and from the world and lead us to behave in rigid, compulsive ways. According to Horney, self-alienation begins as a defense against "basic anxiety," which is a "profound insecurity and vague apprehensiveness" (*NHG*, 18) generated by feelings of isolation, helplessness, fear, and hostility. The invariable consequence of basic anxiety is that the child forsakes his real self and puts "the greatest part of his energies into securing reassurance."⁵He seeks reassurance in his relation to others by developing interpersonal strategies of defense — which we shall examine next — and he seeks to compensate for his feelings of worthlessness and inadequacy by an intrapsychic process of self-glorification. These strategies constitute his effort to fulfill his frustrated, and therefore highly intensified, needs for safety, love and belonging, and self-esteem. They are also designed to reduce his anxiety and to provide a safe outlet for his hostility.

There are three main ways in which the child, and later the adult, can move in his effort to defend himself against a pathogenic environment. He can move toward people and adopt the self-effacing or compliant solution; he can move against people and develop the aggressive or expansive solution; or he can move away from people and become resigned and detached. Each of these solutions carries with it "certain needs, qualities, sensitivities, inhibitions, anxieties, and . . . values."⁶ Each solution involves also a view of human nature, a sense of the world order, and a bargain with fate in which certain attitudes, qualities, and behaviors are supposed to be rewarded.

The conditions that produce any one set of defensive strategies tend to produce them all; but since they involve incompatible character structures and value systems, the individual usually makes one solution predominant and represses the others. When the submerged trends are for some reason brought closer to the surface, the individual will experience severe inner turmoil; and he may be paralyzed, unable to move in any direction at all. When his predominant solution fails, he may embrace one of the repressed attitudes.

The person in whom compliant trends are dominant tries to overcome his basic anxiety by gaining affection and approval and by controlling others through his need of them. His values "lie in the direction of goodness, sympathy, love, generosity, unselfishness, humility; while egotism, ambition, callousness, unscrupulousness, wielding of power are abhorred" (*OIC*, 54–55). He does not hold these values as genuine ideals, but because they are necessary to his defense system. His bargain is that if he is a good, loving, noble person who shuns pride and does not seek his private gain or glory, he will be well treated by fate and by other people. He needs to believe not only in the fairness of the world order, but also in the goodness of human nature. In both areas he is vulnerable to disappointment. In the compliant person, says Horney, there are "a variety of aggressive tendencies strongly repressed" (*OIC*, 55). These aggressive drives are repressed because feeling them or acting them out would clash violently with his need to feel that he is loving and good, and would radically endanger his whole strategy for gaining love, justice, and approval.

The person in whom aggressive tendencies are predominant has goals, traits, and values that are the opposite of those of the self-effacing person. He needs "to achieve success, prestige or recognition" (*OIC*, 65). What appeals to him most is not love, but mastery. He abhors helplessness and is ashamed of suffering. There are three expansive types: the narcissistic, the perfectionistic, and the arrogant-vindictive. They all "aim at mastering life. This is their way of conquering fears and anxieties; this gives meaning to their lives and gives them a certain zest for living" (*NHG*, 212).

The narcissistic person seeks to master life "by self-admiration and the exercise of charm" (*NHG*, 212). He has an "unquestioned belief in his greatness and uniqueness" that gives him a "buoyancy and perennial youthfulness" (*NHG*, 194). His insecurity is manifested in the fact that he "may speak incessantly of his exploits or of his wonderful qualities and needs endless confirmation of his estimate of himself in the form of admiration and devotion" (ibid.). He sees the world as a fostering parent and expects continual good fortune in the form of good luck and the fulfillment of his wishes by fate and by other people. His bargain is that if he holds onto his dreams and to his exaggerated claims for himself, life is bound to give him what he wants.

The perfectionistic person "feels superior because of his high standards, moral and intellectual, and on this basis looks down on others" (*NHG*, 196). He has a legalistic concept of the world order. Through the height of his standards, he compels fate. His claims are based "on a 'deal' he has secretly made with life. Because he is fair, just, dutiful, he is entitled to fair treatment by others and by life in general" (*NHG*, 197). Ill fortune shakes him "to the foundation of his psychic existence. It invalidates his whole accounting system and conjures up the ghastly prospect of helplessness." His recognition of "an error or failure of his own making" also "pulls the ground away from under him. . . . Self-effacing trends and undiluted self-hate, kept in check successfully hitherto, then may come to the fore."

The arrogant-vindictive person is motivated chiefly by a need for vindictive triumphs. Whereas the narcissistic person received early admiration, and the perfectionistic person grew up under the pressure of rigid standards, the arrogant-vindictive person was treated harshly. He has a need to retaliate for all injuries and to prove his superiority to all rivals. In his relations with others, he is at once ruthless and cynical. He trusts no one, avoids emotional involvement, and seeks to exploit others in order to enhance his own feelings of mastery. He believes that might makes right and that the world is a jungle in which the strong annihilate the weak. He wants to be hard and tough and regards all manifestation of feeling as a sign of weakness. He fears the emergence of his own compliant trends because they would make him vulnerable in an evil world, would confront him with self-hate, and would threaten his bargain, which is essentially with himself. He does not count on the world to give him anything, but he is convinced that he can reach his ambitious goals if he remains true to his vision of life as a battle and does not allow himself to be seduced by his own softer feelings or the traditional morality. If his expansive solution collapses, self-effacing trends may emerge quite powerfully.

The basically detached person pursues neither love nor mastery; he worships, rather, freedom, peace, and self-sufficiency. He tries to escape suffering by being independent of external forces, by feeling that nothing matters, and by concerning himself only with those things that are within his power. His bargain is that if he asks nothing of others, they will not bother him; that if he tries for nothing, he will not fail; and that if he expects little of life, he will not be disappointed. The detached person withdraws from himself as well as from others. This is an effort not only to restrict wishes and to repress suffering, but also to escape from the conflict between his aggressive and compliant trends.

While interpersonal difficulties are creating the movements toward, against, and away from people, and the conflicts between these trends, concomitant intrapsychic problems are producing their own defensive strategies. To compensate for his feelings of self-hate and inadequacy, the individual creates an "idealized image" of himself, which he "endows . . . with unlimited powers and . . . exalted faculties" (*NHG*, 22). Since the individual can feel worthwhile only if he is his idealized image, everything that falls short is deemed worthless; and there develops a "despised image" that is just as unrealistic as its idealized counterpart.

With the formation of the idealized image, the individual embarks upon a "search for glory," as "the energies driving toward self-realization are shifted to the aim of actualizing the idealized self" (*NHG*, 24). The idealized image generates also a whole structure of intrapsychic defenses that Horney calls "the pride system." The individual takes an intense pride in the attributes of his idealized self, and on the basis of this pride he makes "neurotic claims" upon the world and his fellows. His claims make him extremely vulnerable, of course, for their frustration threatens to confront him with his despised self, and with the sense of worthlessness from which he is fleeing.

The individual's search for glory subjects him to what Horney calls "the tyranny of the should." The function of the shoulds is "to make oneself over into one's idealized self" (*NHG*, 68). One aspect of the individual's bargain with fate is that if he lives up to his shoulds, his claims will be honored; reality is controlled through an intrapsychic process of self-mastery. The shoulds are impossible to live up to, partly because they are unrealistic and partly because they reflect the individual's inner conflicts and are often contradictory in nature.

Self-hate is the end product of the intrapsychic strategies of defense, each of which tends to magnify the individual's feelings of inadequacy and failure. Self-hate is essentially the rage that the idealized self feels toward the self that we actually are for not being what it "should" be. Horney sees self-hate as "perhaps the greatest tragedy of the human mind. Man in reaching out for the Infinite and Absolute also starts destroying himself. When he makes a pact with the devil, who promises him glory, he has to go to hell — to the hell within himself" (*NHG*, 154).

Analyzing Literary Characters: Shakespeare's *Hamlet*

Not all literary characters are appropriate objects of psychological analysis. Many must be understood primarily in terms of their formal and thematic functions in the artistic whole of which they are a part.

Some are highly individualized, however, and are presented in realistic detail. These "round" or "mimetic" characters are described by E. M. Forster as "creations inside a creation."[7] They have their functions within the larger creation; but they are inwardly intelligible as well, and their behavior can be understood in motivational terms. The study of such characters is one of the least developed areas of literary criticism, in large part because we have lacked a conceptual system that would permit us to see and to talk about them in detail. For many characters, Horney's theory remedies this deficiency. Her theory enables us to understand the characters in all their complexity and to see them, however remote their period or culture, as human beings who are very, very much like ourselves. It enhances our appreciation, too, of the authors' achievements. It permits us to recover their psychological intuitions and to do justice, perhaps for the first time, to their almost unbelievable genius in mimetic characterization.

There is one feature of Horney's theory that makes it especially suitable for the analysis of literary characters, and that is its emphasis upon the present structure of the psyche. A major weakness of psychoanalytic studies of character has been their use of a diachronic mode of analysis that explains the present in terms of the past. Because of their reliance upon infantile experience to account for the behavior of the adult, these studies must often posit events in the character's early life that are not depicted in the text. This results in the generation of crucial explanatory material out of the premises of the theory, with no corroborating literary evidence except the supposed results of the invented experiences, which were inferred from these results to begin with. This procedure has resulted in a justifiable distrust of the psychological study of character.

Horney's theory focuses upon the character structure and defensive strategies of the adult, rather than upon infantile origins. It permits us to establish a causal relationship between past and present if there is enough information, but it also enables us to understand the present structure of the psyche as an inwardly intelligible system and to explain behavior in terms of its function within that system. As a result, we can account for a character's thoughts, feelings, and actions on the basis of what has actually been given. If the childhood material is present, it can be used; but if it is absent, it need not be invented. Because Horney's theory describes the kinds of phenomena that are actually portrayed in literature and explains these phenomena in a synchronic way, it permits us to stick to the words on the page, to explicate the text.

We can see how this works with *Hamlet*. What kind of a person is Hamlet? Why is he so terribly vulnerable to disillusionment and despair, to confusion, turmoil, and paralysis? The facts as they appear would be disturbing to almost any man; but not everyone would react as intensely as Hamlet does. To understand Hamlet's feelings we must try to comprehend his character and enter into his experience. We can do this, I think, without reconstructing his childhood; but we shall have to use our imaginations somewhat and infer from the evidence in the text the attitudes, beliefs, and expectations from life that Hamlet has held as a grown man and that have been so profoundly disrupted by the events following his father's death.

Before his father's death, Hamlet is a man who strives very hard to be good, who believes in the nobility of human nature and of the important people in his life, and who expects virtue to be rewarded, both here and hereafter. He values love, dutifulness, and constancy, and has faith that these qualities will win the devotion, loyalty, and esteem of others. He shuns pride, revengefulness, and ambition, embraces Christian attitudes, and has a religious dread of sin. In order to live up to his moral standards, he has repressed his sexuality. He is fearful of lust in himself and is disgusted by it in others. He has high expectations of himself and strives to be an exemplary human being. He idealizes women and is high-minded and pure in his dealings with them. He has warm relations with men and an ideal conception of friendship.

Life is going well for Hamlet before his father's death. His kind of people are in power, his values are being honored, and the future looks bright. The death of his father and the events that follow upset this situation and threaten Hamlet in a number of ways. His father's death is a shocking, untimely death that deprives Hamlet of a loved parent and sets him brooding on mortality and the "base uses" to which even the greatest of men may return (V, i).[8] When Claudius becomes king, Hamlet is further alienated from the world in which he was formerly so much at home. His own noble qualities have been passed over, and the crown has been given to a man who is the opposite of both his father and himself. His whole demeanor shows that he is feeling abused. His faith in the political order has been profoundly disturbed, and he cannot help feeling that life is unjust. His fair visions of the future have been mocked by events.

The most devastating blow to Hamlet is, of course, his mother's marriage to Claudius. Because of his powerful identification with his father, he feels the wrongs Gertrude has done to the dead king as

163

though they had been done to himself. Hamlet is angry with his mother on his father's behalf. Hamlet's identification with his father may be in part the effect of mourning. But the main reason for his identification is that he has modeled himself upon his father and glorified those qualities in himself that he shares with him. He and his father are similar psychological types. They have similar idealized images, similar claims, and similar shoulds. They both strive to be noble, good, and loving; and they both expect these qualities to be rewarded. They are conscientious, dutiful, religious men who exalt women, are faithful to their oaths, and place a high value upon sexual purity. They have lived up to their shoulds, but their claims have not been honored, and their bargain is in ruins.

The king, instead of receiving fair treatment, is betrayed by his wife, murdered by his brother, and prematurely forgotten by everyone except his son. Virtue is not rewarded. Instead, the evil Claudius is triumphant. He has committed the most heinous of sins, but instead of being punished, he has gained through his villainy both Queen Gertrude and the throne.

Both Hamlet and his father revile Claudius so because he is the opposite psychological type. For the Hamlet type of man it is unbearable for the Claudiuses of the world to gain the love, power, and recognition that should be the reward of virtue. There is something more, I think, to the repugnance Hamlet feels toward Claudius. Claudius represents the sexual and aggressive drives that Hamlet represses in himself. He is what Hamlet is afraid of becoming. Hamlet's father is an external embodiment of his idealized image; Claudius symbolizes his despised self. When Claudius's successes undermine his solution, Hamlet's repression is threatened and he becomes all the more afraid of his forbidden impulses. He cannot help doubting the efficacy of virtue (what has it done for his father?); and he is enraged by Gertrude, by whom he feels betrayed. His taboos are still in operation, however; and he is afraid of becoming a monster. His attacks on Claudius are in part an externalization of his loathing for those parts of himself against which he is struggling and in part a reaffirmation of his own nobility. They reinforce his pride in his virtue and assure him that he can never become like the bestial creature he so thoroughly condemns.

First Soliloquy

The disgust with life and the longings for extinction that Hamlet expresses in his first soliloquy are the reactions of a man whose most cherished beliefs have been shattered and whose strategy for dealing with the world has proved to be totally ineffective. His oppression is the result not only of his disillusionment, but also of his repressed hostility. He is full of bitterness and rage, but he cannot express his feelings directly to Claudius and Gertrude. He mutters asides, quibbles with words, and accuses them with his display of mourning and melancholy.

The wish for death which Hamlet's first soliloquy opens is partly a desire to escape from a world in which he despairs of receiving love and justice and partly a desire to throw off the burden of his inner conflicts. It is also a product of turning against the self, a frequent defense in the self-effacing solution where there is a powerful taboo against violence, especially toward a parent. In this defense "an impulse unacceptable if directed toward some object in the outer world is turned inward against the self, as a child in a rage will suddenly start striking himself, tearing his own hair, or throwing a tantrum."[9] Hamlet's suicidal fantasies provide both an outlet for his destructive impulses and a defense against acting them out. He harbors murderous impulses toward his mother, but he cannot permit himself even to feel them. What he is aware of is that he wants to die. One object of suicide is to make others feel guilty, and this is surely a motive for Hamlet. But self-murder is also a sin. Hamlet can no longer believe that goodness will be rewarded in this world; but he still expects evil to be punished, both here and hereafter. The penalty for suicide is eternal damnation. If he could only melt away without any act of his own, he would at once escape his pain, retain his virtue, and show others how they have destroyed him.

As his death wishes indicate, Hamlet is already in an impossible position for his kind of person. His encounter with the ghost intensifies the pressure on him both to be aggressive and to be good. The ghost's outrage feeds Hamlet's already seething indignation; and he is prompted to his revenge by both heaven and hell, by a righteous desire for justice and a murderous craving for retaliation. Hamlet cannot help feeling ambivalent, however, about being an avenger. It is a matter of love, of loyalty, and of manliness for him to carry out the ghost's commission; and he swears to do so. But there is both in Christianity and in Hamlet's self-effacing defense system a strong taboo against aggressive behavior. "I could accuse me of such things," he tells Ophelia, "that it were better my mother had not borne me. I am very proud, revengeful, and ambitious . . ." (III, i). The ghost himself is not a single-minded revenger. He is protective toward Gertrude and fearful of his son's damnation:

> But, however thou pursuest this act,
> Taint not thy mind, nor let thy soul contrive
> Against thy mother aught . . . (I, v)

Hamlet is supposed to be aggressive, but also to be good; to avenge his father, but not to taint his mind; to stop the incest, but not to contrive anything against his mother. The ghost's conflicting messages correspond to Hamlet's own inner conflicts and contribute to his paralysis. Hamlet will not be a good son if he does not secure revenge; but vengeance is the law of the jungle, the motto of the aggressive types; and to behave in this way, with whatever sanction, cannot help but arouse profound anxiety in a man like Hamlet. To be an avenger is to descend into the arena with the Claudiuses of the world, to become like them, and to experience intense self-loathing and fear of divine retaliation.

When we meet Hamlet in act II, he is in a state of psychological torment. He has sworn to avenge his father, but two months have passed, and as yet he has done nothing. His failure to act violates both his self-effacing and his aggressive shoulds; it makes him feel disloyal, unloving, and cowardly. He is tortured by self-hate. To escape his self-accusations he tries to stir up his passions to such a pitch that he can override his scruples and take his revenge. Any approach to action, however, heightens his fears of being sinful and incurring damnation; and he delays again, thinks up a new plan, or longs to withdraw into stoical patience or the oblivion of death. He oscilates from one defensive strategy to another, but nothing will satisfy his contradictory needs and permit him to escape the hell of his own self-hate. Each side of him accuses and inhibits the other. He is damned whatever he does. We can see the dynamics I have just described very clearly at work in his encounter with the players and in his second and third soliloquies.

Second Soliloquy

Hamlet asks the First Player to recite the description of Priam's murder and the grief of Hecuba in order to stir, to express, and to justify his own emotions. The contents of the recitation, combined with the player's passion in reciting it, have a profound effect upon Hamlet, as we see when he is left alone. His second soliloquy is primarily a series of self-denunciations. He is a "rouge," a "peasant slave," a "dull and muddy-mettled rascal," a coward," an "ass," a "whore," a "drag," a "scullion" (II, ii). There is a massive release of self-hate here. Hamlet's self-accusations are a form of self-punishment, an expression of his profound sense of his own ignobility, and a part of his effort to escape his despised self by rousing himself to action.

Hamlet attacks himself by comparing himself to the player. It makes him feel "monstrous" that the player is so moved by the woes of Hecuba:

> What would he do,
> Had he the motive and the cue for passion
> That I have? He would drown the stage with tears
> And cleave the general air with horrid speech,
> Make mad the guilty and appal the free,
> Confound the ignorant, and amaze indeed
> The very faculties of eyes and ears.

This is what Hamlet has been wanting to do ever since his mother's marriage, but something has forced him to hold his tongue. Can it be, Hamlet wonders, that he is a coward? This is partly self-accusation and partly a search for an explanation of his delay. Hamlet experiences his conflicts; but he does not understand them; and he keeps trying, as we all do, to make sense of his behavior. The accusation of cowardice is most effective and brings him to the pitch of passion at which he has been aiming. Hamlet's pride is now stirred up, and he attacks himself for being content with mere verbal violence, like "a whore," "a drab," "a scullion," instead of acting courageously, like the son of a king.

His bloodthirsty mood quickly gives way, however, to more cerebral activity as he reverts to the plan he had already set in motion to trap Claudius with the play. The play is another device for being aggressive in an indirect way, for torturing Claudius without making an overt assault, either verbal or physical, upon him. Hamlet excuses himself for this further delay by questioning the reliability of the ghost. His doubts are in keeping with contemporary doctrines concerning ghosts; but Hamlet recalls these doctrines at this time because something within him is reacting against his earlier clamoring for vengeance, and he is once again troubled by fear of damnation.

Third Soliloquy

The next time we see Hamlet he is once again subdued by his inner conflicts. His third soliloquy is a rather confused meditation in which three possible alternatives are being considered: compliance, aggression, or withdrawal. Hamlet begins by asking himself whether it is better to be or not to be; but he immediately shifts to the consideration of another question:

> Whether 'tis nobler in the mind to suffer
> The slings and arrows of outrageous fortune,
> Or to take arms against a sea of troubles,
> And by opposing end them? (III, i)

This is the question by which Hamlet is most deeply tormented and that he cannot resolve. He wishes above all to be noble, but does this mean submitting to fate or attacking the evils of life in an attempt to correct them? Hamlet longs to escape from the buffetings of fortune and the agony of his dilemma by withdrawing into the oblivion of death, but suicide would be a sin and he has a dread of the afterlife.

Hamlet cannot come to rest in any solution. Submission will not work because he has sworn to avenge his father's murder and to stop the incest. He is too full of outrage, moreover, to accept the injustices of life; and he has a a need to live up to his culture's conception of manliness. Aggression will not work because it violates his taboos against attempting to master fate (which is pride and rebellion) and exposes him to fears of sinfulness and damnation: "Thus conscience does make cowards of us all. . . ."Hamlet is very much drawn to detachment as a defense; he would dearly love to attain a stoical independence of fate. He envies and admires Horatio:

> for thou has been
> As one, in suffering all, that suffers nothing,
> A man that fortune's buffets and rewards
> Hast ta'en with equal thanks . . . (III, ii)

But Hamlet is much too tormented by outrageous fortune and by his own inner turbulence to achieve such a philosophic calm.

Since he cannot become invulnerable by self-mastery, such as Horatio's, Hamlet's detachment takes the form of a longing for death. In death he could escape both his inner conflicts, with their accompanying self-hate, and the injustices of life:

> For who would bear the whips and scorns of time,
> The oppressor's wrong, the proud man's contumely,
> The pangs of despised love, the law's delay,

The insolence of office and the spurns
That patient merit of the unworthy takes,
When he himself might his quietus make
With a bare bodkin?

These wrongs are very largely those that "good" people suffer at the hands of the aggressive types. Hamlet is "patient merit"; Claudius is "the unworthy."

Hamlet's fantasy of dying is generated not only by his craving for escape, but also by his self-effacing trends. When confronted with the ineffectiveness of his solution, the self-effacing person may be attracted to self-destruction. It provides an outlet for his aggression, shows others what they have done to him, and preserves his moral superiority. As Horney observes, "going to pieces under the assault of an unfeeling world apears to him as the ultimate triumph. It may take the con-spicuous form of 'dying at the offender's doorstep'. . . . Suffering per se appears as the proof of nobility. What else can a sensitive person in an ignoble world do but go to pieces! Should he fight and assert himself and hence stoop down to the same level of crude vulgarity?" (*NHG*, 236). Hamlet cannot commit suicide, however, because of his fear of the afterlife. It is clear that Hamlet fears damnation should he either kill himself or die in the pursuit of vengeance. Conscience, which binds him to this weary life, also prevents him from carrying out his great enterprise; and he finds himself paralyzed, unable to submit, to act, or to escape. This is the last time we see Hamlet as a moody, inert figure. His encounter with Ophelia and the Mousetrap scene release his anger, and he becomes capable of both verbal and physical assault. His self-effacing trends remain in evidence; and he develops a more and more profound sense of resignation; but his aggression is henceforth liberated; and he becomes, at times, a stereotypic avenger.

The turning point in Hamlet's attitude toward Ophelia occurs when she tries to return his gifts, saying that "Rich gifts wax poor when givers prove unkind" (III, i). Hamlet needs Ophelia's goodness to help him cling to his faith in human nature. Her present behavior, however, is false; and his immediate reaction is to feel that Ophelia, too, is a betrayer. In his belief in Ophelia, in her purity and love for him, lay his last hope that he could both maintain his own nobility and escape the fate of his father. His final disillusionment liberates his aggressive side, and he expresses at last the grievances that have been rankling in his bosom for months. His explosion of hostility seems to relieve his oppression, to lift his spirits, and to fill him with energy. In his dealings with others he becomes vigorous, articulate, and combative. He is aggressive toward Gertrude and Ophelia in the play scene; and when the king rises, distraught, and flees the court, Hamlet becomes gay. He has been oppressed with impotent rage, but now he has broken through the defenses of this "smiling, damned villain," and it is Claudius who is stricken. What we see here is the energy of liberated aggression. With the final collapse of his hopes for love and innocence, Hamlet's angry self has risen to the fore and has swept away the constraints that have paralyzed him hitherto. He feels powerful, on top of things, capable of violence. I believe that Hamlet does not kill Claudius in the prayer scene for exactly the reasons he gives. He is in the grip of his vindictive shoulds, which demand not only Claudius's death, but a revenge that is in keeping with the nature of the offense. When Hamlet plots against his schoolfellows at the end of act III, he sounds very much like an Iago: "O, 'tis most sweet, / When in one line two crafts directly meet."

It is difficult to integrate all this with the picture of Hamlet built up in the first half of the play, to believe that the tender-minded prince has turned into a fiendish avenger. His task no longer seems a heavy burden but a source of malicious delight. We must remember that beneath his tender-mindedness there has been an enormous sense of injury and a rage so intense that its repression has produced severe neurotic symptoms. The Machiavellian monster that Hamlet has fought so hard to keep locked inside is now free. From the end of act III to the conclusion of the play, the different sides of Hamlet's personality assert themselves in turn, as well as, at times, simultaneously. He still has inner conflicts and a need to reconcile his various shoulds; but his compliant, aggressive, and resigned trends seem to be compartmentalized sometimes and to manifest themselves in relatively pure forms.

Final Soliloquy

In his final soliloquy Hamlet is in the grip of his aggressive shoulds. He attacks his detached and compliant trends and accuses himself, once more, of delay:

> Now, whether it be
> Bestial oblivion, or some craven scruple
> Of thinking too precisely on the event,

A thought which, quartr'd, hath but one part wisdom
And ever three parts coward, I do not know
Why yet I live to say 'This thing's to do;'
Sith I have cause and will and strength and means
To do't. (IV, iv)

His self-accusations are, in part, irrational. His revenge is not dull, and it needs no spurring. *Hamlet* is a revenge play in which the obstacles that delay the revenge are at first within the hero and then outside of him. Once Hamlet becomes capable of action, no suitable occasion arises, until the end. After the play and the murder of Polonius, he is swept along by events that he has little power to control. What we see in his self-accusations is a new set of unrealistic shoulds. It is no longer perfect innocence, but aggressive potency that Hamlet demands of himself, whatever the obstacles.

Hamlet is not only attacking himself for his inaction, he is also justifying his intended violence by making it seem a matter of reason and honor. The example before him is hardly one that Hamlet in his Christian frame of mind would find admirable. Twenty thousand men are prepared to

fight for a plot
Whereon the numbers cannot try the cause,
Which is not tomb enough and continent
To hide the slain. . . .

In his present mood Hamlet sees this as glorious and Fortinbras as a great man. His glorification of bellicosity, ambition, and honor, and of a readiness to die, is the expression of Hamlet's aggressive shoulds, which are punishing him for his own lack of a fiery spirit. These people are ready to fight and die for "a straw," "an egg-shell," whereas he, whose honor is so much more at stake, has "let all sleep." In order to restore his pride and to gain some measure of glory for himself, Hamlet must think from this time forth nothing but bloody thoughts.

Act V

What is most striking about Hamlet in act V is his resignation, his sense of himself as being in the hands of Providence. The success of his rash invasion of Rosencrantz and Guildenstern's cabin shows that

> There's a divinity that shapes our ends,
> Rough-hew them how we will. . . . (V, ii)

The fact that he had his father's signet in his purse shows once again that heaven is "ordinant." He has profound misgivings about the fencing match with Laertes, but he ignores his premonitions and resigns himself to what will be:

> . . . we defy augury: there's a special providence in the fall of a sparrow. If it be now, 'tis not to come; if it be not to come, it will be now; if it be not now, yet it will come: the readiness is all: since no man has aught of what he leaves, what is 't to leave betimes? Let be. (V, ii)

This speech shows also Hamlet's readiness to die. He expects heaven to direct him to his revenge (he still has no plan); but he also expects to die himself and does not wish it otherwise.

These attitudes are the expression of a defensive posture that begins to develop at the end of act III, when Hamlet reacts to the death of Polonius:

> For this same lord,
> I do repent: but heaven hath pleased it so,
> To punish me with this and this with me,
> That I must be their scourge and minister.
> I will bestow him, and will answer well
> The death I gave him. So, again, good night.
> I must be cruel, only to be kind:
> Thus bad begins and worse remains behind.

By killing Polonius, Hamlet has irrevocably violated his self-effacing shoulds and destroyed his claim to innocence. This liberates his aggressive shoulds, which manifest themselves powerfully, as we have seen. But Hamlet also has a need to assuage his guilt and to reconcile the new state of affairs with his self-effacing side. He does this in several ways.

According to the logic of the self-effacing solution, worldly misfortune is a sign of guilt, a penalty for sin. Hamlet sees his killing of Polonius not only as a sin in itself, but also as a punishment for his basic guilt, a sense of which emerges whenever his pride in his goodness is undermined. It is an act by which he pays for past transgressions and for which he must be punished in the future if his own shoulds and

172

divine justice are to be affirmed. Hamlet has a need to die in payment for the death that he has given. He is self-protective in the interests of his mission, but he is content to die in the enactment of it, and he acts in a way that courts his own destruction.

With the collapse of his idealized image, Hamlet defends himself against total despair and unbearable self-hate partly by switching to an aggressive value system that glorifies toughness and violence, and partly by seeing himself as an agent of the divine plan. His pride in his goodness having been crushed, Hamlet clings to a posture of humble submission, of acquiescence to the demands of a higher justice. He no longer tries to control his fate or to transcend the limitations of human nature: he acknowledges his sinfulness, accepts the fact that he must dirty his hands, and trusts in God to bring about a just resolution of all issues.

There is in Hamlet, from the closet scene on, a strong element of resignation. He has reacted to the shattering of his dreams with terrible cries of pain; but after he assimilates the meaning of his rash and bloody deed, there is nothing left to hope for but the completion of his mission. His fate is settled: he must purge the world of evil and be punished himself for the crimes he commits in so doing. He becomes immune to the slings and arrows of outrageous fortune by developing not only a wish for death, but an indifference to life — "what is 't to leave betimes?"

The ending is like a wish-fulfillment dream conceived from Hamlet's point of view. It satisfies his needs for punishment, revenge, vindication, and escape. The plotters against him are hoist with their own petard. Claudius inadvertently kills the queen and then is dispatched himself with the instruments he has aimed at Hamlet. Evil does not triumph, after all. Laertes is "justly killed with [his] own treachery." The queen and Hamlet are also punished. Hamlet gets his wish for his own death and for that of his mother, but he is guilty neither of matricide nor of suicide. Providence has arranged all. He is forgiven by Laertes for his death and for that of Polonius, and his own death at once justifies and pays for the murder of Claudius. He is still concerned with his nobility, his reputation; and his friend Horatio is there to save his "wounded name." He chooses the next king with his dying breath and then goes to "felicity," while Horatio lives on "in this harsh world . . . / To tell [his] story." He receives tributes from Horatio and from Fortinbras that testify both to his spirituality and to his manliness:

HOR. Now cracks a noble heart. Good night, sweet prince;
      And flights of angels sing thee to thy rest!

. . . .

FORT.   Let four captains
      Bear Hamlet, like a soldier, to the stage;
      For he was likely, had he been put on,
      To have proved most royal. . . .

He was fit, after all, to be the son of his father.

Analyzing the Author: Shakespeare

We must be very careful when we try to infer the historical author from
his artistic creations. We must recognize that the historical person has a
life independent of his works, that many of his attitudes and attributes
may never appear in his fictions, and that those that do appear may have
been disguised or transformed by the process of artistic creation. We
must allow, moreover, for artistic motivations, for generic requirements, and for the inner logic of the individual work. It is possible,
nonetheless, to tell a good deal about the author from his works when
we examine such things as his recurring preoccupations, the personal
element in his fantasies, the kinds of characters he habitually creates,
and his rhetorical stance. In this delicate biographical enterprise,
Horney's theory is again very helpful.

Horneyan psychology can help us to illuminate the author through
his works because in the course of artistic creation the author's defensive strategies tend to express themselves in a variety of ways. His works
are, among other things, efforts to reinforce his predominant solution
and to resolve his inner conflicts by showing himself, as well as others,
the good and evil consequences of the various trends that are warring
within him. He will tend to glorify characters whose strategies are
similar to his own and to satirize those who embody his repressed solutions. His rhetoric will affirm the values, attitudes, and traits of
character that are demanded by his dominant solution, while rejecting
those that are forbidden by it. His plots will often be fantasies in which
his claims are honored in a magical way, while his repressed strategies
are shown to bring misery and retribution. Because he cannot help expressing his subordinate trends also, however, his works will frequently
manifest his inner conflicts. His attitudes, values, and beliefs will often

be inconsistent or self-contradictory. His conflicting trends will lead him to criticize each solution from the point of view of the others and to have toward his characters the same mixed feelings he has toward the aspects of himself that the characters embody. The relationships among his solutions may vary, moreover, in the course of his life; and this will be reflected in changes in the kinds of characters he portrays, in his rhetoric, and in his dominant fantasies. I have shown how all of this works in the concluding chapter of my book on *Jane Austen*. For purposes of illustration here, I shall give a brief account of a basic conflict in Shakespeare's personality that can be inferred from a study of his works.

From *1 Henry VI* to *The Tempest*, a frequent concern of Shakespeare's plays is how to cope with wrongs, how to remain good in an evil world. In the histories and the tragedies, the tendency of the main characters is to respond to wrongs by taking revenge; but this contaminates the revenger and eventually results in his own destruction. In Horney's terms, the aggressive solution, with its emphasis upon retaliation and vindictive triumph, does not work. But the self-effacing solution does not work in these plays, either, as many innocent, well-intentioned, but weak characters perish. Hamlet's problem, as I see it, is how to take revenge and remain innocent. The problem is insoluble and nearly drives him mad. In a number of the comedies and romances Shakespeare explores a different response to being wronged — namely, mercy and forgiveness. Because of the conventions of these genres, with their providential universe and miraculous conversions, wronged characters do not have to take revenge: either fate does it for them or they forgive their enemies, who are then permanently transformed. In these plays, the self-effacing solution, with its accompanying bargain, works very well, but only because the plays are unrealistic.

What I infer about Shakespeare from his plays is that he has strong vindictive impulses, but even stronger taboos against those impulses and a fear of the guilt and punishment to which he would be exposed if he acted them out. He does act them out imaginatively in the histories and tragedies and is purged of them through the destruction of his surrogate aggressors. He also has a fear of his self-effacing side, however; and he shows both himself and us through characters like Henry VI, Hamlet, and Desdemona that people who are too good and trusting cannot cope and will be destroyed. In the tragedies he portrays the inadequacy of both solutions. In some of the comedies and in the romances he fantasizes the triumph of good people and avoids guilt either by glorifying forgiveness or leaving revenge to the gods. In *The Tempest*, through Prospero's magic, he imagines a solution to Hamlet's problem; for Prospero is at once vindictive and noble, vengeful and innocent. He takes his revenge through his magic, by raising a tempest and inflicting various psychological torments; but he does not really hurt anybody; and when he has had his vindictive triumph, he gives up his magic and forgives everyone. Many critics have been uncomfortable with his forgiveness of Antonio, who shows no sign of repentance; and they have, I think, good reason; for it is the product of Prospero's compulsions and is inappropriate to the practical and moral realities of the situation. Like the Duke in *Measure for Measure* and many other of Shakespeare's self-effacing characters, Prospero cannot, in the final analysis, place blame where it belongs and effectively deal with the guilty. The unworkability of the solution that Shakespeare has embodied in *The Tempest* begins to be felt when we imagine the return to Italy.

From a psychological point of view, one of Shakespeare's major projects was to find a way of giving expression to the hostile, vindictive, aggressive side of his personality without violating his stronger need to be noble, loving, and innocent. Recognizing this helps us to understand many of his plays and also, I believe, a number of the sonnets. *The Tempest* is perhaps the most brilliant solution that he ever imagined to this essentially insoluble problem, and it is not surprising that it was his last great play. In *Henry VIII*, which followed, the self-effacing side of Shakespeare is overwhelmingly predominant, and we no longer feel ourselves to be in the presence of a complex and fascinating personality. Shakespeare's inner conflicts have much to do, I suspect, with the richness and ambiguity of his greatest art.[11]

This Writer Reading

Considerable attention has been focused of late upon the reading process, which is coming to be seen more and more as a transaction in which the reader's personality plays an important part. Horneyan psychology can help us to be aware of the influence the reader's defensive strategies have upon his critical perceptions. Since it is a very risky business to psychoanalyze one's fellow critics on the basis of their criticism, perhaps the best way to illustrate the influence of the psychology of the critic upon his criticism is through an analysis of one's own work, especially of earlier work from which the necessary distance has been attained. I should like to illustrate my point here with a consideration of some of the ways in which my personal psychology influenced my critical perceptions in my book on George Eliot,[12] and of how my psychological development has affected my more recent perceptions both of Eliot and of my critical reactions to her.

Experiments in Life examines George Eliot's ideas in relation to her time and her art in relation to her ideas. It shows how her protagonists arrive, through a varied course of experiences, at some version of the Religion of Humanity, in which living for others, for something beyond the self, gives meaning and value to their lives. *Experiments in Life* was originally my doctoral dissertation. While I was writing it, I identified completely with George Eliot's point of view. I not only expounded, but I also believed in her Religion of Humanity. I was convinced that she had solved the value problems of modern man living in a universe without God, and I expected my book to have an important effect upon the way in which enlightened men henceforth thought and lived. When my dissertation director, Hillis Miller, posed marginal questions about why George Eliot believed as she did, I felt that it was silly of him to ask why someone believed the truth.

A strange thing happened after I completed my dissertation. When I was given the chance to teach George Eliot at last, I found that my enthusiasm had disappeared, that her beliefs had lost their magic. I remained convinced that I had understood her correctly, but I was no longer sure of my own relation to her ideas. I was mournful at my loss of fervor and quite bewildered about what had happened.

It was at this point that I first read Karen Horney. Her description of the way in which our value systems are often a function of our defenseive strategies seemed directly applicable to me, and, by extension, to George Eliot. Miller's questions began to make sense. I came to see that my relation to George Eliot had been profoundly influenced by a shaky performance on my doctoral oral, which had hurt my pride, undermined my confidence, and made me turn to my dissertation as the means by which I would show everybody how good I really was. Since the dissertation had to be so good, it became almost impossible to write; and there were long periods when I despaired of ever finishing. My dreams of a glorious academic career were in ruins, and I needed to find a new meaning for my life. It was while I was in this state of mind that I found George Eliot's philosophy absolutely convincing. The way to glory, she proclaimed, is not through personal ambition and triumph, but through goodness, self-sacrifice, and living for others, whose need of us gives indubitable meaning to our lives. Even if I did not become a great critic and scholar, I could be a wonderful husband, father, and friend; and I convinced myself that I was these things, though in truth I was not. The stories of Maggie Tulliver and Dorothea Brooke appealed to me as glorifications of gifted young people, much like myself, who attained a kind of moral grandeur, even though they failed to achieve an epic life. In short, my difficulty in writing my dissertation led me to abandon my expansive ambitions, which I now saw no way of fulfilling, and to embrace the self-effacing solution that I found so powerfully set forth by George Eliot.

The successful completion of my dissertation and its warm reception changed my relationship to George Eliot. Finishing the work in which I had articulated my defense against failure did away with my need for that defense and made it lose its appeal. I was once again focused on personal achievement, and living for others was no longer necessary. Hence my lack of enthusiasm when I had the chance to teach George Eliot. I had been looking forward to having the opportunity to preach her Religion of Humanity, but I found myself strangely indifferent to her ideas.

Looking back on my experience after the passage of twenty years, it seems to me that my personal identification with Eliot's ideas produced a combination of blindness and insight. It enabled me to understand them from within and to give them a full, accurate, and sympathetic exposition. My very responsiveness blinded me, however, to a number of things that I think I see more clearly now that I no longer share all of George Eliot's beliefs. Because I was so intent upon understanding her characters as illustrations of her ideas, I failed to see them as imagined human beings who are fascinating in their own right and who are not always in harmony with their formal and thematic functions. I paid no attention to George Eliot's mimetic achievement, and I had very little sense of the brilliance and complexity of her psychological insights. I did not see the necessity to distinguish between her *representation* of a character, which is usually complex, accurate, and enduring, and her *interpretation*, which is often misleading, oversimple, and confused.[13]

My most striking blindness, I think, was to the destructiveness of the solutions at which her characters arrive as a result of their "education." George Eliot shared with many other nineteenth-century novelists the illusion that suffering, frustration, and bad social conditions can make one, somehow, into a noble person. She depicts for us very vividly all of the conditions in Dorothea Brooke's environment that thwart her healthy development, but she does not see that these conditions have actually hurt Dorothea instead of making her a superior being. She shows Dorothea making a series of terrible mistakes as a result of her compensatory search for glory, but she treats these mistakes as the product of Dorothea's "spiritual grandeur," which is "ill-matched with the meanness of opportunity."[14] As a great realistic novelist, George Eliot shows us the destructiveness of the self-effacing solution that Dorothea had adopted in response to her pathogenic environment; but since she shares this solution herself, her rhetoric glorifies it as a sign of moral nobility and places the blame for Dorothea's mistakes on external factors. Since I also shared this solution when I was writing *Experiments in Life*, I presented it with complete, though tacit, approval.

As I now see it, one of the most serious deficiencies of George Eliot's philosophy is her emphasis upon living for others as the means by which we give value to our lives and her failure to recognize the importance of self-actualization. Since our life has the meaning that other people give to it, we may be driven to satisfy their needs at all costs, regardless of our own, or to live up to their values. There is no way in George Eliot's thinking by which we can discriminate between the legitimate needs of others and their neurotic claims. Her characters can rarely defend themselves when other people make irrational demands upon them, and she tends to glorify their compulsively self-sacrificial behavior.

There are psychological reasons, of course, for my present view of George Eliot, just as there were for my earlier one, though I am not likely to have as clear an understanding of them. My shift from George Eliot's values to those of Horney and Maslow is a reflection of my psychological evolution, as well as of new intellectual influences, and of a change in my vision of human possibilities. I seem to be bothered by precisely those things in George Eliot to which I was attracted before. In being critical of them, I am criticizing my earlier self and am trying to exorcise the self-effacing trends that remain within me and that get in the way of my self-actualization. If I were less threatened by self-effacing tendencies in myself, I would have less need to insist upon their destructiveness in others. The expansive side of me is embarrassed, no doubt, by my former enthusiasm for compliant values; and my detached

179

side derives pleasure from seeing through all kinds of defenses — I take great pride in my psychological insight. For these, and probably for some other reasons as well, it has given me considerable satisfaction to expose the weakness of George Eliot's philosophy and to analyze my previous commitment to it.

Horneyan psychology can help us to understand, then, our own response to literature and that of others as well. As I observed in *A Psychological Approach to Fiction*, "it can identify the conflicts, solutions, and values to which the audience is responding. Then, it can count for partial, biased, or conflicting responses. If a character or a work embodies an aggressive, a detached, or a self-effacing solution, or a particular structure of inner conflicts, readers will respond in terms of their own predominant solution or their own structure of conflicts. Criticism often tells us as much about the critic as it does about the work of art" (pp.288–89). We have seen how this operates in my analysis of my own interpretation of George Eliot. It would be extremely interesting to analyze from a psychological point of view the whole body of criticism on a work or an author. Not only would we learn much about the work and about the dynamics of literary response, but we would also gain insight into the psychological determinants of perception and the inevitability of conflicting interpretations.

R. D. Laing and Literature: Readings of Poe, Hawthorne, and Kate Chopin

by Sam B. Girgus

Throughout the turmoil and change of the 1960s R. D. Laing seemed to embody absolute radicalism. While other cultural critics such as Herbert Marcuse and Norman O. Brown called for radical changes in social and psychological structures, Laing seemed even more extreme in oppugning the credibility of the ideas of reality and sanity in themselves. He extolled a politics of antipolitics based upon a psychology of antipsychiatry. For Laing there were no safe harbors of sanity and maturity from which to view immediate events and the workings of history. There were no privileged perspectives that could enable one to distinguish between the real and the unreal. He espoused a philosophy and psychology that said established barriers between the sane and the mad were artificial social and institutional constructions reflecting society's own prejudices, fears, and hallucinations. For many, Laing's philosophy served as a valuable vehicle for radical protest because it operated without a clear-cut road map or design for change, thereby justifying a form of highly personal dissent that did not demand the creation of new systems of belief and social organization. Thus, there was for Laing's adherents a kind of security to be found in a philosophy of insecurity. Moreover, there was an additional element of security to be found in following Laing. He himself was not only a psychiatrist with medical and scientific credentials, but a psychiatrist experimenting with new ideas and approaches. Along with this professional link to the establishment, he was a critic of culture whose knowledge of modern philosophy added further to his image as a radical leader and to his credibility as a psychiatrist developing useful tools for the study of literature and culture.

In the early seventies Laing was considered important enough to warrant the attention of an entire issue of *Salmagundi*, a leading journal of ideas and criticism that prides itself on identifying and establishing the most significant contemporary intellectual trends and movements. The lead article in the edition, which was published in paperback by Harper & Row, was written by Peter Sedgwick, a psychologist and a student of politics and culture who has been one of the most persistent and valuable observers of Laing and the "Anti-Psychiatry" movement. In his thoughtful and critical reading of Laing's work, Sedgwick predicted that Laing's influence would grow. Sedgwick writes, "The theory and the therapy of mainstream psychiatry are bound to be indebted to Laing, and to similar vangard trends in social medicine, if only because no other rival approach, whether biochemical or environmental, seems to possess any dynamic or momentum of comparable power. Laing's theories of schizophrenia are powerfully aided, in the public view, by the distinguished cultural and philosophical apparatus in which they repose: his popularity rides with the great timeliness of many of these supporting ideas, which often raise vital issues of a kind traditionally ignored by doctors, natural scientists and even social scientists."[1]

In fact, however, Laing's influence has seriously waned in the past decade. As Elaine Showalter says, "Nobody, not even the mad, seems to take Ronald Laing seriously anymore." Showalter goes on to describe from what heights of popular and academic acclaim Laing has fallen. She writes, "Gone and almost forgotten are the days when students in Cambridge or Berkeley went to their therapists carrying copies of *The Divided Self*, when bright young schizophrenics learned how to be crazy from *Sanity, Madness and the Family*, when assistant professors got stoned to read *The Politics of Experience*, and The Living Theatre chanted Laing's incantation ('if I could turn you on, if I could drive you out of your wretched mind, if I could tell you I would let you know') to packed houses. . . . Just at the point in 1970 when Marshall Berman declared in a front-page essay in the *New York Times Book Review* that Laing's work 'has shaked just about everyone and everything it has touched,' the man himself dropped from view. . . . "[2]

R.D. Laing and Literature

Laing's recent book perhaps dramatizes the extent of the intellectual and literary isolation of his inward search. Much of the energy behind *The Voice of Experience* comes from Laing's attack on science and technology for distorting our values and priorities and for constructing barriers of thought and feeling that constrict our experiences of ourselves and others. He writes, "All natural science can say about values is that they do not come within its *domain of investigative competence*. A few of the other modes of existence outside the investigative competence of natural science are love and hate, joy and sorrow, misery and happiness, pleasure and pain, right and wrong, purpose, meaning, hope, courage, despair, God, heaven and hell, grace, sin, salvation, damnation, enlightenment, wisdom, compassion, evil, envy, malice, generosity, camaraderie and everything, in fact, that makes life worth living. The natural scientist finds none of these things. Of course not! *You cannot buy a camel in a donkey market.*"

For Laing, science not only has cut itself off from aspects of experience, it tends to encroach upon and vitiate the joy of all experience. He says, "The obliteration of birth takes its place along with the obliteration of mind, and death, as footnotes to the scientific abolition of our world and ourselves."[3] Largely absent from this voice of experience are the qualities of mysticism and spiritual transcendence that were so prominent in *The Politics of Experience*. The book seems to justify Showalter's claim that "Laing's career exemplifies in a particularly vivid way the dilemma of radical aesthetics in the sixties."[4] While many suggest that Laing's dilemma stems from a turn toward radicalism or mysticism, I believe the origins of his problem can be found in his use and development of the assumptions and principles that provide the basis for his psychiatric theory of the divided self, schizophrenia, and the madness of the dominant culture.

Theory

Laing's theory of schizophrenia and the schizoid condition as first delineated in *The Divided Self* reflects his readings of the European phenomenological school of Binswanger and Minkowski and his study of existentialism and phenomenology in the works of Kierkegaard, Heidegger, Sarte, and Tillich. The result involves his development of "the existential-phenomenological foundations for a science of persons."[5] Throughout his work Laing utilizes the phenomenological idea of consciousness that emphasizes the primacy of individual experience. He writes, "Existential phenomenology attempts to characterize the nature of a person's experience of his world and himself. It is not so much an attempt to describe particular objects of his experience as to set all particular experiences within the context of his whole being-in-his-world" (*TDS*, 17). For Laing the ontological context of most importance involves schizophrenia and the schizoid way of being-in-the world as divided, disembodied, and false selves. Laing believes that the study of schizophrenia and the schizoid provides the key to understanding human experience. The schizophrenic and schizoid way of being dramatically demonstrate the universality of ontological insecurity, a condition in which "the individual in the ordinary circumstances of living may feel more unreal than real; in a literal sense, more dead than alive; precariously differentiated from the rest of the world, so that his identity and autonomy are always in question" (*TDS*, 42).

Since the schizoid, therefore, sees reality as a threat and danger, he develops a way of being-in-the-world that seems to provide protection. Laing writes that "the self, in order to develop and sustain its identity and autonomy, and in order to be safe from the persistent threat and danger from the world, has cut itself off from direct relatedness with others, and has endeavored to become its own object: to become, in fact, related directly only to itself. Its cardinal functions become phantasy and observation" (*TDS*, 137). In this situation, according to Laing, the individual's relationship to himself can be described as disembodiment or transcendence. In order to protect himself, the individual separates a "transcendent" or "inner" self from his body. This "disembodied" self in turn deals with reality through a "false-self system." Laing believes that "what the individual regards as his true self is experienced as more or less disembodied and bodily experiences and actions are in turn felt to be a part of the false-self system" (*TDS*, 78). Of course such a process of self-defense really invites perennial self-destruction. Laing writes, "If the whole of the individual's being cannot be defended, the individual retracts his lines of defense until he withdraws within a central citadel. He is prepared to write off everything he is, except his 'self.' But the tragic paradox is that the more the self is defended in this way, the more it is destroyed. The apparent eventual destruction and dissolution of these in schizophrenic conditions is accomplished not by external attacks from the enemy (actual or supposed), from without, but by the devastation caused by the inner defensive manoeuvres themselves" (*TDS*, 77).

R.D. Laing and Literature

It needs to be remembered that Laing uses the terms "schizoid" and "schizophrenic" in an original and interesting way. Laing writes, "In describing one way of going mad, I shall try to show that there is a comprehensible transition from the sane schizoid way of being-in-the-world to a psychotic way of being-in-the-world. Although retaining the terms *schizoid* and *schizophrenic* for the sane and psychotic positions respectively, I shall not, of course, be using these terms in their usual clinical psychiatric frame of reference, but phenomenologically and existentially" (*TDS*, 17). While in *The Divided Self* he clearly sees important differences between the schizoid or sane and the schizophrenic or psychotic personalities, he notes that a thin line may separate the schizoid from the schizophrenic. He says that "it is, of course, not always possible to make sharp distinctions between sanity and insanity, between the sane schizoid individual and the psychotic. . . . In order to understand the nature of the transition from sanity to insanity when the point of departure is the particular form of a schizoid existential position . . . it is necessary to consider the psychotic possibilities that arise out of this particular existential context" (*TDS*, 137). In effect Laing here establishes what Showalter indicates as "the continuity between sanity and madness."[6]

Laing's generalization of the divided self into a universal situation and a basis for human personality involves other important developments for his psychology of the individual and philosophy of culture. The emphasis in Laing on ontological insecurity involves the use of the language of existentialism and phenomenology as a substitute for Freudian terms and methods. As Showalter says, "Laing set about to substitute existential terms, such as 'being', 'person', and 'self', for psychoanalytic ones, such as ego, superego and id."[7] For Freud these psychoanalytic terms were not just categories of being or theoretical descriptions of functional psychic arrangements. They represented complex interactions between biologically based forces of energy and instinct, on the one hand, and forces of culture, control, and conscience on the other. Thus, for Freud, like Laing, the apparent unity of the individual self really constitutes a dissimulation of a divided field of constantly warring parts and fragments. However, for Freud the tumultuous exchanges between instinctual energetics and cultural dynamics create a barrier of balances and relationships that keeps the individual to some degree distinct from his environment. In Freudian theory some measure of individuality and separation persists for the individual. The vision and language of *The Divided Self* weakens the barrier Freud proposes while leaving little to put in its place. By universalizing the schizoid condition and placing it on a continuum with schizophrenia, Laing creates a situation in which all individuals become victims of their environment and mere reflections of their cultures. "For Laing, " Showalter says, "insanity or psychosis is the intensification of the divisions within the self that mirror the compartmentalization and fragmentation of modern society."[8]

Thus, the theory of schizophrenia and the schizoid that Laing launches in *The Divided Self* evolves in *The Politics of Experience* into a political philosophy. Instead of being a clinical and psychological designation, schizophrenia for Laing becomes a term used by the establishment to justify its oppressive power. It becomes a way for a sick society, as Laing sees it, to place the blame for its ills upon the helpless individuals who compose it.[9] Laing articulates this position powerfully in a famous statement that obliterates meaningful distinctions between sane and insane. He writes, "From the alienated starting point of our pseudo-sanity, everything is equivocal. Our sanity is not 'true' sanity. Their madness is not 'true' madness. The madness of our patients is an artifact of the destruction wreaked on them by us and by them on themselves. Let no one suppose that we meet 'true' madness any more than that we are truly sane. The madness that we encounter in 'patients' is a gross travesty, a mockery, a grotesque caricature of what the natural healing of that estranged integration we call sanity might be."[10] In espousing this position, Laing becomes, as Marion Vlastos says, "a psychiatrist in rebellion against the authority of his own professional power." He cast himself in the role of rebel leader fighting against his own corrupt profession and sick society. "Clearly," Vlastos writes, "it seems absurd for a doctor (a healer of humanity) to adjust an individual to a society adjusted to self-destruction."[11]

Ironically, Laing's form of rebellion, especially as expressed in *The Politics of Experience*, can be seen as a continuation of the spiral, a deepening manifestation of the wider social sickness. While *The Divided Self* demonstrates a vicious cycle through which ontological insecurity breeds a false-self system, so in *The Politics of Experience* Laing fights social madness with schizophrenia. He performs, in Sedgwick's terms, a "sharp turn towards the celebration of the schizophrenic condition" that represents his growing mystical and political concerns.[12] Laing writes, "True sanity entails in one way or another the dissolution of the normal ego, that false self completely adjusted to our alienated social reality; the emergence of the 'inner' archetypal mediators of divine power, and through this death a rebirth, and the eventual re-establishment of a new kind of ego-functioning, the ego now being the servant of the divine, no longer its betrayer."[13] Of course, from a Freudian perspective Laing's amalgamation of Jungian theory with a radical political ideology constitutes a program of perverted psychoanalysis, poor politics, and anti-intellectual religiosity. While Laing appears to create a radical new means through which to engage social evil, it can also be maintained from a psychoanalytical point of view that he effectively disarms the psyche's ability to deal in any meaningful way with reality.

By turning man into an absolute rebel and radical, Laing hopes to overcome Freud's pessimistic conclusions about man's self-destructive nature. Laing writes, "Freud insisted that our civilization is a repressive one. There is a conflict between the demands of conformity and the demands of our instinctive energies, explicitly sexual. Freud could see no easy resolution of this antagonism, and he came to believe that in our time the possibility of simple natural love between human beings had already been abolished" (*TDS*, 11). Of course, generations of neo-Freudians have tried to escape the dilemma of instinctual conflict that Freud devised. In *Civilization and Its Discontents* Freud wrote, "The fateful question for the human species seems to me to be whether and to what extent their cultural development will succeed in mastering the disturbance of their communal life by the human instinct of aggression and self-destruction. It may be that in this respect precisely the present time deserves a special interest. Men have gained control over the force of nature to such an extent that with their help they would have no difficulty in exterminating one another to the last man. They know this, and hence comes a large part of their current unrest, their unhappiness and their mood of anxiety."[14]

Freud would not be surprised to learn that little since his time would mollify his pessimism. However, his own existential choice of the way to be-in-the-world involved a commitment to confront directly and without illusions the dangers, both internal and external, that threatened man. In a way, to Freud freedom meant an intelligent and rational response to seemingly impossible problems and irreconcilable dilemmas. In contrast, it can be argued that Laing adopts a psychological version of a nihilistic pose that resembles Dostoevsky's idea of the absurd and Kierkegaard's "sickness unto death." A flight into schizophrenia as a means for fighting schizophrenia creates a perverse politics of silence and despair.

One also may want to question the success of Laing's attempt to devise a new terminology and understanding of psychic structure. As already noted, Laing substitutes a new language of existentialism and phenomenology for the old Freudian terms. Freud's theory of the id, ego, and superego developed over many years until it achieved its final form in the 1920s. It grew out of an early form of id psychology that concentrated on the unconscious. From this he developed a more sophisticated model of the mind based upon ego psychology. His concerns for the workings and functions of the id, ego, and superego relate to his broader investigations dealing with the reality and pleasure principles and his emerging theory of the instincts. Thus, Freud created an elaborate and complex theory of the human mind and behavior that remains controversial today. In striving to develop his own theory by adding Jungian psychology and radical politics to his existential and phenomenological terminology, Laing in effect imposes rhetoric, politics, and poetry upon his earlier study of ontological insecurity and the false-self system. Such superficiality constitutes an important restriction in using Laing as a means for analyzing literature and culture. Although his work does contain inherent limitations, his theory adds significantly to our understanding of literary and cultural situations and characters.

Praxis

In *The Law of the Heart* I spent a chapter on a Laingian analysis of Poe's characters in the hope of gaining practical insight into their psychological motivations and behavior. In "The Fall of the House of Usher," for example, Poe presents a dramatic version of the confrontation between a "disembodied self" that creates a false-self system in the vain hope of protecting itself against imagined dangers and enemies. In the story a disturbed and morbid narrator reveals in his behavior the fears of a schizophrenic character. The central symbol of the story, the House of Usher, represents such a state of mind at war with itself. The fissure in the house and the sister named Madeline further justify a Laingian interpretation in which Roderick Usher can be seen as operating as the narrator's false-self system. Meanwhile, the image in the "black and lurid" tarn by the house reflects, like Roderick Usher himself, a false-self. The tarn, which is on a line with the mad line of the house, arouses a classic situation of anxiety and fear in the narrator. His emotions resemble those of other Poe characters in such stories as "The Imp of the Perverse" and "The Pit and the Pendulum." His feeling of being over a "precipitous brink" represents the situations of ontological insecurity that are dramatized in these and other stories.

This use of a mirror image to dramatize the schizoid creation of a false self also occurs with great effect and power in Poe's "William Wilson." In this story Wilson sees "mine own image" in a mirror that seems to appear out of nowhere. Wilson's double operates conveniently for a Laingian interpretation in the role of a disembodied self. No one else sees the transcendent self of Wilson, who therefore seems to be totally protected by the false-self system. Wilson is presented in the story in a manner that makes him almost a casebook study of the false-self system as described by Laing. The duel at the end of the story fulfills the Laingian model when the selves manifest their fears by turning on each other. In Laing's view a challenge by the false self to the disembodied self's existence indicates psychosis. Thus, in Poe's story the murder by Wilson of his doppelgänger seems to prove psychosis. The last words of the double upon his death at the end of the story are in italics as though rendered in a hysterical shout to emphasize Poe's anticipation of the modern understanding of schizophrenia. Wilson says, "*You have conquered, and I yield. Yet, henceforward art thou also dead — dead to the World, to Heaven, and to Hope! In me didst thou exist — and in my death, see by this image, which is thine own, how utterly thou has murdered thyself.*"[15] Accordingly, Wilson will survive in a physical sense, but in a manner of being dead to the world such as those characters represented in Poe's "Man of the Crowd."

The process of killing or challenging the self in other Poe stories serves to dramatize the theory of transcendence through death, which provides, according to Laing, "the basic defence, so far as I have been able to see, in every form of psychosis" (*TDS*, 149–50). Laing argues that this "ultimate and most paradoxically absurd possible defence, beyond which magic defences can go no further," involves the self's desire to die so as to avoid death (*TDS*, 149). Laing writes, "It can be stated in its most general form as: *the denial of being, as a means of preserving being.* The schizophrenic feels he has killed his 'self', and this appears to be in order to avoid being killed. He is dead, in order to remain alive" (*TDS*, 150). As noted in *The Law of the Heart*, Laing compares this strategy to Paul Tillich's argument that the failure of the self

189

to integrate into being the anxiety derived from nonbeing constitutes neurosis. "*Neurosis,*" says Tillich, "*is the way of avoiding nonbeing by avoiding being.*" Tillich equates this psychology to a prison mentality in which the neurotic searches for absolute security in an environment that destroys reality.[16]

Such a prison mentality describes the way of being of the narrator in Poe's "The Imp of the Perverse." The narrator claims to feel safe in the world, but as a murderer himself he turns this world into ever smaller prisons of the self. He feels that his only danger comes from an imp. Existentially the inner self feels its enemy not in reality but in the false-self system represented by the imp. Ultimately, the inner self confesses as though to mitigate the power of the imp. The self seems to feel a capacity to transcend the physical death it invites through such confession as long as it can escape the imp. "To-day," he says, "I wear these chains, and am *here*! To-morrow I shall be fetterless! but *where*?"[17] It should be noted that Poe's use of the term "sickness unto death" in the "Pit and the Pendulum" compares to both Kierkegaard's and Tillich's idea of the existentially paradoxical and self-destructive attitude of the self toward death.

As I have discussed elsewhere, Poe's words in "The Pit and the Pendulum" — "I was sick — sick unto death with that long agony" — dramatize to some extent Kierkegaard's "sickness unto death, this agonizing contradiction, this sickness of the self, everlastingly to die, to die and yet not to die, to die the death."[18] Thus, Poe's story also dramatizes Laing's idea of the self imprisoning and attempting to kill itself to protect itself. Laing says that "the place of safety of the self becomes a prison. Its would-be haven becomes a hell." "It ceases," he says, "even to have the safety of a solitary cell. Its own enclave becomes a torture chamber. The inner self is persecuted within this chamber by split concretized parts of itself or by its own phantoms which have become uncontrollable" (*TDS*, 162).

Guilt in this and other Poe stories operates according to a Laingian model. In "The Tell-Tale Heart" and "The Black Cat," for example, guilt functions as what Laing calls a "psychic tourniquet" for the continued division of the self from the body (*TDS*, 133). "The individual," writes Laing, "feels guilty at daring to be, and doubly guilty about not being, at being too terrified to be, and attempting to murder himself if not biologically, then existentially. His guilt is the urgent factor in preventing active participation in life, and in maintaining the 'self' in isolation, in pushing it into further withdrawal" (*TDS*, 157).

Guilt operating in this manner helps to explain the meaning of the narrator's role in "The Fall of the House of Usher." The narrator, we remember, functions as a true self in the process of destroying itself. The narrator, in fact, confesses that guilt over his neglect of Usher constitutes a major source of his motivation in undertaking the journey to Usher. Significantly, the House of Usher also seems to function like a prison for a diseased self. As a self divided against itself, the narrator projects onto Usher all of his own gloom. Created as a means of protection out of the narrator's fears, the false self in the form of Usher assumes the narrator's own darkness and becomes the enemy, which in turn, of course, causes the narrator even greater fear and concern. "And thus," says the narrator, "as a closer and still closer intimacy admitted me more unreservedly into the recesses of his spirit, the more bitterly did I perceive the futility of all attempt at cheering a mind from which darkness, as if an inherent positive quality, poured forth upon all objects of the moral and physical universe in one unceasing radiation of gloom."[19] The narrator grows increasingly frightened of Usher in a manner that once again dramatizes the psychotic process of selves at war with each other. As a perfect sign of this deterioration, Madeline symbolizes the effort to achieve life through death. Returning from the tomb and assuming the aura of a ghost, she really represents on a psychological level the existence of psychic ghosts or selves that are manifestations of one's own fears and dreads.

Thus, Usher's song, "The Haunted Palace," symbolizes the existential truth of the story as a tale of what Laing would term "phantoms." The phantom in its attack on the transcendent self allows for the avoidance of any contact with the real dangers outside the prison of the self. Laing writes, "Moreover, the self-self relationship provides the internal setting for violent attacks upon warring phantoms inside, experienced as having a sort of phantom concreteness. . . . It is in fact such attacks from such inner phantoms that compel the individual to say he has been murdered, or that 'he' has murdered his 'self' " (*TDS*, 158). Interestingly, in the story that the narrator reads to Usher, another kind of imaginary figure, a dragon, must be slain after sharing a house with a hermit, thereby reenacting on the level of a fairy tale the story of the House of Usher itself.

While Poe provides an interesting and important body of work upon which to demonstrate a Laingian approach, the emergence during the past two decades of a new feminism articulating a deep fear of a harsh and oppressive external reality that drives women mad suggests new possibilities for establishing the relevance of Laing's approach. The situation of modern women as seen through the perspective of the new feminism encourages the use of Laing's terminology and method. For example, in an article on "Doris Lessing and R. D. Laing," Marion Vlastos writes: "For Lessing, as well as for Laing, fragmentation, compartmentalization, splitting is seen as *the* essential problem of the makeup of our individual lives and of our society. Thus Anna in *The Golden Notebook* is consciously and perpetually tormented by the conflicts between her different roles as a woman — mistress, mother, friend — and by the painful discrepancies between her aspirations and her accomplishments as artist and as political activist."[20]

Similarly, Elizabeth Janeway uses terminology that resembles Laing's in her discussion of the search for new paradigms of female sexuality. She writes: "Beyond its direct social stigmata, the impact of otherness is psychologically disorienting. Intuitive perceptions of the world cannot be trusted if they are made by an interior self which has learned that it is not considered primary. Its judgments always have to be adapted to those based on male experience. Female priori knowledge, then, cannot be taken as valid by the female self who is required by the laws of otherness to live as a displaced person not only in a man's world but also within herself. As a result, her primary impulses to action are always caught and held on a frustrating brink. Even if the delay is only momentary, the need to overcome it by an act of conscious will changes the quality of female activity by robbing it of the full, playful freedom of spontaneity."[21]

Obviously, Janeway's conception of an interior and spontaneous female self that feels itself to be "displaced" and cast into "otherness" and caught on the "brink" suggests comparisons with Laing's ideas of ontological insecurity, oppression, and the false-self system. Janeway's existentially based language of oppression serves not only to dramatize the condition of women but also to enlighten the reader's understanding of women's feelings of alienation. However, when she goes on to explain the dilemma and paradoxes of sexuality, she adopts Freudian terminology. Also, she uses Freudian ideas of the psychic infra-structure to suggest the need to develop a new sexual paradigm for women that will overcome, eventually, the harsh alternatives the Freudian model presents. Janeway maintains that masculine attitudes toward sexuality project upon women contradictory images of Eve as the sexual figure and temptress, and Mary as the motherly symbol of power and authority of love.

Janeway writes: "Is Mary wife or mother? She is both; hence the oedipal conflict. The Victorian view of 'wife' — and let us not imagine that it has vanished — is of a domesticated mother. The duty of the angel in the house is to accept and sublimate the male sex drive by transforming it into procreation. She allows her husband to fulfill God's commandment to be fruitful and multiply. She will then raise her children according to the norms of male society, and in the process her sons will acquire the double vision of women to which the angel owes her existence. They will experience the classic fears invoked by the myth Freud formulated in the name of Oedipus, whose purpose is the structuring of the psyche into id, ego and the internalized social parental deterrent of superego."

Janeway goes on to argue that the authority of the Mary figure has diminished in modern times with a concomitant strengthening of Eve as symbol of women's autonomy and freedom. She writes: "For us Eve stands not just as a trickster, but as a heroine too, challenging the gods and disrupting propriety and social controls. Where Mary embodied the superego, Eve represents the force of id." Noting that "woman does not live by id alone," Janeway sees the developing pattern of power between id and superego as an opportunity for the invention of "new paradigms" and "new selves" for women. Accordingly, in her interest in the search for "new paradigms of female sexuality," Janeway relates existential models of the female self to Freudian structures of the balance between the psyche and culture.[22]

Cynthia Griffin Wolff puts Janeway's theory into practice in her impressive Laingian study of Kate Chopin's *The Awakening*, a book that has become a classic of modern feminism. Although Wolff insists at the beginning of her piece — "Thanatos and Eros: Kate Chopin's *The Awakening*" — on seeing Chopin's heroine, Edna Pontellier, as more than a character to be defined totally by sexuality, Edna still occupies an unavoidable place in the modern feminist imagination. For many readers she personifies the plight of the modern woman forced into estrangement by the roles imposed upon her by society. *The Awakening* is the story of how Edna, who comes from an old-fashioned Presbyterian Kentucky family, marries a man with Creole blood and moves to New Orleans, where she gives birth to two sons. The husband is an insensitive bore who thinks he possesses Edna, but he is not cruel and her growing disdain for him reveals deeper discontents within her that are brought to a crisis through her love or infatuation with a young man. However, women in the novel, including one who serves as an important mother figure and another who becomes a model for the woman artist, also have a great impact on Edna's decision to abandon her husband and to deny conventional morality and taste by choosing to live for herself rather than for her sons, family, and reputation.

In her analysis of Edna, Wolff says that "by using R. D. Laing's description of the 'schizoid' personality," it might be possible to better "assess the configuration of Edna's personality." Wolff writes: "Laing's insights provide at least a partial explanation for elements of the novel which might otherwise be unclear."[23] An important passage early in the novel provides a key to Edna's personality and an obvious signal of how Laing offers a valuable tool for analyzing her. Chopin writes: "Mrs. Pontellier was not a woman given to confidences, a characteristic hitherto contrary to her nature. Even as a child she had lived her own small life all within herself. At a very early period she had apprehended instinctively the dual life — that outward existence which conforms, the inward life which questions."[24]

Using this duality as the basis of Edna's personality, Wolff argues that there is "an increasingly resistant barrier between the 'real' external world and that world which was most authentic in Edna's experience — the inner world of her fantasies." Wolff argues that Edna devotes her life to devising strategies that will enable her "to maintain the integrity of the two 'selves' that formed her character and to reinforce the distance between them," partly as a reaction to "the apparent terror which genuine emotional involvement inspires" in her. Using Laing's terminology of the self's withdrawal into an inner "citadel" for protection, Wolff says that Edna's selves "are truly betrayed and barren," as she finds freedom only in "isolation and concealment, an increasingly sterile and barren existence."[25]

Wolff's psychological reading of Chopin's novel becomes even more original and interesting through her application of Freud to supplement a Laingian interpretation of Edna's character. Using a developmental model of bodily fixations, Wolff argues that Edna's "libidinal appetite has been fixated at the oral level." She believes that "Edna's preoccupation with the incorporation of food is but one aspect of a more general concern with incorporating that which is external to her." In other words, Edna's oral fixation provides a clue to the continual dissatisfaction and restlessness of her inner being as a frustrated self striving for complete unity and harmony with the mother figure. Wolff writes: "Now in every human's life there is a period of rhapsodic union or fusion with another, and this is the period of early infancy, before the time a baby begins to differentiate himself from his mother. It is the haunting memory of this evanescent state which Freud defines as 'Oceanic feeling,' the longing to recapture that sense of oneness and suffused sensuous pleasure — even, perhaps, the desire to be reincorporated into the safety of pre-existence."[26] Thus, Edna's suicide in the sea can be seen as an act fulfilling her desire for total unity and immersion in an all-protecting and -embracing force. Chopin writes: "The touch of the sea is sensuous, enfolding the body in its soft, close embrace."[27]

A similar use of Laing in conjunction with Freud can help us to understand a female character from an earlier period, Hester Prynne in *The Scarlet Letter.* Standing on the scaffold to face her punishment for adultery in Puritan New England and feeling herself ready to "go mad at once," Hester executes a schizoid strategy of retreating into the self in the manner discussed by Laing. In describing Hester's mental processes of survival on the scaffold, Hawthorne refers to what "possibly" was "an instinctive device of her spirit, to relieve itself, by the exhibition of these phantasmagoric forms, from the cruel weight and hardness of the reality." In Laingian terms, of course we can recognize this "device" as a schizoid defense of herself by placing a false reality between her sense of her self and the oppressive present intruding upon her. Hawthorne writes:

> Yet there were intervals when the whole scene in which she was the most conspicuous object, seemed to vanish from her eyes, or, at least, glimmered indistinctly before them, like a mass of imperfectly shaped and spectral images. Her mind, and especially her memory, was preternaturally active, and kept bringing up other scenes than this roughly hewn street of a little town, on the edge of the Western wilderness; other faces than were lowering upon her from beneath the brims of those steeple-crowned hats. Reminiscences, the most trifling and immaterial, passages of infancy and school-days, sports, childish quarrels, and the little domestic traits of her maiden years, came swarming back upon her, intermingled with recollections of whatever was gravest in her subsequent life; one picture precisely as vivid as another; as if all were of similar importance, or all alike a play. Possibly, it was an instinctive device of her spirit, to relieve itself, by the exhibition of these phantasmagoric forms, from the cruel weight and hardness of the reality.[28]

In marked contract to Edna Pontellier, however, Hester breaks out of the psychic prison of self-defense in order to engage the world that challenges her. She confronts realities as opposed to inventing illusions. Hawthorne writes: "She clutched the child so fiercely to her breast, that it sent forth a cry; she turned her eyes downward at the scarlet letter, and even touched it with her finger, to assure herself that the infant and the shame were real. Yes! — these were her realities, — all else had vanished!"[29]Hester's reversal of the schizoid strategy constitutes a triumph for her reality principle and a victory of her ego over both the internal psychic and external cultural forces that encroach upon her individuality. A more complex and developed figure than Edna, Hester dramatizes a dialectic between the libidinal Eve image of sexuality and a mother image of Mary, an angelic personification of the superego.

Throughout the novel Hawthorne plays off against each other these conflicting ideas of woman as symbolized in the ambiguous meanings of the letter *A* on Hester's breast. The *A* obviously stands for the sexual license and libidinal freedom that was realized in the adulterous act. In a passionate tone and cry of defiance that marks her modernity, Hester even tells her secret lover, the minister Arthur Dimmesdale, that their love "had a consecration of its own."[30] On the other hand, Hester, who devotedly protects the secrecy of Dimmesdale's complicity in their love, renders possible an interpretation of the *A* to mean Able and even Angel because of the artfulness of her independence as a seamstress and woman and because of the role she assumes as a sort of spiritual healer to the lost and lonely of the community.

Through this complex interaction of antagonistic meanings, Hawthorne suggests the dimensions of the challenge to be faced by both men and women in restructuring their relationship and creating new ones. At the end of the novel Hester indicates that "a new truth would be revealed, in order to establish the whole relation between man and woman on a surer ground of mutual happiness," although Hawthorne seems to concede much to the authority of the Mary figure in his tentative delineation of the contours of this new symbolic woman.[31]

In any case, Laing's model of the schizoid-way-of-being-in-the-world and of ontological insecurity has limited value in helping us to understand such a symbolic woman. Understanding the psychological and cultural implications of the tragic failure of Hester's heroic attempt to achieve freedom requires supplementing a Laingian approach with the kind of Freudian reading of the novel that Fredrick Crews provides.[32] Accordingly, such a synthesis of existentialism and Freudianism, somewhat in the manner of Wolff's reading of Chopin, should help us to develop the paradigm that Janeway seeks for a new woman whose integration of the Eve and Mary aspects of personality could create the kind of revolution that even Laingians would admire.

Phenomenological
Psychology
and
Literary Interpretation

by Joseph Natoli

At the core of any psychological approach to literature is people — author, reader, or character. In ways to be discussed further on, a phenomenological approach to literature considers all three. But it begins with characters. Once the assumption is made that characters in literature are reflective of people in real life, it remains only to find a psychology that enables us to probe deeply into a character, a psychology whose emphasis is parallel to that of a novelist, a dramatist, or a poet.[1] And it is phenomenology's emphasis upon a person's own perceptions in relation to a surrounding world that most closely corresponds to the phenomenal experiences generated in literature.[2]

The novelist, for example, is concerned with particularity and action, with description, with the world of appearance and the spontaneity of lived experience. We need a method to trace action and description back to thought (and vice versa), a method that does not accept consciousness as a "black box" but acknowledges the interconnection of consciousness and world through intentionality. A phenomenological perspective takes us out of the armchair of the psychoanalyst attending only to the words a character speaks, and enables us to reconstruct the phenomenal reality of a character by attending to that character's varied interactions with the world. It is not simply a matter of a character's stream of consciousness but what that consciousness tends toward.

For instance, a character may say he loves his Brooklyn neighborhood, but the way in which he transfers to us the actual physiognomy of that neighborhood — the objects and people that comprise that neighborhood — tells us a story different from what he has told us, the simple statement that he loves his Brooklyn neighborhood. If it is true — and I believe it is — that literature is essential to our discovery of " . . . the experiential foundation of our world," then that discovery is made only when we have an approach that confronts consciousness interacting with the world, with human experiences themselves, and not thoughts, feelings, senses, or intuitions extracted from those experiences.[3] It is therefore not the task of novelist, poet, or dramatist to simply present characters who dramatically pour out their hearts and souls and are right in what they say about their hearts and souls. What we find, rather, in the richest literary works are characters deeply embedded in their own phenomenal worlds, their perceptions not commentary upon their actions but inextricably tied to their actions. We must find the physiognomy of their thoughts in the physiognomy of objects and people outside themselves with whom and with which they interact. In any literary text — novel, play, or poem — we find ourselves as readers not outside but inside literary worlds richly brocaded with a variety of interconnecting intentional universes: character's, author's, and our own. What everyone says or does not, what everyone does or does not, how everything is described or is not, how time passes or does not — are all unavoidable components of a literary world. We look to a psychology of a phenomenological bent in order to approach such a world without being seriously reductionistic.

When we assume that literature is reflective of real life, we are suggesting that the two correspond so closely that a great deal of what we know of human nature we know through literature. When we seek to apply any psychological approach to literature, we are further suggesting that what we have discovered regarding human nature through psychology can be effectively applied to literature. When a phenomenological approach to literature is employed, we are calling upon the wisdom of that approach not to translate literature into discursive terms (a psychological case study, for instance) but to achieve a deeper understanding of literature. The fact that we can accept literature as a record of human perceptions tied to the world does not transform literature into "real life." Literature is not life but is reflective of life. It is, as Merleau-Ponty states, an embodiment of truth and it is this "embodying," this patterning, that enables us to re-see the world, to see things in the world more clearly.[4] Maurice Natanson also looks beyond mimeticism, a literary microcosm equatable with the world, and associates a deeper, richer revelation of the foundation of human experiences with aesthetic patterning itself.[5] Thus, the phenomenologist is interested in literature as a record of conscious experience, of consciousness interacting with the world, without ignoring the nondiscursive nature of literature itself.

The phenomenologist also views a literary character as a reflection of a real person and accepts the fact that we, as readers, can come at that character only from life's side of the mirror. We bring what we know of life and people to bear upon the literary work. However, when we initially confront a character within a work, we do so tacitly, prereflectively. I cannot see how the human act of reading or observing art can be anything else. If we impose our own views and predilections upon any part of a literary work before responding to it prereflectively, we do no justice to that work. The phenomenological approach accepts the fact that there is no *Hamlet* unless it is read or observed by someone. But it is most respectful of the integrity of that work, or of any literary work, since it supplies the reader with a method of description that replaces the imposition of a reader's allegory upon the work he or she is reading. We must describe this method more fully.

Toward Methodology

What, then, is a phenomenological literary analysis and what are its basic tenets? It is first of all an analysis of character based on a correspondence rather than identity of character and real-life person. No matter how far a literary character may roam from our sense of what is "real," what is possible, he or she, to the degree that they are artfully drawn, connect in our minds with our own lives, help us in discovering "the experiential foundation of our world." Secondly, the aesthetic structure of a literary work is tied to "what-is-so-structured" and must be taken into account in any interpretation of a literary work.[6] Thirdly, a phenomenological approach is not simply an analysis of what a character says and does but is a description of the total interaction of consciousness and surroundings, an interaction of an internally constituted world, a phenomenal world, and an externally constituted world, what we often call the "real world." In phenomenological terms, what we are describing as an interaction of consciousness and surroundings is a human life-world, a *Lebenswelt*, a world in which a character lives.[7]

In order to successfully describe this world, the world of any one character, we must necessarily come to terms with other characters and with the author. We come to terms with other characters in relation to the perceptions of our chosen character and as the other characters are revealed through their own perceptions. We come to terms with the author only after we have described each character's *Lebenswelt* and extracted some implicit consciousness, the author's, from the interweaving of all phenomenal realities within the work. In considering the author, we're not being "nosy," and we're not looking for a lurking Oedipus complex. We *are* trying to describe a world constituted one step away from the phenomenal worlds of our characters. We are lost within the work unless we have a corresponding sense of what is normative, what is the "real world" as constituted within the work. When we consider a world constituted outside the work, we consider ourselves as readers. And this is our last tenet. The reader who has put aside his or her own reflections and has considered the work prereflectively must finally be accepted as being one step farther from the work and applying his or her own sense of what is "real," what is "normative," in order to achieve significant human understanding of the work. What is constituted as "real" and "normative" outside the literary work, in our own worlds as readers, is an inevitable rod that we in turn apply to the author's sense of "real" and "normative." We stand upon some ground in our final comprehension of what we have so assiduously described, and that ground is our own *Lebenswelt*.

Regardless of how "real" our character perceives his or her world to be, we apply the entire world of the literary work as a corrective rod to any one character's perception. In the conflict or struggle between any character's phenomenal reality and the author's implicit phenomenal reality, we seek understanding from our own base, first bracketing out our own reflections and relying on tacit or prereflective understanding in order to achieve a descriptive understanding of the work. We, as readers, are both active and passive, significant and insignificant, dispensable and indispensable, always onstage while of necessity being offstage. Let me try to describe more fully rather than resolve these paradoxes.

A phenomenological analysis of a literary work can have its fullest effect upon us only if we develop our analysis from within the work, if we approach the struggles that are there in the work and describe them. Among all the incredible struggles within a well-endowed literary world, our struggle as readers must be a backstage struggle, must be defused at the door. In this regard, we must be the least significant. Noncombatants. Our prereflective understanding of what is going on precedes a potential struggle between our own reflections and those extracted from the work. Insofar as we are noncombatants or passive participants, not actively struggling within the literary world, we are backstage. But insofar as a literary work cannot exist until it is perceived by someone, some reader, some observer, we are indispensable. Insofar as we, as readers, are page by page ever watchful, acutely aware, we are active.

How active, how powerful are we as readers? As a phenomenological reader, I see myself as a man holding a phenomenological key on the lookout for the right locks. Admittedly, I sometimes find a lock I can open, but I have gotten a preview of the "treasure" inside and I do not value it. I must not only find a lock I can open but I must be convinced that the treasure inside is worth having. My interest in a literary work, a possible fascination, precedes my phenomenological analysis, but it cannot make the literary work a good one. Or a bad one. It seems to me very possible that the results of a phenomenological analysis and an initial interest or fascination in a work may conflict. In other words, my powers as a reader may be limited.

Let us say that what I have read about a literary work or even a first reading of that work itself corresponds to my own interests, my own experiences, my own beliefs. My interest may extend even to my conclusion that this work could be fruitfully examined from a phenomenological perspective. At that point, the moment I begin to read or reread the work "phenomenologically," I must be open to the possibility that the results of my reading and my initial interest in the work may not wind up reinforcing each other. Interest draws me to the work, but the method I employ demands I "bracket" out that predisposition, all my reflection connected with the work, and approach the work prereflectively, describe it prereflectively. Both the literary work and the phenomenological method are really, then, defenses against the reader's phenomenal reality. We, as readers, are not permitted to project a valuation of good or bad based on our predispositions into our description of a literary work. The range of the reader is thus limited.

And what will this reliance on a prereflective, tacit understanding of a literary work do for us? It is hoped that this reliance will lead to a full description of the varieties of conflicting phenomenal realities within a literary world. The first part of our analysis, then, is description. When we move from this description toward some interpretation of the literary work as a whole, we bring our own *Lebenswelt* more into play. We move from a tacit level of comprehension to a level from which we attempt to put things together on a rational-logical level. We move toward meaning and significance while at the same time moving farther from the work as we approached it prereflectively. The closer we come to the analysis part of our "literary analysis," the closer do we come to our own phenomenal roots as readers. We are fully activated. We do not need our own outside perspective simply to applaud or reject the literary world we have described, to finally take or reject according to our personal needs. We need our perspective, we need to rely on our own human life-worlds, in order to sort the work out on a human level. We humanize the work by accepting our function as perceivers of what is there in the literary work to be perceived. Thus, we complement the work, bring it into a human life-world by the only means at our disposal — we bring it in via our own life-worlds as readers. Specifically, we perform two acts — first, we sort out the variety of phenomenal realities from our reader perspective, and second, we use our own life-world in order to digest as much of the meaning and implications of what we have described as possible. If we have succeeded in our description of coming close to the work and have not merely reproduced our own perceptions, then that description should direct the ways in which our own outside perspective gives final meaning to the work.

In this final stage of analysis we run the risk of losing the work, of saying more about ourselves than about the literary world within our literary work. We run the same risk, in short, that every attempt at literary interpretation does. I do not think this risk is more pronounced in a phenomenological approach. I do think that in that approach we come closest to revealing literary worlds because the exploring of interacting, conflicting phenomenal worlds, even our own as readers, is the primary psychological function. What we have finally via a phenomenological approach is a "personal digestion" of a literary "dish," an act in which neither the ingredients of the recipe nor the tastes of the diner have been ignored.

We first observe what is in a literary world by observing one character, by trying to describe the *Lebenswelt* of one character. That

Lebenswelt is meticulously built up from a character's perceptions of self, others, objects, and time.[8] Therefore, an intrinsic component of a phenomenological analysis is a close scrutiny of the total literary world in which the character has his or her being. In answering the question, What is the nature of such and such a character's being within a certain literary world? We must use what we know of that literary world, determined by other characters and the author, to know that character. And, we must use what we know of that character to know that literary world. We begin with one character and then through that character touch other characters, the physical setting of the work, the time frame — all of which are used to reveal that one character's *Lebenswelt* while simultaneously providing us with an entrance to the entire work. It is phenomenological psychology's recognition of an objectified consciousness, a consciousness interacting with the outside world, that prevents us from becoming imprisoned permanently within any one mind. We range outward into the whole literary world, our mode of travel the intentional nature of consciousness.

The Range of a Phenomenological Approach

A phenomenological approach can be applied to poetry, drama, or fiction, but the most rewarding genre, in my opinion, is fiction (taken here to mean novels and short stories), especially contemporary fiction. Epic poetry is more rewarding here than lyric poetry. If we were to do a conventional character analysis, drama would be as fertile a source as fiction. But since a description of a character's *Lebenswelt* is based on that character's interaction with the objects of his world and other people in that world, the narrative descriptions of fiction and of epic poetry are rich resources not shared by drama or lyric poetry. If we think of Heidegger's sense of the world as a workshop in which we work out our individual identities, then fiction and epic poetry are larger workshops in which characters function.[9] And the larger the workshop and the more work we see characters perform, the more able are we, with our phenomenological method, to reach a full descriptive understanding.

However, in my Praxis section, I have not excluded drama or poetry as illustrations of the phenomenological approach to literature. In choosing William Blake's "The Sick Rose," I have chosen a poem that is part of a very detailed series, *The Songs of Innocence and of Experience*.[10] A good part of this work's power lies in its use of various speakers, none of whom can be blithely equated with Blake. In choosing Shakespeare's *Hamlet*, I have chosen a play whose language resonates into every corner of every possible *Lebenswelt*.[11] I have confined myself to the character of Hamlet, a description that lies of course at the core of the play, and, as a description of character, at the core of the phenomenological method. Although I describe Hamlet's *Lebenswelt* by means of his own perceptions of self, others, objects, and time, I do not achieve a complete description of Hamlet the character because I do not, for brevity's sake, seek what Hamlet is unaware of but lies in the consciousness of other characters as well as in Shakespeare.

The last work I will consider is a novel by Joan Didion, *Play It As It Lays*.[17] I believe that a reader situated within the same "real world" as an author, say the author of a novel, has a good chance of distinguishing what are phenomenal realities and what are implied normative realities. The basis of this ability lies in a mutual sharing by reader and contemporary author of the objects, events, ideas, values, etc., of the present. A reader of contemporary literature not only has a good chance of recognizing the accoutrements of his or her own age but also a good chance of knowing what these accoutrements are supposed to mean or have been interpreted to mean. I therefore consider contemporary fiction to be most accessible to the phenomenological approach, a view I will explore in my discussion of Didion's novel.

When I say that by choosing a contemporary novel I believe I have maximized the virtues of the phenomenological method, I am in effect saying that certain literary works are more "vulnerable" to the phenomenological approach than are others. Formalist critics recognized the same variation in the accessibility of texts by staying clear of Dickens, Dostoevsky, and Blake, and making a home where they knew they would be welcome. Are works that we cannot get a hold of phenomenologically inferior to works that we can? Are works that lend themselves nobly to such an approach necessarily good or great works? Unless we are ready to state categorically that a phenomenological approach encompasses every aspect of a literary work — and, rightly employed, can lead us to a complete critical evaluation of the work — we must use our approach in a fashion I have advocated previously, as if it were one key to a treasure bound by many different locks. We cannot condemn those writers and works in which we, with our approach, are not at ease. The phenomenological method is not equal to the total literary work; the range of the method is limited. Let us consider, for example, William Blake's "The Sick Rose":

O Rose thou art sick.
The invisible worm,
That flies in the night
In the howling storm:

Has found out thy bed
Of crimson joy:
And his dark secret love
Does thy life destroy.

The design in which the words to this poem are encased pictures the worm in human form. Two other figures are pictured in lamenting postures. In "The Sick Rose" it is possible to discern two "characters" almost immediately — worm and rose. It is also possible to discern a speaker, who may or may not be the poet, and somewhere behind it all, the poet. Neither worm nor rose are true characters since they do not reveal their own perceptions. Focus must be placed upon the speaker of the poem, who reveals himself or herself in comments about worm and rose. In spite of a conventional perception regarding a rose as beautiful, the speaker finds, in the very first line, that this rose is sick. The rose is sick because her life is being destroyed by the dark secret love of an invisible worm. The design reveals to us that the worm is a human male. We know therefore that this is not a poem about gardening. Our real landscape is human life.

In the mind of the speaker of the poem, the worm is obviously someone quite specific, since the speaker refers to the worm as "The invisible worm." It is someone up to no good, someone evil. And that evil has been created not through hate but through love, although a dark secret love. Almost immediately, we perceive the dichotomy in the mind of the speaker: a bright, open love is a love that can be displayed in society without fear or censure, while a dark secret love is a shameful love leading to evil, to death. A dark secret love is that sexual love which must go on behind closed doors, which cannot be lawfully witnessed. We label this dark secret love "sexual" because the speaker has revealed traditional Judaic-Christian moral categories in which the dark side of love is "secret sexuality," sexuality not institutionally sanctioned. Since the worm bringing this death through sexuality to the rose is "The" invisible worm and not "a" invisible worm, we place him within the speaker's mind as the Devil or a Devillike figure. Our own perspective as readers now defines a significant uneasiness in us: something is wrong with the speaker, something is wrong with the way he or she perceives the world. The speaker's perceptions are "sick." The speaker is "sick." And we know this not because we categorically assume any follower of a Judaic-Christian ethic must be sick, but because the speaker reveals to us a sick world, a world unrelieved by any of the virtues we, as readers, know the world holds in abundance. This speaker sees a ravished, dying world, and "his" or "her" poem is a cry for help from somewhere in that fragmented world.

Where is the poet? The *Lebenswelt* we can distinguish as Blake's is not, first of all, restricted to this one poem but extends to the entire work — *The Songs of Innocence and of Experience*. Whether Blake's or any literary artist's *Lebenswelt* develops throughout his or her career or remains consistent throughout can be determined only by describing the *Lebenswelt* revealed in each separate work. In my discussion here of "The Sick Rose," I consider that poem to be only a part of the whole collection of *Songs*. "The Sick Rose" is a song of Experience. Most often the speakers within poems of Experience are themselves victims of what Blake considered to be the "evils" of Experience.

In another song of Experience titled "The Garden of Love," a speaker returns to the garden of love that previously bore so many sweet flowers and discovers that it is filled with graves, that priests have bound with briars the speaker's joys and desires.[13] This bound speaker is the generic speaker of many of the songs in Experience. The roots of the speaker in "The Sick Rose" lie in the Garden of Love. Once we, as readers, enter the Garden of Love, we learn that the worm of our poem may, in the poet's view, be a priest, a priest "binding with briars, my joys & desires." The words "his dark secret love" indicate to us that perhaps we should go one step beyond the priest to the god, Blake's Nobodaddy, whom he serves. This god's love proves fatal. Once we free ourselves of the speaker's perception and take on Blake's, we begin to see the cause, in Blake's view, of the speaker's illness. The speaker has constructed for himself a god who binds and shackles and is then considered in a very perverse way as loving because of those acts. By virtue of such beliefs, the speaker is cut off from a good part of himself or herself. Such a fragmented intentional consciousness permeates the world of the speaker and finally achieves the most masterful perceptive act in all of the songs of Experience, the most consummate displacement of beauty there for the perceiving by a sick mind—the transfiguration of a red rose into a sick, dying object.

It is yet another song of Experience that enable me to conclude that in the poet's view the god lurking behind the songs of Experience is a construct of a sick mind, that the speaker's worm is indeed invisible since it is a terrible product of his own mind. The poem I refer to is "The Human Abstract," where the tree of mystery and deceit is discovered to be growing in the human brain.[14] The entire poem "The Sick Rose" is a particular kind of mental construct whose very enigma compels us to ask: Whose mind is here described? Whose mind is doing the constructing? Where are the phenomenal perceptions? Where are the normative perceptions? We wound up identifying five "characters" — worm, rose, speaker, poet, and reader. Initially, we identified the speaker's perception of sexual love as a destroyer of life. The speaker's depressed view of the world made us feel uneasy as readers. Seeking the poet's view, we discovered, by considering other poems in the work, that a repressive religion was a destroyer of life.

We further discovered that in the poet's view, repressive religion was solely a product of man's own mind. Our own views of rose and worm altered from victim and ravisher, from real symbols acting out a universal drama, to objects invested with the speaker's own sickness and acting out no drama but the speaker's own internal tragedy. The rose and worm are the speaker's objects, presented in the guise he has chosen for them. It is only a repressive religion (Blake's worm) that causes the speaker to see his worm as unlicensed sexuality and to foresee the rose's death by means of a sexual act. "As a man is, so he sees," Blake wrote.[15] Or, in the words of Shakespeare's Hamlet, " . . . there is nothing either good or bad but thinking makes it so" (II, ii, 251–52).

Hamlet's *Lebenswelt*

The characterization of Hamlet has been the subject of numerous interpretations, and yet Hamlet's life-world remains elusive; the man behind the thoughts and the actions has been variously described. Any attempt at responding to the heart of the question as to why Hamlet procrastinates invariably leads to an exposure of a critical approach's strengths and weaknesses. It is in the hope of revealing most dramatically the phenomenological approach to drama that Hamlet has been chosen for discussion.

There is, Hamlet tells Rosencrantz, " . . . nothing either good or bad but thinking makes it so." And indeed, Hamlet's thinking makes it so, makes the play, makes the action and inaction of the play. What is Hamlet's thinking? Can we describe Hamlet's life-world, his *Lebenswelt*? And is that world and the good or bad it imposes upon time, others, self, and objects substantially different from the "real world," the good and bad evaluations in the play that are not Hamlet's? How great is the discrepancy between Hamlet's phenomenal reality and the phenomenal realities of other characters? Is there implicit in this play a "normative" reality that we can call Shakespeare's? We know at the start that this is the tragic history of Hamlet, Prince of Denmark. If the tragedy is with him, is it in his perceptions? Is there any way that it cannot be in his perceptions? If the tragedy is with him — is his tragedy — where is the nontragedy in this play? Are there, in other words, nontragic perceptions in this play? Where is the nontragic counterpart that enables us to see Hamlet's tragedy? Is it explicit, implicit in the play? Is it in us and nowhere in the play? If there is a Shakespearean "normative" view of things implicit here, perhaps the nontragic counterpart of the play is within it. Perhaps the tragic counterpart is not in Hamlet after all but in the world of Elsinore, and the play is his tragic history only insofar as he has the misfortune of being in such a world. If we cannot really be sure of the location of a tragic and nontragic dimension, we can be sure of a dimension that is opened by a phenomenological method — Hamlet's world and outside Hamlet's world.

When we describe Hamlet's being-in-the-world, his *Lebenswelt*, we approach the world outside his mind through his mind, specifically through his perceptions of self, others, objects, and time. This is all he is conscious of. If we wish to connect Hamlet the character to the play *Hamlet*, we must consider not only Hamlet's being in the world but simply being in the world of Elsinore. The passage between Hamlet's mental landscape and the world of Elsinore is partially through what he himself is not conscious of and therefore does not possess. The play as it exists outside Hamlet's mind — T.S. Eliot's "facts of the play" — is not all known to Hamlet; some of the facts of the play lie in the consciousness of other characters. What has traditionally been found in the unconscious of Hamlet is in a phenomenological view found in the world around him.

In the phenomenological view there are no layers to life. Life may be rich, deep, mysterious, but what is not conscious for one lies accessible in others. Such is the case in *Hamlet*. Within what Claudius, Horatio, Laertes, and everyone else in the play reveal to us on the conscious level is what Hamlet is unaware of, cannot perceive. Some of what they know comprises his "unconscious," not hidden within him at all but out there and not perceived by him, available to us as observers-readers. By attending to the world of the play, the conscious themes of *Hamlet*, we discover what is not in Hamlet's *Lebenswelt*. We find the passage between Hamlet's *Lebenswelt* and the play that is *Hamlet*. Thus, a complete phenomenological study of *Hamlet* would go beyond the *Lebenswelt* of the character Hamlet and consider the phenomenal worlds of other characters. My discussion here is limited to Hamlet's being-in-the-world.

Once we have described Hamlet's being-in-the-world, we can make some attempt at answering questions this play raises, particularly the question of why Hamlet procrastinates. In order to describe Hamlet's *Lebenswelt*, we automatically range into the play, making our encounters through Hamlet's eyes, noting where and when the "facts of the play" support or negate his perceptions. We, as readers, are not part of Hamlet's tragedy, though we realize very quickly that all of Shakespeare's art is unleashed to make us so, to make Hamlet's tragedy " . . . speak loudly for him . . ." (V, ii, 403). It is the compelling force of the tale in the telling that both enables us to view the depths of Hamlet's *Lebenswelt* and threatens to submerge us within the tragedy itself.

In regard to self, Hamlet, before he even meets with the ghost, refers to himself as the opposite of Hercules, the performer of miraculous feats (I.2.129-159). He refers to himself as a rogue and peasant slave (II, ii, 553), a dull and muddy-mettled rascal (ibid., 571), an ass (ibid., 587), a man of weakness and melancholy (ibid., 606). The act of revenge that the ghost calls upon Hamlet to perform obviously cannot be accomplished until Hamlet re-creates his own self-image, somehow altering a perception of himself that determines how he will act.

Hamlet's view of himself extends to a cynical view of all men. We are all arrant knaves who should not be believed (III, i, 128–30). While waiting for the appearance of the ghost in act I, Hamlet's attention is drawn to Claudius's late-night revels. Hamlet then expresses the view that particular men are corrupted by a particular fault. One effect, the result of chance or the nature of things, is sufficient to bring down infinite grace and virtue. Hamlet thus perceives a world in which goodness is overwhelmed by the slightest flaw. At this point in the play Hamlet knows nothing of his father's murder. Has his mother's hasty marriage to Hamlet's uncle Claudius engendered this pessimism?

There is a phenomenal world here that is Hamlet's, a world not explainable in terms of events we as readers perceive.

Hamlet thinks his mother is less than a mindless beast for not mourning his father but immediately marrying Claudius (I, ii, 150). Again, this is his opinion before the ghost tells him of the murder. Premature marriage and a brief mourning have not created Hamlet's disposition but have been met by it, have been absorbed within Hamlet's intentional world, have been met and transformed by intentional consciousness. Claudius is called a satyr before he is known to be a murderer (ibid., 140); Polonius, after being killed by Hamlet, is called a foolish, prating knave by Hamlet (III, iv, 215); Rosencrantz and Guildenstern are fanged adders and summarily brought to their deaths by Hamlet (ibid., 203); all women are hypocrites and married women are whores (III, i, 146–49); even Man-Thinking is despised by Hamlet, since three-quarters of thought engenders cowardice (ibid., 84–88).

In the last act (Hamlet at the grave of Ophelia) Hamlet expresses views of men that are even more bitter and cynical than previously expressed. Politicians who circumvented God, courtiers who bowed and scraped, clever lawyers and financiers have all undergone a fine revolution from something to nothing. Yorick, who had had wit, is now a jawless skull. Alexander, who had conquered the known world, is nothing more than a stopper for a bunghole; and Caesar himself is a bit of clay. From the world as un unweeded garden in the beginning of the play to the world happily turned to rotting corpses in the last act, Hamlet's perceptions have never permitted him to see a world in which one act of revenge would mean anything, would be significant. One act of revenge does not alter such a world peopled by such people. Hamlet's world does not give him that one ounce of optimism, of faith, hope, and charity, of love, necessary for him to attempt a good act in a bad world. We are all arrant knaves, and it is Hamlet's thinking that for him makes it so.

What is on Hamlet's mind, or more precisely, how the world is perceived through Hamlet's eyes, is revealed by the way he speaks not only of himself and others but of the objects in the world surrounding him. First of all, he perceives according to intentions that prevent him from seeing certain things and direct him toward seeing others. The things he does see are seen not as under a microscope but in accordance with his determining predisposition. His thinking invests the object — any object, say Yorick's skull or the ghost of Hamlet's father — and we know by seeing them through Hamlet's eyes what their significance to him may be. We can reconstruct a part of his life-world by so viewing the things of his world as he views them.

Hamlet perceives his surroundings as a prison (II, ii, 253) and an unweeded garden:

> O God! God!
> How weary, stale, flat, and unprofitable
> Seems to me all the uses of this world.
> Fie on 't! ah, fie! 'tis an unweeded garden,
> That grows to seed; things rank and gross in nature
> Possess it merely. (I, ii, 132–37)

And he relates his mental disposition to the world he perceives,

> I have of late, — but wherefore I know not, — lost all my mirth, forgone all custom of exercises; and indeed it goes so heavily with my disposition that this goodly frame, the earth, seems to me a sterile promontory; this most excellent canopy, the air, look you, this brave o'erhanging firmament, this majestical roof fretted with golden fire, why, it appeareth nothing to me but a foul and pestilent congregation of vapors. (II, ii, 299–307)

Hamlet reveals his *Lebenswelt* more in what he says about people and himself than about the world of objects around him. Dialogue reveals the former while narrative reveals both. The matter of time, however, is as available in drama as in fiction, and in *Hamlet* we learn much about Hamlet's view of time.

It is Hamlet's perception of time that reveals to us that his father's death has triggered a clash between internally constituted reality and externally constituted reality. The death is an event outside Hamlet that has come inside and literally been encased within internal, existential time. Time in a mechanistic sense cannot continue for Hamlet until the death of his father is made sense of in his own mind. At the point that the death makes sense (and in Hamlet's view it can make sense only if he revenges that death), it can be propelled outward again into external time; existential and external time can join. But that congruence in time does not take place. Indeed, there is no evidence that such a congruence has ever taken place in the young Hamlet's life thus far. An aspect of tragedy in this play is certainly that the young Hamlet runs out of time,

time in which an inner sense of time could have developed, matured outwardly. Hamlet comes out of existential time only at the moment of his death, an event that does not bring together internal and external time but explodes both, ends both. For Hamlet, from the very first act of the play, time stands still; there is no past or future but only the ever-present moment in which he is transfixed, wriggling on his back like Kafka's Samsa but getting no place.

The death of Hamlet's father and the ghost's cry for revenge stand like viral invaders within an organism that cannot expel or destroy them. The attack Hamlet mounts against this invader is ineffective; it misses the mark. It is designed for other purposes. The time is truly out of joint. Nevertheless, the invader, the act of revenge, remains. There is nothing for Hamlet to do but exhaust the resources he has, to fight an externally constituted reality with an internally constituted reality. And that fight goes on internally, hidden energy creating fitful sparks of unconnected action. We see Hamlet act but get nowhere. His is not today's or tomorrow's plain of battle but a plain of mind within a fixated moment outside time as we conventionally conceive it. He perceives all his acts as futile and himself as imprisoned within one moment.

In act I, Hamlet questions the two months since his father's death and concludes that it feels more like a month. In act III, he refers to the time since his father's death as two hours. In act V, he asks the clown at Ophelia's grave how long since his father overcame Fortinbras, and the clown answers:

> Cannot you tell that? Every fool can tell that. It was that
> very day that young Hamlet was born. . . . (V, i, 150–52)

The event occurring on Hamlet's birthday would normally be significant, but is not significant for Hamlet because all time has been usurped by the death of his father and the necessity for revenge in the present, a present that, for Hamlet, remains present throughout the course of the play.

But perhaps, as Hamlet tells Horatio in act V, there is special providence in the fall of a sparrow. Perhaps all time, internal and external, lies in the power of this special providence. Perhaps the existence of such a special providence will not only guide Hamlet's revenge but by its very existence enable him to resolve his internal dilemma satisfactorily. I mean by this last statement that perhaps the existence of a special providence is a justification for Hamlet to perceive the world and himself differently, and with such renewed hope revenge his father's murder. Is time and our actions within time guided by a special providence? Does Hamlet really believe this? What we know of Hamlet's view of time enables us to comprehend Hamlet's words regarding a special providence.

We know that actions in the past fixate him in an immovable present and rob from him all possibility of a future. Time does not move for Hamlet. For example, Hamlet looks upon the play within the play, his mousetrap for Claudius, as a "show-stopper," as a provocation that will cause Claudius to perceive that the murder-marriage is a "show-stopper," an event that stops time for him as it has for Hamlet. If Hamlet cannot stop real time and cause Claudius to be fixed in a never-changing moment, he can at least construct a play and force Claudius to stop the course of the play, to stop time within the dramatic world. When Claudius stops the play, he justifies for Hamlet Hamlet's perceptions of himself, objects, others, and time. Thus, when Hamlet comments upon the apparent movement of time and its relationship to events in the following speech,

> There is special providence in the fall of a sparrow. If it be now, 'tis not to come; if it be not to come, it will be now; if it be not now, yet it will come—the readiness is all. (V, ii, 208-11)

he is saying nothing more than that providence guides some in a changing course of time and they need only be ready.

Unfortunately, Hamlet is not in a situation where time changes. For Hamlet, time stands still in Elsinore. A special providence must find a special place to be providential, certainly not Elsinore. For Hamlet, a special providence is special because it has nothing to do with the world Hamlet perceives himself to be in. Since we know that Hamlet's *Lebenswelt* is partially based on his perception of others and the world, we know that he is incapable of perceiving a special providence acting in the lives of others, acting in the world. I think Hamlet's derisive opinion of a special providence is revealed in the lines themselves, lines that require a reexamination since, upon first hearing, they sound like nonsense.

Analyzing Our Description of Hamlet's *Lebenswelt*

There are two dimensions of reality that we have defined in *Hamlet* via his own perceptions: one, the external dimension of the play, a dimension that we have gained through Hamlet's eyes and that has been corroborated in the play itself; and the other, the phenomenal reality that is Hamlet's. The first involves murder, Gertrude's precipitous marriage to her recently dead husband's murderer and a vow of revenge by Hamlet to his father's ghost. The second involves a reality in which we are arrant knaves all, in which even the great become bunghole stoppers. The dilemma here is for Hamlet to move from a phenomenal reality to an external reality, to put aside his own perceptions and assume perceptions outside himself.

Hamlet obviously agrees with Rosencrantz's estimate of the importance of that ". . . spirit upon whose weal depends and rests / The Lives of many . . ." (III, iii, 14–15). Something is rotten in the state of Denmark, the state outside Hamlet's mind, and it is he who, as prince, is born to set it right, to kill the usurper and thus avenge his father. It is important to reiterate at this point that Hamlet does not know all "the facts of the play." The external world he has constituted for himself, the world he perceives, has for us, as readers, its full dimensions only when we free ourselves of Hamlet's *Lebenswelt* and probe other characters. A full view of the world of Elsinore as it is constituted outside Hamlet's mind is essential to our full phenomenological description of the play. However, in considering Hamlet's *Lebenswelt*, we describe and analyze from the perspective of that *Lebenswelt*, in terms of that *Lebenswelt*. We get to see it all from Hamlet's view and then analyze what we have before turning elsewhere in the play.

Hamlet's external state as he perceives it does not determine his personal acts. This external state includes the requirements of revenge, of the "lives of many," of princely duties. And yet for Hamlet a personal act, like the murder of Claudius, is dependent upon personal perceptions, upon a human life-world personally constructed. It is Hamlet's phenomenal reality that must sanction the murder. In other words, for Hamlet to act as the situation constituted outside himself demands he act, he would first have to become someone else.

The force by which Hamlet is bound to perceptions that keep him from acting creates the tension in Hamlet and may be viewed as

Hamlet's true antagonist. This is not to say that Hamlet's view of what must be done, what actions should be taken, resolves the rottenness in Denmark. We cannot trust his sense of what "normal behavior" would be under the circumstances abiding in the play as a whole. It is possible that action on anyone's part in this play resolves nothing. Or that Hamlet's own *Lebenswelt*, as difficult as it makes things for Hamlet, is the only *human* life-world in the play. In other words, to be in any other dilemma in this play except the one Hamlet is in would imply a lessening of one's humanity, a step backward into the evil that permeates the play. But from having described Hamlet's *Lebenswelt*, we know that if he is able to resolve the force by which he is bound to his perceptions, he is, in a sense, free to act as the external situation demands. This is the dilemma he has described for himself, and we know that regardless of whether his internal or external views can be verified, they remain real for Hamlet. Unfortunately, he moves farther and farther away from resolving his dilemma and plunges deeper into his own human life-world, from whose perspective he can only consider too curiously the world about him.

The tragedy we see in Hamlet is the tragedy of all those whose own human life-world becomes deeply at variance with the world around them. The coinage of Hamlet's brain is no longer even a passable counterfeit for the coinage of the world. Hamlet has been caught within a world of intentions that give meaning to the world in a way antithetical to the fulfillment of his vows to revenge his father's murder. The struggle Hamlet makes in the course of this play is a struggle to give up personally constructed meaning and take on societally constructed meaning. This struggle ensues throughout the play: a mind is continually in the throes of freeing itself of a task it cannot perform while contemporaneously trying to free itself of a life-world that makes that task, the act of revenge, impossible. Hamlet's hesitancy is thus defined in this way in the phenomenological view.

If Hamlet's *Lebenswelt* were not malleable, he would make no struggle to act. But he does struggle. He is not the man so bound by pathological determinants that he sees nothing of his situation in the way other people see it. Hamlet sees the necessity for revenge at the same time that he considers suicide, at the same time that he considers the futility of all human life. But suicide and cynicism are the true products of his *Lebenswelt*, and they do not collapse but grow in strength as the play progresses. Hamlet's own *Lebenswelt* — the view we have described of his perceptions of others, self, objects, and time — wins the day, and thus Hamlet loses the struggle.

It is Claudius who really arranges his own death. Hamlet, in the play's final scene, is simply an actor without internal motivation, without intentions. At the moment of his death, Hamlet is farther away from acting in accord with the demands of a reality constituted outside his own mind than ever before in the play. His feigned madness is indeed a feigned madness, but one in the service of a mind struggling to put aside its own intentions and perceptions and take on the world's. That feigned madness is then a dissimulation in the service of a mind struggling toward societal perceptions. Had that feigned madness been constructed by a mind not convinced that the world and its creator were mad, a mind not constructing according to an intentional system at odds with society's, it could have been an effective, though roundabout, means of Hamlet taking revenge.

But feigned madness comes to naught because Hamlet's own dissociation from conventional perceptions and actions increases. He cannot function in the "real world" except according to his own *Lebenswelt*, and from that perspective, murder serves no purpose. Only death mercifully saves Hamlet, resolves his dilemma. We have thus developed a view of Hamlet as a man who toils mightily for five acts to bridge the gap between his own *Lebenswelt* and the demands of an outside world. And it is his tragedy to fail.

Because Hamlet's tragedy is at the core of the play, a great deal of the play is revealed through our description and analysis of Hamlet's *Lebenswelt*. Through description we have achieved some understanding of Hamlet's plight. If we move back from the play, from our close-up of Hamlet, we try to take in other characters as they are and not as they are perceived by Hamlet. We add this descriptive detail to our Hamlet description and modify it accordingly. If we move back still farther, we perceive the play as a gestalt, as a dramatic interweaving of perceptions. Finally, what is not in the consciousness of any one character is in our consciousness. We become aware of the richness of Shakespeare's design as we probe deeper into the variety of phenomenal realities in the play. We become aware of the consciousness that has not only created Hamlet's consciousness and those of every other character in the play, but has guided our own consciousness toward an understanding of the play.

In order to demonstrate a phenomenological approach that extends beyond one character and toward meaning in the work as a whole, we shall turn to a contemporary novel.

Joseph Natoli

Joan Didion's *Play It As It Lays*

Before moving in close to this novel, I would like to stand, in Northrop Frye fashion, several steps away from both myself as reader and the world of Maria Wyeth, the protagonist of this novel, in order to see how I, armed with a phenomenological perspective, make connections with this novel and what those connections mean in regard to my eventual interpretation.

First of all, Joan Didion and I are in the same "real world." The number and kinds of contacts we make with it are not the same; our phenomenal worlds differ. And yet what she writes and has written has become for me and for other readers part of the experiential foundation of our world. In other words, part of that "real world" that I sporadically make contact with has been constituted for me, not discursively but experientially, by my reading of Joan Didion's novels. And when she creates the objective consciousness of her characters, minds interacting with the objects of their literary worlds, she is presenting both minds and objects that are reflective of a "real world" both she and I share. And what her own perceptions are as distinguished from those of her characters also touches base with a uniformly shared "real world."

What does all this amount to? To a critic leaning toward an objective, empirical literary analysis, the commingling of my world and Joan Didion's world would be a lamentable drawback, an obstacle to critical analysis. To a phenomenologically oriented critic, aiming to draw a full descriptive analysis through the delineation of consciousness as revealed in the physiognomy of objects, and also through the delineation of objects through the physiognomy of consciousness, his being in a world from which both are derived is a definite asset. In a phenomenologically oriented psychology, we have, for the very first time in literary history, an approach uniquely designed to tackle contemporary works. Indeed, if literature can contribute to the experiential foundation of our world, the world we are presently experiencing, then an approach that makes that literature available to us increases our understanding of the world in which we live and simultaneously increases literature's present and future effect upon that world. Each in his or her own phenomenal world, we move in literature through the varieties of phenomenal worlds of characters, adjusting our own worlds and paying heed to the author's implicit sense of what a "normative" world is like.

Maria Wyeth, in a mental institution at the novel's beginning, recalls a variety of incidents that present her as a young woman hurt by memories of her mother's desperate life and suicide; by the institution-alization of her retarded daughter, Kate; by the sudden collapse of her own acting career; by her husband's interest in another woman; by a sordid abortion — all events that she cannot quite bring together in any way that enables her to continue living a "normal" life. There are features in *Play It As It Lays* that make the book susceptible to a phenomenological approach. Maria Wyeth's present life is revealed through brief scenes in which her perceptions of herself, others, the world around her, and time are vividly presented. Maria is in a neuropsychiatric ward when the novel begins, and what ensues as flashback is a particularized depiction of events leading to her collapse. The virtually plotless nature of this novel, its dwelling on sick people within a sick society, the author's refusal to intrude and comment upon either behavior or perceptions, are common rather than idiosyncratic qualities of contemporary fiction. And, as in much contemporary fiction, character analysis reveals a psychopathology. The phenomenological approach is well suited to tracing a pathography, a *Lebenswelt* whose components — perceptions of self, others, time, and objects — are pathological.[16]

Hamlet's *Lebenswelt* was so obviously superior to the rotten state of Denmark, to the world around him, that we, as readers, are ready to condemn as mad the world rather than Hamlet. In the case of Maria Wyeth, we perceive a soul without noble dimension, buffeted about in a world made rotten not by clear acts of murder and the necessity for revenge, but rotten beyond human proportions, beyond human acts. What we discover in Didion's novel is a world that seems to run without human involvement, that is stale and mechanical and senseless. It seems not to be a human life-world, and to what degree it is or isn't, to what degree our contemporary world as protrayed in this novel is or isn't, can be described by our approach.

Besides Maria Wyeth's view of things, we are given in two brief chapters the views of two other characters: her present husband, Carter, and a friend, Helene. Both accounts respond reasonably to Maria's behavior. Carter simply testifies to the erraticism of her behavior by describing a few incidents; and Helene believes Maria's actions stem from selfishness, willfulness, and irresponsibility. Both accounts are "true" and objective; these onlookers do not lie. But an outside perspective filled with established notions of normal behavior, of value and response, does not reach the phenomenal experiences of Maria herself, what we as readers perceive. In constructing Maria's *Lebenswelt*, we must ignore consensually validated accounts by other characters if we wish to determine how the world is actually seen by Maria. Van den Berg describes in the following manner a patient's dilemma in regard to the world outside himself:

> His existence is about to disintegrate; everything around him is old and dilapidated. He is living with the relics of a past time, and he is a living anachronism. That the streets and squares seem fearfully wide and empty is the literal expression of his "subjective," i.e., personal condition. He is a lonely individual; the objects are far away and hostile. There is no better way for him to describe his condition; he tells the truth of his mental illness. *He is right.*[17]

We are treated to Maria's commentary on "objective" descriptions of her behavior. Carter has done a documentary of her life, *Maria*, a picture that ". . . showed Maria doing a fashion sitting, Maria asleep on a couch at a party, Maria on the telephone . . . Maria cleaning . . . Maria crying. . . ." Maria does not like the film. "She never thought of it as *Maria.*" She does not see herself and yet the film does not lie. It is "objective." But it, too, has missed her, and therefore, for Maria, it does lie. The film she does admire is one in which she plays a girl who " . . . seemed to have a definite knack for controlling her own destiny." But, as we discover, this is the one thing she cannot do.

Events in the present, her daughter's commitment and an abortion, put the present outside Maria's control and conjure up a past reconstructed by her troubles in the present. What will become viable for her in the present is determined by these events, events that in Maria's case are filled with sickness and death. What may be wholesome in both her past and her present is, because of her present interests, not available. Specifically, there is only a past, present, and future made significant by one's intentions — intentions that are themselves modeled by events, regardless of when they occurred, that remain significant, that are present events.

A hypnotist with obvious Freudian leanings attempts to locate Maria's present trouble to her prenatal life: "Your worries may date from when you were a baby in your mother's womb." But since that life is not in Maria's present consciousness, has not been deemed significant from her present perspective, it does not exist for her. Maria does have memories of her mother's death and her father's troubles, memories that are transformed by her perspective in the present. Thus, we see that only a "present-past" is really important. What is significant in the past will be operating in the present, will be a part of present consciousness, will compose the very fiber of present consciousness. There is no past that is not a present-past. Any effort to conjure up a past-past, a personally nonexistent past, will be useless. To the hypnotist's questions regarding what she is doing, seeing, hearing at some time in the past — a past to which he has wished to transpose her via hypnosis, Maria responds with a detailed description of experiences in the present:

> I'm driving over here . . . I'm driving Sunset and I'm staying in the left lane because I can see the New Havana Ballroom and I'm going to turn left at the New Havana Ballroom. That's what I'm doing.[18]

Maria's future means one thing: an opportunity to have Kate, her daughter — an opportunity that grows progressively less realizable, making the future as a real future less realizable. An abortion in the present is the immediate impetus to Maria's desire to have Kate with her in the future. An event in the present (an abortion) brings an event in the past (loss of Kate in a mental institution) to life and determines a future event (getting Kate out). But it is the present's perspective that determines both past and future. The sordid aborting of a child makes it imperative for her to "find" her living child, to regain Kate. Maria feels that what she can recall from the past and what she sees in the present and what she hopes for in the future can be transformed by Kate. Unfortunately, Kate's psychiatric treatment relies on chemicals, is behaviorally oriented, and succeeds in keeping her out of Maria's world as well as her own.

Maria's visits to Kate are discouraged; success in this form of therapy depends on a violation of a basic interpersonal relationship — that of mother and daughter. Kate has the power to transform reality for Maria, and Maria therefore seeks desperately to reach Kate through an understanding of her treatment. But chemicals have put Kate out of Maria's reach. Human life-worlds have been aborted.

> "You keep talking about the new medication. I mean *what is it*." Kate screamed. The nurse looked reproachfully at Maria. "Methylphenidate hydrochloride." Maria closed her eyes. "All right. Your point."[19]

Once Kate is not available to Maria as a transforming agent, as a means to make the present and future less frightening, Maria loses track of herself. Her human life-world is one in which she perceives only ". . . hacked pieces of human flesh . . ." in the plumbing and ". . . fetuses in the East River, translucent as jelly fish. . . ." This "real world" becomes understandably hard to hold on to. It is a continuous nightmare. The world consensually validated by other characters in the novel is a world different from the one Maria is permitted by her own perspective to see.

An attempt at comforting her is a failed attempt at transforming her world, a world only Kate can transform. Maria comments sarcastically at such attempts:

> In the past few minutes he had significantly altered her perception of reality: she saw now that she was not a woman on her way to have an abortion. She was a woman parking a Corvette outside a tract house while a man in white pants talked about buying a Camaro. There was no more to it than that.[20]

Rather than act as transforming agents, the people Maria sees symbolize for her the ". . . quintessential intersection of nothing." They anesthetize her (". . . there had come a time when she felt anesthetized in the presence of Ivan Costello and now that time had come with Carter . . .") or revolt her (". . . everywhere Maria looked she saw someone who registered on her only as a foreigner or a faggot or a gangster . . ."). One expects that Maria will run into people who fit into her *Lebenswelt*. "I don't know if you noticed, I'm mentally ill," a woman tells Maria at a snack counter, and we, as readers and observers, know this is the only kind of person Maria can notice.

But Maria Wyeth is not locked into an unwholesome vision within a society noted for its wholesomeness. Through Maria's interaction with other characters, we get some sense of a world constituted outside herself. But in this novel, we also find a positive note that Maria has missed, that is not part of Maria's world. What we find is a woman with whom Maria sits and to whom she listens disinterestedly. This woman has made a decision:

> "I made my decision in '61 at a meeting in Barstow and I never shed one tear since." "No," Maria said. "I never did that."[21]

In the middle of a desert, this woman whose husband has left her for ". . . a girl down to Barstow . . . ," runs a coffee shop with posted hours and lives in a house that she manages to keep clean. While she speaks to Maria she characteristically sweeps sand off her porch, though the wind blows new sand as she sweeps. Her decision, it seems, is to "play is as it lays," to persevere regardless of the odds. Thus, we begin to move from Maria's view of things to another character's view. And this character's view is a still point in the midst of turbulence, not only Maria's but every other character's.

Is this character representing Didion's view? Is this "play it as it lays" attitude — perseverance in the face of recurrent, inexplicable misfortune and setbacks — Didion's "normative" view that opposes Maria's phenomenal misconstructions, Maria's eventual breakdown? Implicit in any character's misconstructions of reality is the author's values. We can often find a character with whom our initial character, our protagonist, interacts who represents a life-world contrary to our protagonist's. The implicit values of the author emerge. We get, in other words, a look at the "meaning" of a work in the author's view. I make this qualification because "meaning" shines forth from the work and not from our sense of the implicit values of the author. An author's implicit values inhering within a novel are contributive to and not equated with what a reader ultimately determines to be the "meaning" of the novel. The implicit human life-world of an author is not synonymous with the total novel. On our way to exploring the life-world of the total novel, our exploration reveals the life-worlds of characters as well as author.

When we juxtapose Maria's life-world with those of other characters, we search for a life-world that is in some way, through the art of the novelist, potent, arresting. Where, we ask, is the world that is not Maria's, that is not tragic? If the novel is rich as life is rich, if the novel is not simply a guise for rhetoric, we, as readers, stand on different grounds and receive different views of the literary world we are in and yet not in. One of the views we search for is the author's. In this particular novel, we find a character who seems to be presenting the author's view.

When we approach Maria's description of the "physiognomy of objects" in her world, we despair or not depending upon the nature of our experiences, as readers, of the world she describes. We struggle toward a prereflective understanding of her "objectified universe." Certainly for Maria the world is both loathsome and perilous.

> She could not read newspapers because certain stories leapt
> at her from the page: the four year olds in the abandoned re-
> frigerator . . . the infant in the driveway, rattlesnake in the
> playpen, the peril, the unspeakable peril, in the everyday.[22]

She dreams of ". . . opalescent mussel shells . . . ," but awakes and realizes ". . . the mussels on any shore . . . were toxic." Tulips look dirty, plants consumed needed oxygen, food arranged itself into ominous coils, fetuses filled the plumbing. We know what events have taken hold of Maria, determining what in time is available to her, determining her relationship with others. We also know how she sees the world. From her description of her world we could surmise the existence of certain determining events, events that the novel reveals. A complete view of her human life-world emerges. We are not surprised to discover that Maria is dissociated from her body, that she neglects it, loses considerable weight, feels pathologically dirty, sleeps throughout the day, loses all sexual feelings, becomes almost catatonic. In short, her view of herself is what we would expect after having described her perceptions of what is significant in time, others, and the world around her. Our phenomenological method takes us far into this novel, toward meaning based on description.

Constructivist Interpretation: The Value of Cognitive Psychology for Literary Understanding

by Henry D. Herring

Although the dominant mode of psychological interpretation in literature has continued to be psychoanalytic — the system of thought originated by Sigmund Freud — several conceptual systems in psychology that differ from the Freudian have now emerged and reached a state of development to make them useful for literary interpretation. One of these fields is cognitive psychology, a disciplinary area within general and social psychology that emphasizes the constructing capacities and processes of human thought. It concerns itself, too, with how thought relates to feeling and action. The purpose of this essay, therefore, is to set out the initial elements of what I will call a constructivist approach to literary criticism — a designation I have chosen to emphasize the role of construction in cognitive processes and that seems justified by the frequent use of terms such as "construct of thought" or "construction of reality" by cognitive psychologists, even though they do not designate themselves "constructivists."

The existence of cognitive psychology with its emphasis on the conscious and constructing capacities of human thought as a significant component of learning, meaning, feeling, and behaving has a long history in the development of psychology. Some of this knowledge has come from people who began within the psychoanalytic context but modified their positions substantially — among them Alfred Adler, one of Freud's earliest and most prominent associates; Karen Horney, who emphasized strategies related to the individual's desire for security and revised many psychoanalytic conceptions of women;[1] and R.D. Laing, who leavened his original psychoanalytic training with Sartrean existential thought. Yet cognitive theories have emerged even more importantly out of the experimental fields of psychological study that have not ordinarily attracted the attention of literary critics. The origins of these ideas can be found in the learning theories of the cognitive behaviorist, Edward Chace Tolman, who rejected the notion of learning as a simple stimulus-response syndrome and introduced the concept of intervening variables to designate the cognitive — or thinking — processes that cannot be observed but can be carefully inferred to intervene between the stimulus and the actual response made.[2]

Another source can be found in the efforts to assess and describe the cognitive development and constructing capacities of human beings as carried ourt by psychologists such as Jean Piaget and Jerome Bruner. In social psychology, the experiments of attribution theorists in particular have stressed cognitive abilities in their efforts to determine how persons assign causes for events, and the effects of those attributions on their actions.[3] Finally, within clinical psychology, the branch of the discipline that has many of its early origins in Freudian thought, one finds the clinical evidence of Aaron Beck and Albert Ellis, both of whom have emphasized the role of belief systems in disturbed behavior.

Clearly, one of the characteristics of this psychological tradition is the diversity of its sources and the absence of a dominating figure, such as Freud or Jung, to help provide unity. In part, the first task to make it useful for literary criticism must be to pull the ideas together. However, at the same time that this diversity poses problems for unifying the concepts, it also provides a much wider range of evidence, drawing upon experimentation, observation of normal behavior, and information from clinical sources. Its epistemological base offers the possibility of a firmer, if somewhat less systematic, grounding. The loss of system, however, will be a gain if an interpretational model emerges that allows for a more flexible and valuable conception of literature in human experience.

In attempting to pull these ideas together into formulations useful to literary thought, I shall group them into four interrelated conceptual categories: (1) the goal-oriented character of action, (2) the need to construct interpretations of experience, (3) the influence of the interpretations on feelings and actions, and (4) the complexities of developing and using interpretational constructions. From this explanation an evaluation of the general implications of the cognitive/constructivist perspective can be made for experience and criticism.

Basic Concepts of Cognitive Psychology

The Goal-Orientation of Action

The first component of cognitive psychology is the belief that behavior is goal-oriented. Fundamentally, this concept means that actions do not merely represent controlled responses, whether simple or complex, to some stimulus that precedes the action or to some reinforcer that follows it, regardless of whether the stimulus or reinforcer is a simple electrical shock, the shattering death of a friend, a learning pattern deliberately induced by a parent, or even the reading of a poem or novel. Although any of these events may influence the actions taken, the choice of action arises from the desire to attain a goal related to the individual's beliefs about such matters as the value of the goal, the effort required to achieve success, and the probability that available strategies will work. In human behavior Thomas Lidz calls this characteristic the person's ability to project himself or herself into the future and to take purposeful action.[4]

What is fundamental to the cognitive position is the person's desire to move into a conceptualized future in a way that he or she believes will achieve goals. This desire leads the individual to acquire, structure, test, and use information that he or she thinks will be useful and effective. Evidence for this component of the constructivist perspective comes from the entire spectrum of psychological investigation: Tolman's animal experiments, J.B. Rotter's research on the use of strategies in human interaction in social psychology, and George Kelly's conclusions from clinical observations that individuals try to anticipate the future and act in relation to those anticipations.[5]

Mary Gordon's novel *Final Payments* (New York: Random House, 1978) offers a clear sense of a character struggling cognitively toward goals. Isabel Moore, who emerges at thirty to make a life of her own after years of caring for her invalid father, moves toward two common ends: she gets a job and starts an intimate relationship. However, Hugh, her lover, is married; and when his wife, Cynthia, humiliates Isabel in public, Isabel's perception of herself as "above reproach" (p. 230), developed during her years of caring for her father, is shattered. To regain her goodness, she decides to renounce herself by living with and taking care of Margaret Casey, the housekeeper from her childhood whom she hates. She discovers, though, that her expectations of life — her goals — have changed; and she desires the risk of love even though the threat of loss made life "monstrous" (p. 294). Recognizing that she no longer believes in renouncing the self to care for another as the goal of her life, she activates a new plan, calling her friends Liz and Eleanor to come get her and writing to Hugh that in time she will return. The novel sets out how one cognitive goal — goodness and self-sacrifice — changes, however difficultly, to another — risk and fulfillment — and hence how Isabel's actions shift gradually to accomodate her new purposes.

The Construction of Interpretations of Experience

The second and most important characteristic of the cognitive/constructivist position arises from the acquisition and testing of information: the individual construes information into an interpretation of experience that he or she attempts to use to make sense of existence and to enable choice and action. Tolman's notion of the cognitive map constitutes a rudimentary form of the process. A more developed form comes in the observations of and experiments with children that led to Jean Piaget's descriptions of cognitive development.[6] Although Piaget's work is complex, several of his ideas have fundamental relevance here. His basic theory suggests that the individual progresses cognitively from simpler to more complex abilities that allow him or her to function in the world. For a child the removal of an object from sight is the same as its disappearance from the world; he or she has no sense that it has been put, for example, under the rug. Eventually, the child can conceive of the permanence of the object, that its removal merely means it can no longer be seen.[7] With the development of symbolic and linguistic modes of thought, a form of action in Piaget, the individual achieves the most complex levels of cognitive operations. Throughout his or her experience, the individual uses cognitive skills for adaptation by assimilating elements of the external world to present activities and also by accommodating his or her activities to the requirements of the surrounding world. In addition to adaptation, however, the second major cognitive function, especially as the child acquires symbolic and abstracting powers, is to organize experiences. Beginning with simple acts like subordination (grasping comes to be understood as a component of pulling), the child moves to more complex and relatively complete structurings of the knowledge that will enable actions designed to acquire what he or she values.

For Piaget, who conceived of his ideas as structuralist, the structure neither comes from predetermined sources nor remains fixed, but rather is being "constructed" all the time because of the continual processes of adaptation and organization that force the individual to "restructure" previous operational sets into new ones. These sets take account of the person's continuing experiential encounters and the continuing development of new transformational (organizational) schemata to use in thought and action.[8] Intelligence and behavior, then, are constructing and active.

Piaget's descriptions of cognitive development concur fundamentally with those of Jerome Bruner and Ulric Neisser. Bruner conceived of knowledge as structuring information about one's environment, the process of "learning how things are related."[9] Neisser contends that the enormous information that an individual receives must undergo active cognitive structuring in order to become useful for acting within the world. Neisser describes a continuously interactive process in which individuals use schemata to organize information and to direct perceptual explorations of objects and the environment, which then modify the original schema.[10] As Bruner summarizes the cognitive process, it allows for simplifying information but also for generating new concepts that make knowledge more manipulable.[11]

For many attribution theorists and for the clinical psychologist George A. Kelly, the purpose of structuring knowledge is to gain understanding and to make sense of experience, for example by attributing causes to events so that one can use these understandings — "constructs," to use Kelly's term[12] — as a way of predicting (or at least gauging) the outcome of events and consequently acting with some assurance even when one has only imperfect knowledge. As Kelly notes, however, the meaning assigned to an event comes from the individual rather than from the event itself; the meaning comes from the way the event fits into the person's constructions (pp. 9–10). As Kelly argues, a person generally tries "to improve these constructs through experience or education" in order to get better "fits" between what he or she believes and what happens (p. 9); but the important recognition for the constructivist scheme is that an individual actively constructs an understanding of the world (however correct or incorrect) based upon a complex wide-ranging, and constantly evolving body of information that he or she tests in multiple ways (primarily through experiences, but also through the shared constructions of other people). Eventually, the person must use this construction to make decisions and to act until it is altered, perhaps as a result of the information gained through its active use. As indicated in Piaget's model, the process continuously and actively structures and restructures experience, usually in increasingly complex ways. Ideally, from this process emerges an interpretation of experience that gives rise to a competent set of beliefs that can serve as a useful guide for goal-directed action, albeit a guide that must be subject to revision as new information becomes available and new goals arise.

Hester Prynne in Nathaniel Hawthorne's *The Scarlet Letter* (1850)[13] provides a compelling instance of an individual who must reconstruct her interpretation of her experience. Condemned by the Puritan society she lives in for the sin of adultery and sentenced to wear the scarlet *A* on her breast as a constant reminder, Hester's experience causes her former characteristics of lightness, gracefulness, attractiveness, and passion to become "withered up" (p. 163). In her world, with her experiences, she can no longer interpret her existence in a way that might allow these qualities to belong to her and to be used by her in her actions. Denied the traditional interpretation of herself as a woman in the community who might marry and share love, Hester has to construct a different interpretation of her existence that will "fit" her circumstances better. She does; and though its details are far too complex to be fully analyzed here, some of the prominent elements can be pointed up. Most importantly, her circumstances turned her life "in great measure, from passion and feeling, to thought." In an age when the bold thought of men had "overthrown and rearranged . . . the whole system of ancient prejudice . . . [,] Hester Prynne imbibed this spirit." In her thought, "The world's law was no law for her mind" (p. 164). Because Hester cannot construct her world around passion and feeling, then, she turns to thought so radical that she rejects the common laws of the world as appropriate to her; and hence she reinterprets her action not as sin, telling Dimmesdale in the forest that " 'What we did had a consecration of its own' " (p. 195).

By turning to thought, by coming to construe her intimacy with Dimmesdale as a consecrated act rather than as a sin because she, rather than the society, defines its meaning, Hester reinterprets her experience in a way that enables her to see herself as a person of value instead of as a sinner without worth. Consequently, she can act within the community as a valuable member, aiding especially those who suffer. Her reinterpretation also explains her decision to return to the community after having left for years, apparently without necessity, in order to comfort suffering women. She especially reassures them that "a new truth . . .

would be revealed, in order to establish the whole relation between man and woman on a surer ground of mutual happiness" (p. 263). In the end, her interpretation of her experience in order to make sense of her world and to reject its condemnation of her becomes the construction that gives her life meaning, that guides her decision to return to the original place of her pain in order to assist others in reconstruing their worlds in ways that will be more satisfying to them.

The Influence of Interpretations on Feelings and Actions

The third element of a constructivist psychological model concerns the important relationship between the person's construction or interpretation of his or her experience and his or her emotions and actions. In much of Western thought the tendency has been to separate emotions from thought, as in the Renaissance attitude that the passions threatened to dominate an individual's life unless reason could tame and govern them. In much popular psychology today, a reversed attitude exhorts people to abandon inhibiting intellection in order to "get in touch" with their feelings. Since the nineteenth century, literature itself has often been associated with the emotional rather than the intellectual dimensions of human experience.[14] A cognitive/constructivist analysis, however, offers a much clearer conception of the intricate interplay between thought and feeling, recognizing that they overlap and reinforce one another, but perceiving, too, that the origin of the emotional response usually comes from the belief system that the individual has constructed. Albert Ellis summarizes the process most succinctly: "when a highly charged emotional consequence (C) follows a significant activating event (A), A may seem to, but actually does not, cause C. Instead, emotional consequences are largely created by B — the individual's *belief system*."[15] Inevitably, too, the belief system has a strong connection to action, either through the path of triggering emotions that shape actions or by independently shaping a person's decisions about how to act (as in the example of Hester above).

Shakespeare's *King Lear* (c.1606)[16] suggests how intricate and powerful connections between belief, emotion, and action can be. In the opening scene of the play, Lear conveys at least three crucial components of his conception of love, its expression, and its connection to his daughters: love must extend beyond the mere fulfillment of obligations; its expression requires extravagance; Cordelia represents his ideal embodiment of love, justifying the implicit assumption that she should meet his beliefs about love even more than Goneril or Regan. Cordelia's response of "Nothing" to Lear's question of what she might say to gain more of his kingdom than her sisters, a response broadened only to the "duties" of obedience, love, and honor, activates Lear's great rage because his beliefs conflict with Cordelia's, a conflict exacerbated by his stronger love for her than for her sisters. If he had shared her conception, however, of love as an unqualified bond not needing extravagance (a belief expressed in her aside, "What shall Cordelia speak? Love, and be silent"), then agreement rather than rage would have been his response and her sisters might have been the objects of his anger or his amusement in their attempts to flatter him.

Tragically, however, his beliefs set off both his rage and his action, causing him to reject Cordelia as his daughter and banish her to France. In the reconciliation (IV, vi), Lear's interpretation has changed. He still believes that Cordelia does not love him, but now he believes she has good reason because he mistreated her by casting her out just as her sisters have now mistreated him. His belief that he has wronged her sets off both his acceptance of her and his remorse, a remorse so deep that he would drink poison at her request. Lear's feelings arise from the interpretation he makes of what the events mean. His change of feelings toward Cordelia come about as a result of the intervening events and the reconstructed meaning he has come to, a change too complex for complete discussion here.

The Interactive Complexity of Cognitive Elements

These fundamental concepts of a cognitive psychology must be recognized as describing a complex system of interlocking elements that rarely take identical shapes in each individual. Indeed, as Aaron Beck emphasizes throughout *Cognitive Therapy and the Emotional Disorders* (New York: International Universities Press, 1976), one of the necessities of a cognitive therapy is to enter into the conceptual system of the person seeking help for the purpose of understanding that person's belief system and consequently how the world makes sense to him or her, however bizarre the individual's throughts, feelings, and actions may seem from outside the system.

The intricacies of a constructivist psychological approach evolve essentially from the effort to understand the interpretation of the world that the individual has made and the connections between that interpretation and the feelings and actions of the individual. This effort encounters many complex difficulties: determining the particular constellation of important experiences that an individual has had, the habits and processes of thinking that have been developed on his or her own and through the encouragement and instruction of others, the intermix of ready-made meanings that have been handed on by the culture and may be wholly unexamined, the conclusions that he or she has reached previously and now acts on automatically without explicit thought, and the interpretations that have been left incomplete or stand in contradictory relationships to other interpretations that may be held simultaneously. The cognitive approach to understanding the human mind, its thoughts, its feelings, and its role in actions — and to understanding its literary creations — demands a rigorous examination of the ways in which people think and act.

Elements of a Contructivist Aesthetic

Although cognitive psychologists have not offered the explicit comments on literature and its role that Freud did, I believe that certain important inferences about the interrelationships between literature and cognitive concepts can be made convincingly. The most significant implication is that literature serves a valuable cognitive/constructivist purpose rather than serving as merely a comfort or a pleasing aesthetic artifact — the limiting roles assigned to it not only in the Freudian psychoanalytic system but even in other critical approaches that are more conventionally literary in their origins and that recognize the role of literature in making sense of experience.[17] Literature as knowledge or as a mode of acquiring valid knowledge about the world functions in two ways from a constructivist perspective: (1) the literary work provides an imaginative working out of the genuine complexity of belief sets about the world, and (2) the literary work corresponds to the human act of constructing experience.

The Imaginary Working Out of Belief Sets

In the first of these functions, literature embodies the major conceptions of the constructivist mode — goal-directed behavior guided by a deliberately constructed interpretation of experience that shapes feeling and action. In the character of the persona or even the "voice" of literary works where familiar structures such as plot or character are not used, we get constructions of experience by one or more perceivers.

Consequently, in literature we find the working out of possible belief sets about the world — how they are constructed within a given person (or voice), how they interact or conflict within that person, how adequately they serve the character as a set that enables him or her to move toward goals successfully or unsuccessfully. Like constructivist psychology, the literary work traces out the individual process of putting together a world in such a way that one can think, feel, and act within it; and a critical approach using constructivist principles guides the reader to the evidence within the work as a means of understanding how these particular sets of beliefs interact effectively or destructively. In most instances, in fact, the literary work achieves through the constructing imagination a complex interaction of beliefs, thoughts, feelings, and actions that the experimental mode of the psychologist cannot reach directly because of the need to constrict the focus of an experiment and to control it. Literature explores imaginatively the genuine complexity of human thought, feeling, and action that other disciplines also investigate, but under restricted conditions. The significant point, however, is that the literary work need not be seen as an aesthetic comfort or as a disguise that guards us artificially and temporarily against the painfulness of experience. Instead, the events of the work can be understood as one mode of investigating and undergoing the ways in which belief sets are constructed, are used in the evolution of feeling and action, and undergo change as a result of experiences, circumstances, and choices.

Henry James's intricate novel, *The Portrait of a Lady* (1882),[18] gives incisive cognitive portrayals of numerous characters and of four in particular — Ralph Touchett, Madam Merle, Gilbert Osmond, and the central figure, Isabel Archer. As a result, the novel offers rich material for a constructivist analysis. An indication of how a constructivist interpretation can illuminate the imaginative complexity of belief sets in a novel and help to clarify major problems in the understanding of a character can be shown in an analysis of how Isabel, a woman of imagination and independence, comes to marry Gilbert Osmond, a man of limited capacities who tries ruthlessly to control others. The predicament that a cognitive understanding helps to explain comes late in the novel when Isabel has decided to go to England to visit Ralph, her dying cousin to whom she has a deep attachment. She discovers, however, that faced with Osmond's opposition to her trip, "the resolution with which she had entered the room found itself caught in a mesh of fine threads" (pp. 471–72). Her state of uncertainty and conflicting feelings reveal the enormous changes that have occured in Isabel's understanding of her world and herself. The amazement of the reader that Isabel could feel such equivocation and the intrigue of understanding how she has arrived at it goes back to the characteristics Isabel possesses at the beginning of the novel and the interpretations — the beliefs — she has about her world then. In the first half of the novel, we discover a young woman who is pretty, confident, curious about life, and imaginative. More importantly, her beliefs about herself in the world and her desire to explore it in her own terms allow her to turn down the marriage proposal of Lord Warburton, a powerful and wealthy man who by the standards of the times and the novel represents the ideal husband. Isabel can refuse him because she believes, in Ralph's judgment, that she is "some one in particular" (p. 35); and she realizes herself that to marry Warburton would mean acceding to a place in his world, thereby denying the murmurings within her that "she had a system and an orbit of her own" (p. 37). As she says to Warburton in the letter rejecting him, "We see our lives from our own point of view; that is the privilege of the weakest and humblest of us" (p. 101). Consistent with this interpretive scheme, Isabel not only denies Warburton personally but rejects the necessity of marriage in general for women (although she does not rule it out absolutely).

Her marriage to Osmond thus seems the more puzzling and inconsistent, especially because those people close to her opposed him as much as they endorsed Warburton. Ralph even tells her Osmond's critical flaws, that "he's narrow, selfish" (p. 302). Yet, a careful cognitive analysis allows us to understand precisely how Isabel chose to marry Osmond. For in our recognition of Isabel's forcefulness, her very capability of interpreting her world in a way that rejects the usual values imposed on young women, we must not fail to give full weight to certain elements of her circumstances, of her beliefs, and of her very way of constructing beliefs that make her act understandable. In the first instance — her circumstances — she has had little experience in the world and so remains ignorant of many of its qualities, especially duplicitousness, since guile does not exist in her nor in the people who have been close to her. In the second place (partly because of her inexperience), she holds some naive beliefs, such as her idea that people allow themselves to suffer too easily, that "It's not absolutely necessary to suffer; we're not made for that" (p. 40).

As these elements of experience and belief reveal, Isabel's powerfully appealing interpretation of the world that sets her apart from its conventional dimensions also rests on a set of experiences still impoverished because of her age, and especially lacking in components, such as suffering and deceit, that can shatter beliefs. Yet, the most important of the three qualities has to do with the very processes she uses to construct her beliefs; for we have learned early on that her imagination has close links to her being "a young person of many theories" (p. 41). Indeed, her version of her world that appeals to us so strongly has emerged from her capacity to imagine different possibilities for a young woman and to combine that with her theory of her personal worth, thereby making her freedom possible. Even so, we know that she has the capacity to reimagine, to construct a new theory to guide her actions — a capacity inherent in a constructivist conception of reality.

What becomes crucial in a cognitive understanding of Isabel, then, has to do with why she alters her interpretation of her life in a way that not only enables her to marry Osmond, but to overlook those qualities in him that will destroy her and especially her ability to maintain her independence, her ability precisely to continue to construct new theories. The first alteration of Isabel's intention to remain independent and stay free of marriage emerges from her experiences, mostly traveling to different countries, after inheriting a fortune from Ralph's father (an inheritance Ralph arranged to enable her "to gratify [her] imagination" [p. 159]). She has not found a valuable way to spend her time, confessing to Ralph that she changes her plans nearly every day. She believes her life, now, to be "frivolous" and that "One ought to choose something very deliberately, and be faithful to that" (p. 231). Implicitly, her experiences have changed her interpretive focus from freedom to dedication.

The second part of the change — why decide to marry Osmond — involves a number of complicated perceptions (many of them misperceptions) of Osmond that cannot be fully elaborated here, but include his apparent preoccupation with the arts, a worthy interest in Isabel; his "wilful renunciation" of the world and the decision "To be content with a little" (p. 231), appealing to Isabel's idealism; and lack of money, a circumstance her fortune can correct to laudable ends. Remembering, however, those qualities of Isabel that persist and that come to be the genuine sources of conflict with Osmond — her love of ideas, of personal independence, and of independent thought — there are two dimensions of Osmond that make her especially vulnerable: she believes that he "wants me to know everything" (p. 300); and — although we learn it after the marriage we may assume that it worked on Isabel, too — Osmond is particularly adept at deceiving people into believing that he cares only for "intrinsic values" (p. 345).

For Isabel, then, in her new construction of purpose — to dedicate herself to a specific life — she finds that Osmond meets her requirements and especially the two she values most, the seeking of ideas (knowledge) and the fundamental insistence of the self alone as the source for determining values. She is wrong in both assessments, but her cognitive error arises from her inexperience with deception, from Osmond's master skills as a deceiver, and from her own ability to imagine and construct a theory that guides her actions. As Ralph notes, Isabel's imagination had "supplied the human element" (p. 232) that had been missing in Osmond; and "She was wrong, but she believed; she was deluded, but she was consistent. It was wonderfully characteristic of her that she had invented a fine theory about Gilbert Osmond, and loved him, not for what he really possessed, but for his very poverties dressed out as honours" (p. 305)

The "mesh of fine threads" in which Isabel finds herself at the beginning of this analysis becomes clear; we can know the belief sets and their complex shifts and interweavings that have brought her to the point of irresolution as she confronts Osmond about her perfectly reasonable desire to go to London to see Ralph. She remains the woman who desires independence, who thinks for herself, whose self cries out against the injustice and suffering of her marriage; but she remains, too, the woman who came to believe that she should choose and dedicate herself to something permanent (marriage), and so she cannot glibly ignore her beliefs and her commitment. As we know, she goes to London and then returns.

As readers, we may resent her suffocation in marriage or applaud her faithfulness to her obligations; but, as importantly, a constructivist analysis enables us to understand how Isabel has come to her predicament — how her thinking has led to her feelings and her actions. In recognizing how her beliefs come from her interpretations, the analysis reveals how the interpretive strategies that she (or anyone) uses may lead her into conflicts, or may even be so distorted as to be self-defeating or self-destructive. The constructivist analysis yields precise knowledge for us about the details of how belief sets are constructed and then guide a person's feelings and actions. This interpretation also allows us to understand how Isabel's own way of thinking leads her to marry Osmond, thereby clarifying one of the major critical problems of the novel without resorting to categories such as chance or tragic fate that do not genuinely explain her actions.

The Literary Work as a Cognitive Construction

The second function of literature within the constructivist approach comes in the correspondence of the work itself, perhaps especially in its creation but also in the act of reading it, to the human act of constructing experience. Jerome Rothenberg, a psychoanalytic investigator, has already reported that literary creation resembles the complexity and careful development of what the Freudians call secondary process thinking (the conscious and the rational) much more than the chaotic thinking that psychoanalysts characterize as primary processes (the unconscious and the intuitive).[19] Yet in the constructivist approach, where the entire process centers on adaptation and organization consciously moving toward some interpretation of experience that will make sense of the world, the creation of the literary work needs no special explanation. Literary form, in all of its intricate manifestations, serves in the way it seems to serve: (1) to gain control over its materials and to structure them to reveal some understanding of the world (even when, as in Samuel Beckett, that may be to emphasize the senselessness of our ordinary patterns of thought and action), and (2) to serve as models for interpreting experience (as opposed merely to representing or imitating experience). The literary work, both for the author and for the reader, as the one creates and the other comes to understand how the work fits its world together, functions as the cognitive act, serving as one realization of the constructive processes that we continually use to guide our actions. The literary work thus remains always in keeping with what it has been recognized to be — a deliberately constructed expression in which design and subject function as an ensemble.

As one complex instance of the use of a work as an ensemble in which the cognitive understandings of literature emerge in conjunction with its expressive manifestations, we can turn to John Berryman's long sequence of poems, *The Dream Songs*.[20] Although many concerns run through the poems, one of the persistent preoccupations of Henry, the persona, arises from his interpretation of the world as threatening for a number of reasons — including his father's suicide when he was young, his frequent feeling of rejection, and the deaths of his friends. As a result, he believes he lives in a "horror of unlove" (song 74). One particular threat that emerges from Henry's interpretation of the world is madness — a state that attracts him because it promises relief from his pain, but one that repels him because it spells his death as a poet since his song could no longer be understood. In a number of songs, Berryman poses this dilemma and the reality of its threat by carefully constructing a poem that reveals Henry's collapse into madness: the poem in the disintegration of its language becomes the cognitive act itself, demonstrating the disintegration of Henry's language, his loss of song, and his fall into madness.

As one example, song 368 reveals the union of understanding and expression in the poem as cognitive act. In essence, the poem seems to be a dream of monsters sweeping through a city; but the images suddenly give way to the comment, "Thought of his kind ground & lurched to a halt, / all nouns became verbs." Abruptly, the continuity of images, of who is speaking, and even of the consistency of language, as nouns and verbs reverse themselves, are interrupted and questioned. In the final stanza, the interpretational question comes up: "Was all this the result of a failure of love, . . ." Immediately after, a new image of a girl with "several legs" enters the poem, and she shouts to "Your Majesty," an unidentified person. In the last line, a "he," ambiguous as to whether he is Henry, Your Majesty, or someone else, "hunkered down & begs." Although the poem can be understood in certain basic ways, its fundamental construction and expression serve to suggest the breakdown of coherence, the fear that often accompanies ambiguity, and the belief that a world without love encourages collapse and doubt. The poem constructs a moment of severe anxiety and perhaps even madness by coming close to being incoherent itself. A constructivist analysis allows us, then, to link all of the information — formal and propositional — that the poem contains to develop an understanding of its meaning. In this poem, we come to know the characteristics of a moment when the ability to hang on to a world that makes sense falls apart.

Conceived from the constructivist perspective, the literary work not only corresponds more closely to what it seems to be, but takes on an even more serious role than other, more traditional, critical approaches, such as formalism, allow it. The work, instead, effects a construct of beliefs that interpret the world in a plausible, but perhaps quite individualistic, way, and then validates the construct through the thoughts and actions of its personae. Literature, then, need not be taken as a comfort or as a language construct that constitutes a unique entity set apart from existence or other forms of knowledge; but rather, it can be recognized as an actual means of gaining information about how we come to construct versions of our world, what those differing versions are, how they interact and conflict with one another, and how as human beings we continually adjust and revise those constructions.

This reconception of the function of the literary work does not deny the validity of other ways of conceiving literature. For example, while it does offer a means of recognizing the ways in which a work functions that are not solely aesthetic, it certainly does not deny the possibility of studying the work as an aesthetic entity. Nor does it so alter the aesthetic function, as in the psychoanalytic position, that the examination of form in traditional ways becomes merely self-deception. Literary form illuminates a thinking/feeling construction in a verbal mode that refers to parallel human experiences outside the literary work. Consequently, rather than becoming temporary but pleasurable escapes from an unbearable world or unconscious desires, the form and subject of the work serve to grapple with and shape the activity of human thought as it tries to understand human experience in order to take actions directed toward goals. No longer must the literary work be conceived of either as an object constructed only to delight us and to be admired by us or as a disguise for what we cannot bear and need comfort for. The literary work becomes a complex vehicle for exploring the multiple ways, successful and unsuccessful, of getting hold of experience.

In the same way, a constructivist criticism brings its focus to the cognitive strategies created in the work — to discerning their main lines and their points of intersection with other systems of belief in the work, to determining the directions of change, and to assessing the effectiveness of a character or speaker's construct from within his conception of his world. Such a criticism focuses understanding on how the basic interpretational strategy of a character or persona is created in a work and its implications for the feelings and actions of the individual. The constructivist approach should also enable comparisons of several works to determine the strategies that predominate in an author's canon, in the works of a particular time period, or in works from different periods. These second two efforts might yield insight into the similarities or differences in strategies for construing experience and the consequent effects of those strategies on feeling and action for the periods under consideration, such as the connection between beliefs of widespread corruption and the portrayal of characters who go mad in early seventeenth-century English drama.

A Comparative Critique

Although a complete comparison of the ways in which a psychoanalytic interpretation and a constructivist interpretation might differ in the reading of a literary work cannot be undertaken here, an effort should be made to suggest the major points of difference between this proposed new approach and the one that has long been more prevalent. In order to make the comparison, I will use the "Tomorrow and tomorrow and tomorrow" speech from Macbeth,[21] which follows:

> Tomorrow, and tomorrow, and tomorrow
> Creeps in this petty pace from day to day
> To the last syllable of recorded time.
> And all our yesterdays have lighted fools
> The way to dusty death. Out, out, brief candle —
> Life's but a walking shadow, a poor player
> That struts and frets his hour upon the stage
> And then is heard no more. It is a tale
> Told by an idiot, full of sound and fury,
> Signifying nothing.

The Freudian interpretation of the speech that I will use for comparison is Norman Holland's in *The Dynamics of Literary Response* (106–14),[22] still one of the best theoretical statements of the psychoanalytic position. Holland basically attempts two things: (1) he wants to show that John Crowe Ransom's attempt to make logical sense out of the lines as an isolated poem fails because logic must fail when confronted by a passage motivated instead by fantasy;[23] and (2) he wants to show that the disguised fantasy in the lines is the primal scene, the fears of children about adult sexuality, especially sexual relations between their parents.

In the case of Ransom, Holland has no problem in the basic argument; for Ransom himself claims that the passage lacks unity, especially the unity of a coherent set of images that logically follow one another. What is most interesting in Holland's discussion of Ransom is that he finally argues that the poem does not appeal to Ransom because it either does not suit Ransom's way of defending himself against his unsavory fantasies or because Ransom's usual forbidden fantasies do not happen to be about the primal scene. The significant implication of this argument is that statements about a literary work do not illuminate the knowledge to be found in the work itself, for indeed the work does not embody knowledge. Instead, it serves for the critic as an inkblot, without meaning in itself, but as the instigation for remarks that tell us about the psychological makeup of the critic. In a parallel way, the work reveals the psychological makeup of its author as well — in this case, Shakespeare — because its expression embodies fantasies. In neither case does the substantial knowledge to be gained from *Macbeth* reside in the play or in references to experience in general.

The second part of Holland's interpretation concerns the particular fantasy that he discovers in the speech. Because the speech conceals a fantasy, it does not have to be logical; indeed, he argues, images of a player on the stage have been well documented in psychoanalysis to refer to primal scene fantasies, and Macbeth's image of hearing rather than seeing the actor emphasizes the fear of these sexual moments; but the images of daylight — the tomorrows — defend us, letting us know that it is not our days that will end but these frightening nights instead, and so we need not be afraid of our fantasies about parental sexuality.

The effect of Holland's reading is twofold. It removes the literary work from central importance, and it shows us how ingeniously one can manipulate assumptions about fantasies and the unconscious since they are by definition invisible and disguised to anyone but the qualified interpreter (analyst or critic). A speech that seems to be about despair and disillusionment in the face of death and defeat becomes one that in fact offers us the opposite — a comfort against one of our most deep-seated sexual fears.

The objection to this interpretation certainly has nothing to do with its virtuosity, but rather with its circuitousness, its inefficiency, and its unconvincingness. In brief, to understand the speech as a comfort for our fears about our parents' intercourse is farfetched, an objection Holland foresaw (p. 112). A constructivist analysis removes many of these problems. It makes the work the central focus. It offers some plausible connections between the images that reveal a logic interior to Macbeth's thoughts at least, and it does so without appeal to farfetched fantasies.

In a constructivist approach, lifting the speech from the context of the play does pose difficulties; for by definition the speech represents a point in the set of beliefs that Macbeth has used to guide his actions — in particular, the recognition of loss as the outcome of his efforts, immediately in the death of his wife and impendingly in the defeat of his monarchial designs. Even so, an analysis of this speech as a separate entity yields an interpretation of experience quite similar to the one that would be made by using the full context.

In the play Macbeth's speech comes the moment after he is told of Lady Macbeth's death. The evolution of the play has shown Macbeth to be a man singularly dominated by his efforts to take an interpretation of experience and to use it as a guide for constructing his future, most fatally the witches' version of it. Yet, he has also been a man who shared the traditional moral injunction that forbade murder, especially of the king; and he holds on to remnants of this opposing line of thought. His interpretive sets conflict (even more complexly, of course, than here suggested), and so he has at times wavered between them. Significantly, Lady Macbeth has bolstered his new design on the world and supported the acts required to complete it. In this way in particular, his wife has been the reinforcer of his actions, the only person to whom he could speak in full honesty and the only person who does express (or even could express) belief in the validity and justness of his murdering the king and arranging the death of his friend Banquo in order to advance his personal ambitions.

At the very moment, then, when his design will either be established or defeated, he has lost his wife, and just as importantly, his only true ally. Macbeth's dominant system of belief, his effort to shape his future to accord with the witches' prophecy and set himself and his heirs up as kings, has just suffered what he must know to be his greatest loss. Thus, since despair is the emotion usually felt when loss is interpreted as the meaning of the event, despair — the state of mind and feeling dominated by images of loss, hopelessness, and futility — descends on Macbeth. Consequently, while the images of the speech may not follow the logic of ordinary thought processes, they follow the logic of one who has just lost the person who was his only intimate, reliable, and unwavering supporter. Tomorrows become endless and slow, a hopeless weight. Yesterdays reflect futility because of the single fact of death that has either prevented or wiped out all accomplishment, rendering achievement absurd. The candle snuffed out reemphasizes death and the brevity of life, which becomes a shadow, a player on stage for an hour and then gone. All of these images are linked by a cognitive apprehension of the overwhelming weight of effort that stretches out interminably through all one's days but that comes nonetheless in a brief hour to nothing.

As the speech concludes, the futility becomes overwhelming — the tale Macbeth has tried to enact, that Lady Macbeth has tried to enact, his version of how he wanted the world to be, might as well be an idiot's tale, for it has lost its meaning in the moment that the conception of the future embodied in it becomes impossible and pointless. Lady Macbeth and her acts mean nothing; Macbeth's acts to gain the kingship — the point he gave to his life — have come to nothing. What the speech explores, without the consolations of either psychoanalysis or of traditional critical interpretations, is the moment when a person must confront the inexorable evidence that the way he has chosen to act and believe in the world will not work out, even approximately, in the way he expected it to.

What many misinterpret as comforting in this moment of the play is instead our recognition that we have understood fully the set of beliefs that Macbeth used in his actions and that we feel pain at their defeat for having been able to put ourselves inside them, even though they were beliefs whose defeat we would seek. Yet, our sadness should not be confused with comfort; for instead the play dramatizes genuine futility and hopelessness, the full movement from misconceived idea to wrenching enactment to brutal destruction of the way Macbeth tried to organize his existence, to direct himself toward a goal. Macbeth has construed the world evilly and cruelly, but for him his defeat creates the same distress, futility, and hopelessness that might come from more praiseworthy but equally crushed conceptions of how one might live one's life. In this modeling of the beliefs of the character, of the consequences of feeling and action in their enactment, and of the exploration of what this outcome means within his construction of the world, we have the point of connection for the reader, the point of entry into someone else's perspective and way of construing events. From the point of view of a psychological interpretation, the literary creation provides a means of comprehending the conceptual and emotional experiences of the other in order to evaluate them, accept or reject them, or use them to modify our own conceptions and actions. Even though the particular construction he follows leads him to hallucinations, we need no startling fantasies to use Macbeth's construction of internal and external experience as a means of comprehending better the relationships among ideas, feelings, and actions in human experience.

Indeed, as I have suggested, perhaps the most important promise in a constructivist perspective comes from beginning to understand how the literary work gives knowledge rather than simply comfort or pleasure. Those possibilities seem to lie in the potential of literature for tracing out with complexity the intricate individual and collective sets of beliefs that activate our emotions and our actions as we move toward our goals. It may well be that this knowledge will not be unique to literature in the way we have come to insist upon. In fact, it may be knowledge that often can and should be corroborated through disciplines other than literature, such as psychology. Yet, it will be knowledge gained through the special qualities of literary expression that can activate imaginative complexity to come to parallel understandings both of experience and of the many forms we use to construe it — multiple forms rather then single ones, forms that reveal the singular and intricate connection between interpretation and belief, thought and feeling, and ultimately, action.

An Empirical Approach
to the
Psychology of Literature

by Martin S. Lindauer

The empirical approach, as used in science generally, and as it applies to psychology, requires that the phenomena under study be observable; and if this is not possible, that they then at least be closely tied to observables.[1] The question of whether literature is "good," and similar normative questions of what should be the case are not empirical questions — but people's beliefs and feelings about literature are (when suitably verbalized, expressed by ratings, or recorded in some way).

Empiricism in its public meaning can be useful in examining matters relevant to the psychology of literature. These include: (1) the content of literature (e.g., motives of characters in novels, emotions in poetry, and values in short stories); (2) the personality of authors (including childhood sources of creativity and differences between dramatists and painters); (3) the preferences of readers (and whether younger and older ones differ); and (4) the role of the social context in which authors produce (and an audience receives) a literary work (and how styles change over time and between cultures). These and other aspects of the psychology of literature have proven amenable to empirical attack.[2]

Despite the apparent usefulness of tying psychology and literature together through empiricism, the method is largely unknown, unappreciated, or misunderstood.[3] The psychology of literature is largely defined by intuitive rather than empirical methods; by speculation rather than facts; and by concepts that are historical, critical, and philosophical rather than scientific. Psychology is mainly represented by the clinical and case studies of psychotherapy, psychoanalytic and related "depth" psychologies, and psychiatry. These, at best, are marginal examples of the empirical method.

In order to balance the underrepresentation of the empirical approach, this chapter discusses the relevance of scientific methodology to the study of literature. The goals of this chapter are to encourage the reader to seek out empirical studies of literature and to appreciate their strengths (and weaknesses).

The first section introduces the empirical method against the backdrop of alternatives, and their advantages and disadvantages. The second section translates the characteristics of literature into empirical terms. The third section provides the theoretical and practical context in which empirical research takes place, along with designs that direct research. The fourth and final section presents six brief studies that illustrate the empirical approach to literature (and asks the reader to evaluate them).

The General Nature of Empiricism

Its Public Character

The empirical study of literature relies on procedures and provides data that are specifiable and concrete; facts and the means used to obtain them, literally speaking, can be pointed to. This public nature of empirical inquiry is its distinguishing feature, and is really what the term "objective" means. The denotable requirement of empiricism raises a basic question: How can subtle psychological qualities, especially those so aptly represented by literature (emotions like love and hate, values like freedom and choice, and similar reflections by sensitive observers), become observable objects of study? After all, psychological states are subjective, private, and hidden.

The dilemma can be reduced in several ways, although none completely resolves it. Readers' and authors' verbalizations about (or tests of) mental, personal, and inner states can be observed and recorded, as can their written accounts. So, too, can the behavior that results from

247

otherwise covert processes. (Imagination and thought are spoken about and acted upon.) The psychological meaning of a literary work, while less accessible, can be made observable by the judgments of readers. Even highly abstract phenomena (imagery, attitudes, and personality) can at least be indirectly approached. The covert can be linked to measurable sources of input (i.e., stimuli) and concrete forms of output (i.e., responses).

Alternative to Empiricism

Most studies of literature, even though "psychological," are not empirical. Scholars have different sorts of questions, concepts, interests, and styles, and these lead to historical, critical, or philosophical forms of inquiry about psychological phenomena. Evidence is sought along intuitive, personal, revelatory, and experiential lines; and logic, internal consistency, and what experts have said in the past are valued. These nonempirical views do not seek disconfirmation, in the way the sciences do, mainly because the public criterion, discussed above, is not paramount.

Psychoanalytic and similarly clinical perspectives have many contacts with literature. But "tender-hearted" clinicians, say the "toughminded" empiricists, fall short of most scientific standards. Their observations are based on a few specially selected cases, examined from therapeutic-helping rather than a scientific-discovering perspective, and offered in qualitative rather than quantitative terms. Clinical evidence is judged to be biased in unknown ways and hence unreliable. Nevertheless, the dramatic appeal, personal relevance, and anecdotal detail of the clinical case study make it the dominant voice in the psychology of literature.[4]

Scientific ventures into literature, few as they are, have usually been greeted with condescending skepticism or defensive hostility. Science and the humanities are typically thought of as incompatible: each defines a topic in its own way, pursues its unique path, and looks toward its particular goals. Scientists speak of "proof," and humanities of "personal encounter."[15] This "conflict between the two cultures" has been debated by many, in diverse disciplines, and for a long time — and with little discernable progress. The attempt to join the empirical method to the literary domain, promoted here, is one possible way of advancing this issue. Literary revelations, suitably recast in the form of predictions (i.e., testable hypotheses), could be studied empirically; and clinical insights could enrich quantitative analyses.

An Empirical Approach

Limitations

The empirical approach is not without its own limitations. These help account for its tenuous position in the study of literature, and for its place being usurped by clinical practitioners.

One striking shortcoming is the circumscribed character of empirical research. Empiricists study only what is studiable (i.e., observables). Inquiry thereby becomes rather molecular, in contrast to the relatively all-encompassing character of scholarly and clinical research. It is easy to be incredulous over empiricism's claims to relevance, no matter how impressed one may be by its technical competencies. The questions seem unimportant, the answers look trivial, and the interpretations appear timid.

But the circumscribed nature of empiricism is not necessarily a disadvantage, may indeed be purposely sought, and in any event, is only temporary. A study is designed to be small in scope in order to make it easier to carry out, to pinpoint errors, and to take remedial action. The capacity of an empirical study to be proved wrong, and therefore improved, is a possibility enhanced by its manageable brevity.

Empirical studies are restricted in scope for another reason. A single study is usually part of a series, most of which has not yet been done (but eventually will). Thus, connections are not apparent. Since relatively few empirical studies in literature have been done, it may be a while before they approximate the broadness of nonempirical efforts.

Applying Empirical Criteria to Literature

The application of the empirical method to literature should offer few surprises to those familiar with the social and behavioral sciences. The key concepts (e.g., observability) do not change as different topics are investigated. The empirical method is adaptable, varying with who or what is studied (readers or books, contemporary or historical authors) and the type of data collected (experiential or behavioral).

But empirical transformations of the literary domain appear awkward and hence are naturally usettling to the nonempirical scholar. One finds frequency counts of multiple sets of truncated and quasi-literary passages, randomly drawn, and judged by consensus; there are ratings of experiential introspections and the use of undergraduates-*cum*-writers. These among other characteristics discussed below are some of the signs of literature treated empirically.

Martin S. Lindauer

Examining Conscious Experience

Readers and authors can be directly questioned, interviewed, and tested about their feelings, thoughts, and reactions to literature, or on matters related to literature. But what they say is full of uncertainties: they may be unwilling or unable to communicate (or are not specific or exact enough); and introspective and retrospective accounts are likely to be inaccurate, distorted, or only partially available.

The ambiguities of reports on mental life are unavoidable. But they can be reduced. Inner states can be verbalized to some extent; and test scores and performance can indirectly reflect them. Or pitfalls can be solved by avoiding them and leaving the psychology of literature in speculative hands.

These difficulties challenge the ingenuity of the empirical researcher. The fragility of subjective data requires procedures, controls, and designs that anticipate and minimize error. Nevertheless, despite the best efforts, psychological research in the arts and humanities, compared to biological and animal-comparative areas, will remain "soft." The results of any one study must therefore be tentatively and cautiously evaluated. The expectation is that further clarifying and corrective studies will be done.

Locating and Specifying the Literary Experience

The readers' literary experience poses additional difficulties beyond those associated with the study of conscious experience in general. The reaction to literature unfolds over time, and is cumulative. Hence, it is hard to specify which passage led to what effect, and the nature of that effect (e.g., whether it was primarily cognitive or emotional). One simple rule is that if there is a relatively immediate effect, then sensory-perceptual processes were involved; but if the effect takes some time to unfold, then the response is more complicated. It includes not only perception, but at least memory and thinking as well. It is therefore simpler to study the immediate effects of literature.[6]

To expedite the partitioning of the literary experience, and thereby narrow its locus, brief literary passages are ideal. Reactions can then be more clearly associated with specific sections. To this end, extremely simple materials — like vowels, consonants, and letters — have often been used as surrogates for literature. Somewhat less rudimentary, but still hardly literary, are titles of books, names of characters, and one-line literary epigrams.[7]

Such simplifications of a literary work and response are obviously far removed from real literature. These reductions, it is hoped, will enable the researcher to capture a hint of the basic processes at work. Armed with such clues, complexities can be added. These lead to research that is closer to real literature and the actual literary experience. At this time, however, research in literature is largely at the simplest levels.

Studying Authors

Empirical research should ideally take place under laboratory conditions where interviewing, testing, and recording of responses can be controlled (e.g., uniform). Assuming authors would be willing to come to a laboratory and be studied (and funds were available), the artificiality of the setting might stifle, change, or interfere with whatever is being studied.

These logistical and conceptual problems have limited the number of investigations that have actually used professional (full-time) authors. Instead, approximations have been sought — which usually means the study of undergraduates, often but not always English or writing majors, and occasionally professors of English.[8]

The few studies that have been done with authors, contrary to the popular stereotype of the nonconforming artist, have found them cooperative. Few if any difficulties were reported with the testing circumstances, and their work is said to be similar in quality to their usual efforts.

Despite these encouraging signs, the problems of contacting and studying professional authors have led to their infrequent study. One practical strategy that has not been explored is telephone interviews of authors at home.

Extracting Psychological Information from Literature

The psychological meaning of literary material is neither obvious nor easily accessible. Literature is not data; it is fiction, written in the past, and for reasons unrelated to research. There are, therefore, obvious difficulties in extracting the motives of literary characters, their conflicts, and the kinds of interpersonal relations they have.

The major procedure for transforming literary content into observable data is content analysis.[9] Literature is treated like any other kind of historical, archival, or written material (such as newspapers, diaries, and autobiographies).

There are several steps to content analysis. First, the researcher develops (and tests) a set of categories into which the literary material is to be placed. The exact nature of the categories depends upon the purpose of the study, the kind of material used, and perhaps the expertise of the judges who will be using them. The categories can be as simple as types of nouns (human or not) or personal pronouns used (e.g., references to "I" and "you"); or scales of "interestingness" (or "excitement") can be developed. More complex categories include lists of personal traits and types of relationships. The second step is training a group of judges on using the categories. The third step is the selection of materials whose content is to be analyzed. The sample chosen could be a single work or a series of works; and these could be by the same author or different ones. The lines, paragraphs, or pages would be randomly selected. Fourth, and finally, judges would examine the literary material according to the predetermined categories, and record their judgments (e.g., as ratings or by underlining the passages).

The outcome of content analysis is a frequency tally of the number of times certain categories of material were found in the literature. Consensual validation — the amount of agreement among judges' assignments — establishes the empirical meaning of the content anaysis. For example, if 80 percent of the judges assigned a literary character to the category "friendly to women," the investigator would feel confident about that set of judgments. Agreement (consensus) means that some common attribute of the material can be pointed to — despite its complexity, the diversity of the judges, and the difficulties of the task in general.

Content analysis allows literature to be described in specific and quantitative terms. Consequently, different or related works and authors (and types of content analysis and judges) can be compared.[10] Subsequent studies, using a work whose content has been defined by content analysis, can investigate other aspects of literature. These might include the responses of different kinds of people, the sorts of conditions that facilitate the works' understanding or enjoyment, and the type of authors that produce certain kinds of work. Content analysis's capacity to define input is often the first step in the study of literature.

The Individual and Grouped Data

Statistical measurement of groups of readers, authors, and works means that individual responses, characteristics, and qualities are lost; they are merged into averaged data. Yet, the study of literature is supposed to highlight individuality, uniqueness, and the special case. There therefore seems to be a paradox in using literature to obtain collective results.

The dilemma is generally known as the ideographic-nomethetic (individual-group) issue.[11] Psychologists in the clinical and personality areas are especially troubled by the problem. Like their humanistic colleagues, they consider the person (and differences between people) of primary interest, rather than generalizations, abstractions, and pooled data about groups.

The most frequent solution is to use individual and qualitative reports (from a case study and interviews) to supplement aggregate and quantitative findings. Information from the single case can illustrate, enhance, parallel, and extend grouped data, and perhaps even initiate a more general study.

Obtaining Many Examples: Sampling

One does not simply collect the largest mass of cases in order to obtain a group to study. The selection of literary material, authors, or readers has to be done with great care. An inadequate sample is either too small in size (one, two, or a few instances) or it is chosen in a biased way.[12]

A study with too few cases provides insufficient data for statistical analysis; it cannot have quantitative precision. (The mean of the scores 10, 100, and 1,000 is an unrepresentative 370). Too small a sample also makes it impossible to draw inferences to the larger population of authors, readers, and books from which it was taken.

The size of the sample does not have to be huge. Political polls and TV ratings typically rely on twelve hundred to fifteen hundred (or fewer) respondents; these have a 5 percent (or less) error range with which to predict the opinions of millions. It is therefore wrong to believe that the bigger the sample, the more accurate the results. As a rule of thumb, a typical empirical study will use about twelve to twenty-five subjects (or examples) per group or condition, and at least two groups or conditions.[13] But even if the size of the sample is adequate, the way it is selected has to be correctly done.

If the cases in the sample were selected in an idiosyncratic (or biased) way, the results of a study would be distorted. The selection of a good (unbiased) sample begins with an exhaustive list of whatever one wants to study (authors, books, readers); this is the population. Next, a much smaller set of cases is drawn from the population; this is the sample. It is absolutely crucial that this selection be done randomly. (You might use special tables for this, a dart board, or take names from a hat.)

Let's say you're interested in some question about poetry. First you would collect (from reference works) the names of all the recognized poets who ever lived. From this population, a sample composed of 10 percent of the total (an arbitrary but manageable total) would be randomly chosen. Then a list of these poets' works (or biographies, depending on your purpose) would be compiled. This is the population from which you would again draw a random sample.

To narrow the initial number of cases to be taken from a population, you might use a stratified sampling procedure. The poets chosen would be limited to, for example, those from English-speaking countries who lived in the last two-hundred years. Your results and generalizations would be restricted to the more limited population, rather than to all poets (as was true of the previous sample).

A random (or stratified-random) sample is, by definition, representative (if it is done properly). However, a sample purposely drawn to be "representative"—perhaps because the cases are special, important, or best in some way (or simply available)—is unrepresentative or biased. The results of a biased sample would not be generalizable, but would hold only for the sample drawn. This could be the purpose of the study. But then the uniqueness of the results—whether the findings are special to this group or not—could not be evaluated.

A practical and less controversial (but still questionable) procedure is to select a "representative" sample (on whatever basis), and then randomly draw from this group.

Numbering and Counting: Measurement and Statistics

For literature to be empirically treated, it has to be measurable and countable: What is happening, to whom, where, when, and how often? If we want to know, for example, whether certain works, authors, or readers are "optimistic," then ways of measuring and counting optimism are needed in order to indicate exactly how optimistic they are (and compared to whom or what). An empirical study, unlike others in literature, is therefore marked by a fair amount of numbers (i.e., tables and graphs).

There are many ways of measuring; some are standard and others are constructed just for that study.[14] The measure chosen depends on the researcher's purpose, whether people or texts are of interest, and the kinds of phenomena or behavior being studied.

In general, the less known (perhaps because the topic is new or very complex), the broader the measurement needed (e.g., open-ended and unstructured questions, fill-in's, and checklists of adjectives). If a measure is too restricted (e.g., a three-point rating scale for "liking"), the richness of the phenomena would be lost. On the other hand, when a phenomenon has already been well explored, and many of its relevant properties are known, then more rigorous and circumscribed measures are appropriate (e.g., multidimensional scales that lend themselves to computer analysis).

The empirical study of literature, at this time, is probably more suited for global rather than analytic measures. Most research is still at the formulative and exploratory stages of inquiry. Hence, relatively holistic, experiential, and phenomenological measures are probably best for many studies. However, even when the most sophisticated psychometrics are used, they can still be usefully augmented by qualitative measures.

An adequate measuring instrument leads to a set of numbers. While useful, these still have to be organized. This is the task of descriptive statistics: means and medians, frequencies and percentages, correlations, and graphs and tables. Instead of vague amounts and crude comparisons, there are quantitatively exact descriptions. Nevertheless, the researcher still cannot claim that some literature, author, or readers are "more" optimistic (or whatever) than others.

There is another level of analysis, inferential statistics, which builds upon and goes beyond descriptive statistics. Formulas like the t-test, F-test, and *chi-square* (computations learned in the first statistics course) allow probability statements to be made about the data. If book X is 40 percent better (in readability) than book Z, this large descriptive difference may or may not be statistically meaningful. Neither large nor small numbers, as such, necessarily reveal their statistical significance. Apparent differences may be due to chance (usually expressed as $p > .05$), which means they are normal, expected, and not unusual. Hence the differences can be disregarded, as if nothing happened or no differences were found. On the other hand, small, apparently negligible differences may reflect a real change, effect, or difference (expressed as $p < .05$). The finding is beyond chance and "something really happened"; the results of the study should be attended to. Statistical significance tells the researcher that the psychological significance of numbers has to be interpreted.

Aside from remembering that "data" are plural (datum is singular), one of the greatest sources of confusion in statistics is correlation. The term is often mistakenly treated as if it meant causation. For example, a hypothetical correlation between people's IQ scores and the number of "good" books they read in a year describes a relationship. Contrary to intuition, though, nothing is said about whether IQ causes people to have good taste in their reading habits, whether the reverse is true, or whether both are due to something else (e.g., their education or values). There is a causal basis for a correlation, but the correlation, as such, only describes a relationship.[15] Although correlations do not reveal causes, they do make predictions. Knowing how many good books people read in a year can (in this hypothetical example) be a basis for estimating their IQ's.

Putting Literature Under Controls

Empirical studies are said to have or use "controls." The term has two related meanings. One, as in "control group," refers to the inclusion of a set of subjects, materials, or conditions against which to compare the data of primary interest (from the experimental group).

For example, information about authors' creativity is difficult to interpret in isolation: are they high, low, or average; have they increased, decreased, or stayed the same over time; were their happy (or unhappy) childhoods unique to them? The inclusion of one or more control groups — noncreatives, a different kind of creative group, famous but noncreative authors, authors with different literary styles, younger and older authors — would provide a baseline or perspective. Differences, changes, effects, and trends in the creative-author group would be evaluated by comparing them against the control group.

Consider another example. Suppose you want to study the effect of taking a literature course. At least two groups are required: those who take the literature course (the experimental group) and those who don't (the control group). Without the control group, it would be difficult to know whether changes in the experimental group would have occurred anyway, even without the course. (Perhaps some dramatic news event was carried in the mass media for several weeks.) A more complex study might use several experimental and control groups with different kinds of literature classes, extending over various periods, using different kinds of students, and taught in different ways.

An Empirical Approach

The second meaning of control refers to the care with which a study is done, thereby decreasing its ambiguity and increasing its clarity. The researcher excludes (controls for) extraneous and unwanted variables (e.g., age, sex, training) and manipulates those of interest (e.g., time, place, and amount of exposure to literature). Control is exercised over the selection of subjects, the presentation of materials, and the recording of responses.

Consider the above example of the literature course. If the experimental and control groups were not comparable at the outset of the study (e.g., in the number of previous literature courses taken), then any differences between them at the end of the study could have been there initially rather than the result of taking the course. Control in this instance would be achieved by randomly drawing participants from the same population, and then randomly assigning them to the experimental and control groups. (If this were not possible, two existent groups could be matched as closely as possible on as many variables as seem relevant, e.g., sex and age. There are also statistical controls.) The variables controlled in one study could be the experimental variables in a subsequent study (e.g., age, sex, and the number of literature courses taken).

A study with no, few, or poor controls is meaningless: its findings could be due to the variables of interest, other (and unknown) factors, or both (confounded). In a well-controlled study, the investigator is fairly certain that whatever was supposed to be done, was; and whatever was not supposed to happen, didn't. The results are therefore not open to alternative explanations. Facts are real rather than apparent, i.e., reliable; and the findings are germane to the question addressed, i.e., valid.

Reliability and validity are key criteria in the study of human phenomena, particularly in a literary context. Two general indicators of a study's reliability are its repeatability (replicability) and the internal consistency of its results. Indicators of validity generally depend on successful predictions. For example, if authors receive high scores on a test of creativity, we then expect their work to be judged as creative (concurrent validity); or we expect them to achieve this status some time in the future (predictive validity). Content validity is another check: the results make intuitive sense on the "face of it" (e.g., authors judged eminent score high on creativity). Construct validity indicates that a study's results follow from a particular theory.

257

The Nonliterary Qualities of Research Reports

Empirical research concludes with a report. In exhaustive (and tedious) detail, the report communicates what was done and what was found. The report has to be complete in order to allow others to replicate the study (as a check on reliability). The inclusion of detail also permits researchers to build upon and extend the findings. But the criterion of completeness does not make for an attractive style of writing.

There are other unattractive features. A particular order of topics is followed, each containing certain required information: the hypothesis is stated in the introduction, the subjects are described in the method section, and the results are kept separate from the discussion. The reader therefore knows what to expect and where to find it, and can distinguish fact from interpretation. Adding to these predictable qualities is an impersonal and spartan writing style. Not only is valuable space saved, but the ambiguities of language are also supposedly minimized.

In short, the qualities that often describe the best nonempirical essays—felicity of expression, the wise use of examples, the judicious selection of quotes, and the impact of metaphoric language—are avoided. There are consequently few scientists with "poetry on their pens."[16]

Empiricism in Perspective:
Theory, Practice, and Design

Theory and Hypothesis

Empirical research leads to reliable data. While valuable, the psychology of literature needs more. Empiricism is given its context and direction by theory. Theories generate hypotheses that guide the researcher toward the sort of facts to look for, where to possibly find them, how to measure them, and what they mean once they are found. Hypotheses can come from either empirical or nonempirical sources in psychology, as well as from literature, philosophy, or from personal roots.

The most developed theory in the psychology of literature is Freudian, although there are many other clinically oriented contributions (e.g., Jung, Adler) and post- and neo-Freudians.[17] Nearly all, however, depend on discursive arguments and illustrative examples, rather than empirical sources of validation.[18]

On the other hand, many empirical studies are done with no, little, or a restricted theory. The research tends to be of the "shotgun" variety without an overall plan, and isolated from the work of others.

The abundance of empirically untested ideas (from psychoanalysis and literature), and the technical skills of the research psychologist (interested in hypotheses to test), need to be joined.

Practical Considerations

Certain practical requirements of research have to be anticipated and met (e.g., the limited availability of time, money, subjects, and material). While these should not stop a good idea from being tested, they will reduce the scope of research.

Research will also be delayed by library research and the pilot study. A literature search (see the *Psychological Abstracts*) indicates the work (and thinking) that has preceded your own. A pilot (or exploratory) study relaxes some of the rules of empiricism. It gives the researcher a concrete sense of (or "feeling for") the phenomena, procedures, materials, and data. (The studies reported in part IV are pilot studies.)

Research Designs

The overall plan within which hypotheses are linked to facts-to-be-discovered is the research design. The qualitative-descriptive (1) and descriptive-quantitative (2) designs describe things as they are; the experimental design (3) attempts to explain why things are the way they are.

Qualitative-descriptive. Qualitatively rich descriptions are most useful when a researcher is not sure of what to look for or what might be found; or when interested in the broad or overall picture from which to plan further research.

The interview fulfills these goals. Interviews have various degrees of structure, i.e., the specificity of the questions asked, their order, and whether responses are provided from which to make selections. An unstructured interview is open-ended and free-responding with respect to the style of questions asked and the types of responses encouraged. This design provides detailed, rich, lengthy, experiential, and personal information. It is probably best suited for the study of authors, or more generally, in the pilot work preceding any type of inquiry. But the volume and subtlety of the information obtained make it difficult to treat quantitatively. Thus, most empirical work in the psychology of literature usually falls within the next design.

Descriptive-quantitative. A questionnaire is more specific than an interview. It provides ready-made responses from which a respondent can make selections that describe his or her feelings, thoughts, and beliefs. It is therefore quantitatively easy to describe people's responses to one or several items, or to the entire questionnaire. (The most highly structured questionnaire is a test.) When questionnaires are used in survey research, they are administered to a large sample.

This design also includes observational methods: participant observation, controlled observation, and naturalistic (or field) observation. Most are unobtrusive and nonreactive.[19] In observing authors at work, or in studying "everyday" behavior in the classroom or library, they reduce the possibility that those being studied may be reacting to the study, and thus biasing the finding.

Any method can provide two (or more) sets of numerical data. Relating them to one another is called the correlational method (in contrast to the experimental method, discussed next). (The correlational method is also confusingly referred to as the "statistical method.") Correlations, like all the other methods discussed so far, describe. They do not explain the basis for the observations, descriptions, or relationships.

For some problems, especially at the outset of research, description is as much as can be expected. Description does provide a great deal of information, especially when little or nothing is known, or when what is known is casual, anecdotal, or unsystematic. But for the methods that reveal underlying causes, or suggest how things work, the experimental design is needed.

Experimental designs. Experimental designs are possible only when the variables that define a phenomenon are known, and in addition, are also manipulable (i.e., being able to vary the degree to which something is present or not). Controlled manipulations of known variables can reveal causes, i.e., "what leads to what."

In the simplest experiment, only one factor (the treatment or condition) is studied, e.g., the effect of reading great (or classical) literature. The experimental group receives several types (or levels) of this factor, e.g., different types of great novels are read. A control group receives no treatment (or they may read a popular novel with the same subject matter and length as the great literature read). Both the experimental and control groups are equivalent in all respects except for the type of literature read. Thus, any measured difference between the two groups at the end of the study (e.g., in their "appreciation of human frailties")—given their initial equivalence and keeping everything else "constant" during the study—can be due only to the treatment. The reading of great literatures does (or does not) affect readers' appreciation of human frailties.

More complicated experimental designs (factorial) ask several questions (factors) simultaneously: Does the reading of great literature (factor A), which includes novels of four different types (levels 1–4), affect readers differently? Does the effect depend on the amount of literature read (factor B), in which one, two, or three examples of each type of great literature is read (levels 1–3)? Does the effect depend on sex (factor C, with two levels, male and female)? Each factor could be effective by itself ("a main effect") or in combination with others ("an interaction," in which the effect depends on the type of literature, the amount read, and/or the sex of the reader). The experiment could include any number of other factors (and levels), such as education, age, and background in literature. Usually, though, no more than three factors are studied at a time. (In this experiment, several control groups would be needed, each perhaps given popular versions of the different types of great literature [e.g., best sellers], or a neutral or time-filling task.)

Experiments are difficult to do, especially with literature.[20] The investigator has to know enough about a phenomenon to manipulate it, and to prevent other known phenomena from happening (i.e., control). Thus experiments are rare.

Quasi-experiments are often substituted for "true" experiments. Some empirical criteria are given up or only approximated. This is likely when an experiment can be done only under real-life or field conditions (e.g., in the school, classroom, workplace, or home, where the strict controls of the lab are not possible). Two of the most difficult criteria to meet, and in some cases, not even possible, are the random assignment of subjects of the various conditions of the study, and the establishment of a control group.

For example, in trend (or time) analysis, there may be neither a control group nor a random assignment of subjects. Instead, an effect is signaled by an abrupt change in a group's behavior when a treatment is introduced—compared to the behavior shown earlier, and at a later time. For example, in a literature class, a new mode of instruction (or type of poetry) may be introduced, following which the class is less restive and more participatory; when the new treatment is removed, the previous behavior is reinstated.

Quasi-experiments must be interpreted cautiously, since the presence of uncontrolled (but unavoidable) factors makes alternative accounts of the findings possible. Nevertheless, their findings can be tentatively accepted, and improvements and checks designed into the next quasi-experiment. Thus, two or more quasi-experiments may approximate a true experiment. Quasi-experiments are at least more suggestive about causes than descriptive designs.

The experiment is the ideal for research because it embodies, at its best, most of the criteria of empiricism. Even when a problem is best studied with another design, the experiment sets a standard to follow. The experimental design, though, depends upon further progress from other designs, e.g., in describing a phenomenon fully enough to know what to manipulate. If the psychology of literature is to become scientifically acceptable, more experimental studies are needed.

Examples of Improvable Research

This last section presents six brief summaries of unpublished research conducted by students in a psychology and art course.[21] The studies are about the reader (and more generally, any art audience), authors (and especially poets), and the literary work(s). The studies exemplify attempts to meet empirical criteria—attempts that often fail. Their failures are understandable: they were conducted by untrained students, in less than a semester's time, and as part of a course. But although limited, these efforts suggest what might be done as a start; they can therefore serve as pilot studies. They also fulfill a didactic purpose. The reader is encouraged to locate a study's methodological errors, and of equal importance, to suggest improvements. The task of applying the lessons of empiricism to these studies is an appropriate conclusion to this chapter.[22]

The Reader-Audience

Does literature work? The question addressed by this quasi-experiment was whether exposure to an artistic event, as most people believe, affects an audience's experience (in a measurable way). A theatrical event was used, although the design is applicable to the reading of literature.

A small group of volunteers (only seven), from an introductory theater course, was tested immediately before and after a performance of Puccini's opera *Gianni Schicci*.[23] The students were given a self-descriptive checklist of twenty-seven adjectives from which they selected those that described their experience. They also assigned a meaning to the event on nine scales anchored by bipolar adjectives (e.g., "good-bad").

The results suggested that "something happened." More adjectives were chosen from the self-descriptive list after the show than before it (mean: 11.0 and 9.3, respectively). Most were emotional and arousal words ("excitement," "moved"). Before the show, most of the words were cognitive and calming ("contentment," "contemplation").[24] The ratings on the bipolar scales did not change over the performance. But the theater experience in general (i.e., combining pre- and post-opera ratings) was evaluated as "good, beautiful, and active" (rather than "bad, ugly, and passive"). (The ratings on the remaining six scales were undistinguished.)

What is your evaluation of the study?[25]

Who enjoys poetry? A correlational study was aimed at the reader of poetry. High school and college students were asked about their preferences for poetry, and their reading ability and imagery were tested. Is enjoyment of poetry linked to reading ability and imagery? (Before you read further, you might guess.)

A standard reading test (of comprehension and rate) was given to thirteen upper-class high school students. They also read and rated (on a six-point scale) their liking for three short, contemporary, and traditional poems. (The three separate ratings were combined into one overall score.) In addition, they were asked if they generally liked poetry.

Five of the six slow readers (i.e., their rate of reading scores fell below the group's median score) said they liked poetry in general, while five of the seven fast readers did not. (Are slow readers better able to "savor" poetry? No relationship was found between poetry preference and the reading comprehension score.)

The question of whether poetry was liked or not was asked of fifty-seven lower-division college students. As a measure of imagery, they were also asked if they heard voices (either their own or others') while reading poetry.

Preference of poetry and imagery were related: Of the thirty-five students who said they liked poetry, thirty-two reported hearing voices;

and of the twenty-two who said they didn't like poetry, only two said they heard voices.

What do your "voices" say about this study?

The Author

Do poets have a "gift for nonsense"? One reason poets (and other writers) may be effective is because of their ability to attribute imagery to words easily. In this naturalistic study, using a checklist format, the issue was whether poets' facility with language extended to unfamiliar and highly unusual words—namely, nonsense syllables (e.g., "guz", "zup"). Do poets differ from nonpoets in their ability to assign meanings to meaningless verbal material?

At a reception given for writers at a conference, five nationally recognized poets and five undergraduate students examined a thirteen-page booklet. It contained six-hundred three-letter nonsense words of different degrees of rated associative value (randomly dispersed) taken from standardized tables. In a self-paced task lasting about half an hour, the subjects checked those nonsense words that "remind you of another word."

As expected, the poets as a group indicated familiarity with more nonsense words than the nonpoets did (mean: 173.20 and 127.80, respectively). Furthermore, the poets chose more low associative value nonsense words than did the nonpoets.

What sort of "nonsense" is in this study?

Are writers aesthetic? A test and questionnaire were used to answer a seemingly straightforward question: Are creative-writing students more aesthetic than journalism students? (The former value harmony while the latter value practicality?)

Two classes of college students, sixteen from a creative-writing and a journalism class (each with more men than women, a total of twenty-two and ten, respectively), were studied. They were given an aesthetic test containing thirty-six items with which agreement or nonagreement could be indicated.[26] (E.g., "The Bible can be treasured for its beautiful prose and literary style.") The items ranged across a broad spectrum of subjects, from architecture to sunsets. (A high score indicated a high aesthetic value.) They also received a questionnaire that listed twenty artistic-aesthetic activities (e.g., "Read great literature"). Respondents indicated (1) those activities they engaged in, and (2) the degree to which they were involved (on a three-point scale).

The aesthetic test did differentiate the subjects—not by the type of writing course taken, but by their sex: women in the journalism class were more aesthetic than their male classmates (mean: 22.67 and 19.40, respectively). The sexes were not appreciably different in the creativity class (mean: 22.17 and 21.05, respectively). The two classes (and sexes) did not differ in the number or degree of artistic-aesthetic activities engaged in.

Should male journalism students feel upset by these results?

The Work

Does a writer's style change? A writer's work may be easier to read at the beginning of his career than at the end, since public acceptance may be more important then than later, when a reputation has already been established. On the other hand, the early work may be harder to read, since a writer may be less skilled than later in his career. One might also wonder about the interestingness of works written at the early and late points of a a writer's career, and its relationship to reading ease.

Two short stories by Chekhov, his first ("Late-Blooming Flowers") and last ("The Fianceé"), were studied by content analysis. Samples of every tenth paragraph of the two stories were selected, for a total of eighteen passages to be analyzed. Readability formulas were applied to the material, resulting in two measures:[27] (1) reading ease (RE), e.g., the average number of words per sentence; and (2) human interest (HI) e.g., the average number of personal pronouns used. (In the formulas, 0 = difficult RE and dull HI, and 100 = very easy RE and dramatic HI.)

Chekhov's first story ("Flowers") was more difficult to read than his last story ("Fianceé") (mean: 69.59 and 81.96, respectively). Although "Flowers" was more difficult, it was also more interesting than the easier "Fianceé" (mean: 78.64 and 70.33, respectively).

Do you accept the general rule suggested by this study that "harder prose is more interesting" (and its corollary, "easier prose is duller")?

Are writers more expressive on creativity than are other creative types? In another content analysis study, the number of autobiographical statements on creativity by writers, musicians, and painters were compared.[28] Differences between these creative types, if any, might suggest whether writers' creativity is distinguished from others.

A library's entire collection of autobiographies (115) by three types of creative artists was examined. Some 501 one-sentence autobiographical statements on creativity (e.g., its sources, its relationship to hard work, and the difficulties encountered) were identified by two judges. They were counted for each of the three creative types. (Frequencies were also obtained for the last three centuries.)

Writers wrote fewer autobiographies than either musicians or painters, at least in this sample (13, 30, and 72, respectively). (Perhaps writers' fiction is sufficiently autobiographical.) Writers also made fewer statements about creativity than did painters, but not fewer than musicians (119, 260, and 122, respectively). Painters seem to have the greatest need to give verbal expression to their creativity. Their similarly nonverbal (professionally speaking) musician colleagues do not seem to have this urge. However, in relative terms, writers did make more statements than did either musicians or painters (mean: 9.15, 4.06, and 3.61, respectively).

Writers therefore say more (on the average) than other creative types, even though they do so with fewer autobiographical opportunities. (Perhaps they are less self-conscious than other creative people about revealing themselves.) Henry Miller said more than anyone else (thirty-four statements), followed at a distance by Wolfe, Wordsworth, and Lowell (eighteen, fifteen, and ten statements, respectively). Among painters and musicians, Picasso and Copland had the most to say (with twenty-one statements each).

The twentieth century was the most prolific century for statements on creativity—with the exception of musicians. Inexplicably, the number of statements peaked in the nineteenth-century autobiographies. (Were the writers relatively indifferent to the influence of Freud, did they have a higher birth rate then, or is modern music somehow autobiographical?)

How does this content analysis study of creativity "count" with you?

Notes

Introduction—*Natoli*

1 Leonard Tennenhouse, Introduction to *The Practice of Psychoanalytic Criticism*, ed. L. Tennenhouse (Detroit: Wayne State University Press, 1976).

2 Frank Lentricchia, *After the New Criticism* (Chicago: University of Chicago Press, 1980).

3 Frederick Crews, "Anaesthetic Criticism," in *Psychoanalysis and Literary Process*, ed. F. Crews (Cambridge, Mass.: Winthrop, 1970).

4 Gerald Graff, "Deconstruction as Dogma; or, 'Come Back to the Raft Ag'in, Strether Honey!' " *The Georgia Review* 34 (1980): 404–21.

5 J. Hillis Miller, "The Critic as Host," in *Deconstruction and Criticism* (New York: Seabury Press, 1979).

6 William Kerrigan, "Psychoanalysis Unbound," *New Literary History* 12 (1980): 199–206.

7 Paul Brodtkorb's *Ishmael's White World* (New Haven: Yale University Press, 1965) is a fine psychological study utilizing a phenomenological perspective, but its methods have been largely ignored.

8 Geoffrey Hartman, Preface to *Deconstruction and Criticism* (New York: Seabury Press, 1979).

9 Robert Coles, "Commentary on 'Psychology and Literature,' " *New Literary History* 12 (1980): 207–11.

10 Susan Suleiman, "Introduction: Varieties of Audience-Oriented Criticism," in *The Reader in the Text: Essays on Audience and Interpretation*, ed. S. Suleiman and I. Crosman (Princeton, N.J.: Princeton University Press, 1980), 6.

11 Paul Roazen, *Freud and His Followers* (New York: Knoph 1975), 224.

12 Sigmund Freud, *On the History of the Psychoanalytic Movement*, standard ed. (London: Hogarth Press, 1957), 14: 54–55, 57–58.

13 E. Ragland-Sullivan, review of Jacques Lacan, *Ecrits: A Selection, Sub-stance* 21 (1978): 166.

14 Ibid.

15 Ibid., 167.

16 Suleiman, "Introduction," 4.

17 Michel Grimaud, "Recent Trends in Psychoanalysis," *Sub-stance* 13 (1976): 136.

18 Roy C. Calogeras and Toni M. Alston, "On 'Action Language' in Psychoanalysis," *Psychoanalytic Quarterly* 49 (1980): 663.

19 Richard H. King, preview of Roy Schafer, *A New Language for Psychoanalysis, The Georgia Review* 31 (1977): 255

20 Marion Vlastos, "Doris Lessing and R. D. Laing: Psychopolitics and Prophecy," *PMLA* 91 (1976): 250.

21 Robert Magliola, "The Phenomenological Approach to Literature: Its Theory and Methodology," *Language and Style* 5 (1972): 81.

22 Brodtkorb, *Ishmael's White World*, 152.

Jungian Theory—*Snider*

1 René Wellek, "The Main Trends of Twentieth-Century Criticism," *The Yale Review* 51 (1961): 103.

2 See, for example, Garland Otho Gunter, "Archetypal Patterns in the Poetry of Tennyson, 1823–1850," Ph.D. diss., University of Maryland, 1966; Douglas Wayne Cooper, "Tennyson's *Idylls*: A Mythography of the Self," Ph.D. diss., University of Missouri, 1966; and Nadean Hawkins Bishop, " The Mother Archetype in Arnold's *Merope* and Swinburne's 'Atlanta in Calydon,' " Ph.D. diss., University of Wisconsin, 1972. In the body of this essay I shall be discussing articles that employ Jungian theory.

3 Alfred Adler, "Sigmund Freud and His Historical Setting," in *The Spirit of Man, Art, and Literature,* vol. 15 of *Collected Works* (Princeton, N.J.: Princeton University Press, 1966).

4 Howard Maynadier, *The Arthur of the English Poets* (Boston: Houghton Mifflin, 1907), 374.

5 The first two realizations of the Self for Tristram are his two periods of happiness with Iseult (in cantos 2 and 6). These are less mature stages in Tristram's process of individuation, the process that leads to full psychic balance.

6 A contemporary example of such a work is William Peter Blatty's *The Exorcist.* Speaking of the film version of this novel, Dr. Thayer Greene, a Jungian analyst, says: "Modern consciousness has become so rationalized . . . that the reaction to this kind of movie is a compensatory upthrust of irrational forces—not necessary

evil." Quoted in *Newsweek*, 11 February 1974, 63. I think also that the demon-possessed child in *The Exorcist* represents the collective shadow—an archetypal image of the evil that modern society often prefers to ignore. As an aesthetic whole, however, *The Exorcist* is not satisfactory, being, at its worst, blatant sensationalism.

7   Ronald Crane, *The Languages of Criticism and the Structure of Poetry* (Toronto: University of Toronto Press, 1953), 191.

8   In *Psyche and Symbol in Shakespeare* (Bloomington: Indiana University Press, 1972), Alex Aronson points out that for some the "fullest and most intense self-realization can only be found in death."

9   See Aronson, *Psyche and Symbol*, 191–92 and 258–59, for a further Jungian interpretation of Caliban and his relationship to Prospero.

10 For an extended Jungian analysis of Stevenson's story, see Barbara Hannah, *Striving Toward Wholeness* (New York: Putnam, 1971).

11 I have capitalized the Self throughout this essay in order to distinguish it from the non-Jungian use of the word.

12 Aronson points out, however, that the union achieved in Shakespeare's comedies "is never the result of a mature longing for self-realization. The hero is still in his early manhood, quite unaware of the need to strive towards completeness" (*Psyche and Symbol*, 32). Nevertheless, a level of Selfhood is reached that may pave the way for future development.

13 All references to the novel are from the 1951 "omnibus" edition, *The Ballad of the Sad Café: The Novels and Stories of Carson McCullers* (Boston: Houghton Mifflin, 1951). References to the play are to the New Directions edition, 1951, but my central concern is the novel, which is the superior version. In the play, John Henry is seven.

14 Carson McCullers, "The Flowering Dream: Notes on Writing," *Esquire*, December 1959; reprinted in Carson McCullers, *The Mortgaged Heart*, ed. M. Smith (Boston: Houghton Mifflin, 1958).

15 Oliver Evans, *The Ballad of Carson McCullers: A Biography* (New York: Coward-McCann, 1965), 98. See also Virginia Spencer Carr, *The Lonely Hunter: A Biography of Carson McCullers* (Garden City, N.Y.: Doubleday, 1975), 121. Carr notes that as McCullers and Lee 'walked silently back to the house, Carson was trembling. She was certain now of the style and theme of her book. Its focus had sharpened at last."

16 Laurens van der Post, *Jung and the Story of Our Time* (New York: Vintage Books, 1975), 118.

17 C. G. Jung, *The Archetypes and the Collective Unconscious*, vol. 9 of *Collected Works* (Princeton, N.J.: Princeton University Press, 1969), 1. Frank Baldanza, in an examination of the similarity of the ideas of Plato to those of McCullers, points out that in *The Member of the Wedding*, "love is synonomous, almost mathematically, with wholeness." "Plato in Dixie," *The Georgia Review* 12 (1958): 160

18   Jolande Jacobi, *The Psychology of C.G. Jung* (New Haven: Yale Univesity Press, 1968), 108.

19   In the play version, she is described as "a dreamy, restless girl, and periods of energetic activity alternate with rapt attention to her inward world of fantasy."

20   Carson McCullers, *The Square Root of Wonderful* (Boston: Houghton Mifflin, 1958), viii.

21   C. G. Jung and C. Kerenyi, *Essays on a Science of Mythology* (New York: Harper & Row, 1963).

22   Eleanor Wikborg, *Carson McCullers' "The Member of the Wedding": Aspects of Structure and Style* (Goteberg, Sweden: Acta Univesitatis Gothoburgensis, 1975), 7.

23   Her "crimes are not all that unusual for a girl her age: "She took the pistol from her father's bureau drawer and carried it all over town and shot up the cartridges in a vacant lot. She changed into a robber and stole a three-way knife. . . . One Saturday in May she committed a secret and unknown sin. In the MacKean's garage, with Barney MacKean, they committed a queer sin, and how bad it was she did not know" (p. 626).

24   Frieda Fordham, *An Introduction to Jung's Psychology* (Middlesex, England: Penguin Books, 1953), 61.

Adlerian Theory—*Huber*

1   R. Rom and H. L. Ansbacher, "An Adlerian Case or a Character by Sartre?" *Journal of Individual Psychology* 28 (1972): 76–80.

2   Alfred Adler, "Individual Psychological Remarks on Alfred Berger's *Hofrat Eysenhardt*," in *The Practice and Theory of Individual Psychology* (Totowa, N.J.: Littlefield, 1959); Alfred Adler, "Preface to the Diary of Vaslav Nijinsky," *Archives of General Psychology* 38, no. 7 (1981), 834–35.

3   In 1982 this journal merged to form a new quarterly, *Individual Psychology.*

4   Leon Edel, *Stuff of Sleep and Dreams: Experiments in Literary Psychology* (New York: Harper & Row, 1982).

5   Phyllis Bottome, *Alfred Adler* (New York: Vanguard, 1957), 195.

6   See H. Ellenberger's *The Discovery of the Unconscious* (New York: Basic Books, 1970) for a discussion of the association of Freud and Adler.

7   Carl Rogers, *A Way of Being* (Boston: Houghton Mifflin, 1980); *On Becoming a Person* (Boston: Houghton Mifflin, 1961); Abraham Maslow, *Motivation and Personality* (New York: Harper & Row, 1970).

8   Alfred Adler, *The Problem Child* (New York: Capricorn Books, 1963).

9   M. E. Skorburg, "An Adlerian Interpretation of H. G. Wells," *Journal of Individual Psychology* 31 (1975): 85–96; E. Sachs, "*The Fall* by Ablert Camus: A

Study in Adlerian Psychology," *Journal of Individual Psychology* 28 (1972): 76–80.

10 See J. J. McLaughlin and R. R. Ansbacher, "Sane Ben Franklin: An Adlerian View of His Autobiography," *Journal of Individual Psychology* 27 (1971): 189–207.

11 Thomas Aldrich, *The Story of a Bad Boy* (Philadelphia: Winston, 1927) 224.

12 William James, *Principles of Psychology* (New York: Holt, 1890).

13 H. L. Ansbacher, "The Concept of Social Interest," *Journal of Individual Psychology* 31 (1968): 131–49.

14 R. J. Huber, "Social Interest Revisited," *Character Potential* 7 (1975): 64–77.

15 Alfred Adler, *The Individual Psychology of Alfred Adler* (New York: Basic Books, 1956); *Superiority and Social Interest* (Evanston, Ill.: Northwestern University Press, 1964); *Cooperation Between the Sexes* (New York: Doubleday, Anchor, 1978).

16 W. C. Alee, *Cooperation Among Animals* (New York: Schuman, 1951); R. J. Huber et al., "Evolution: Struggle of Syneray?" *Journal of Individual Psychology* 34 (1978): 210–20; E. O. Wilson, *Sociobiology: The New Synthesis* (Cambridge, Mass.: Harvard University Press, 1975).

17 Alfred Adler, *What Life Should Mean to You* (New York: Capricorn Books, 1958).

18 Ibid.

19 J. J. McLaughlin, "The Dynamics of Power in *King Lear*: An Adlerian Interpretation," *Shakespeare Quarterly* 29 (1978): 37–43.

20 Adler, "Individual Psychological Remarks," 267.

21 Philip Mairet, "Hamlet as a Study of Individual Psychology," *Journal of Individual Psychology* 25 (1969): 71–88; McLaughlin, "Dynamics of Power"; R. C. J. Endres, "Understanding the Life Style of a Medieval Literary Character," *Journal of Individual Psychology* 30 (1974): 251–64; Adler, "Individual Psychological Remarks"; S. Osherson, "An Adlerian Approach to Goethe's *Faust*," *Journal of Individual Psychology* 21 (1965): 194–98; Rom and Ansbacher, "An Adlerian Case"; Sachs, "*The Fall*: A Study"; Skorburg, "An Adlerian Interpretation"; McLaughlin and Ansbacher, "Sane Ben Franklin"; J. Irving, "*The Catcher in the Rye*: An Adlerian Interpretation," *Journal of Individual Psychology* 32 (1976): 81–92; R. J. Huber and G. Ledbetter, "Holden Caulfield, Self-Appointed Catcher in the Rye: Some Additional Thoughts," *Journal of Individual Psychology* 33 (1977): 250–56.

22 See as an example, L. Unger, ed., *American Writers: A Collection of Literary Biographies*, vol. 3 (New York: Scribner, 1961).

23 Adler, *What Life Should Mean to You*, 14.

24 J. D. Salinger, *The Catcher in the Rye* (New York: Modern Library, 1951).

25 Adler, *Superiority and Social Interest*.

26 Ibid., 103.

27 Adler, *The Individual Psychology*.

28   Ibid., 21.

29   Adler, *Superiority and Social Interest*, 117.

30   Ibid., 117.

31   Adler, *The Individual Psychology*, 253.

Reichian Criticism—*Efron*

1   David Boadella, *Wilhelm Reich: The Evolution of His Work* (London: Vision Press; New York: Dell, 1973); W. Edward Mann and Edward Hoffman, *The Man Who Dreamed of Tomorrow: A Conceptual Biography of Wilhelm Reich* (Los Angeles: J. P. Tarcher, 1980). A good brief introduction to Reich's overall theory is given by Jerome Greenfield, *Wilhelm Reich vs. the U.S.A.* (New York: Norton, 1974) 41–54. Reich's own "Introductory Survey" in the opening pages of his *The Function of the Orgasm* (c. 1942; New York: Noonday Press, 1961) is still the best brief introduction by Reich himself. The volume was originally published by Reich's own Orgone Institute Press.

2   William Reich, *The Bioelectrical Investigation of Sexuality and Anxiety* (c. 1937; New York: Farrar, Straus & Giroux, 1982), 6–7.

3   Ursula K. LeGuin, *The Dispossessed* (New York: Avon, 1974), 258. Descriptions that to the popular imagination are terribly sexual, frequently prove otherwise with Reichian insight. See, for example, my *"Story of O as Anti-Sexual Fantasy,"* *Paunch* 48–49 (1977): 144–22; trans. and rev. in *L'Arc* 83 (1982): 43–49.

4   In the 1928 volume *Die Funktion Des Orgasmus*, not to be confused with the 1942 book cited above, Reich noted that his conclusions about orgasm and neurosis were originally based on two surveys: (1) the 338 cases seen at the Vienna Psychoanalytic Outpatient Department in the course of a year, 1923–24; (2) on the forty-one male and thirty-one female patients that he had treated personally. See Reich, *The Function of the Orgasm*, pt. 1, 168. Reich's general theory of the relationships between armor and energy blockage are nicely described by his student Morton Herskowitz, "The Concept of Armoring," *Journal of Orgonomy* 9 (1975): 158–70. Philosophical dimensions of the mind-body linkage involved in Reich's theory are given in my article, "The Mind-Body Problem in Lawrence, Pepper, and Reich," *Journal of Mind and Behavior* 1 (1980): 247–70.

5   See Eleanor Leacock, "Women's Status in Egalitarian Society: Implications for Social Evolution," *Current Anthropology* 19 (1978): 247–55. See also pp. 255–75 for debate and discussion with over twenty commentators. Leacock makes a strong case for the widespread and lengthy existence of a pre-patriarchal egalitarian society.

6   See Robert A. Dew, "William Reich's Cancer Biopathy," in *Psychotherapeutic Treatment of Cancer Patients*, ed. Jane Goldberg (New York: Free Press, 1981) for a good restatement of Reich's theory, which is long overdue for consideration.

7   See Wilhelm Reich, *Ether, God and Devil* (c. 1949, New York: Farrar, Straus &

Giroux, 1973) for his most extensive statement on theory of science.

8   Mann and Hoffman, *The Man Who Dreamed,* 152.

9   Frederik L. Rusch, "Of Eidolons and Orgone," *Walt Whitman Review* 13 (1967): 11–15. The poetry of William Blake, with the famous emphasis on energy as "eternal delight," would seem to allow elucidation through Reichian ideas (and vice versa), but the opportunity is rejected by Diana Hume George, *Blake and Freud* (Ithaca, N.Y.: Cornell University Press, 1980), 19. This may be due in part to George's misunderstanding of Reich's concept of the orgasm, which she takes to be a call for "explosive" climax. She thus confuses Reich's emphasis on a series of phases in the orgastic process, ending not with explosiveness but with the peaceful experience of gratification as energy returns from the genitals to the whole body. The return is felt as "streaming." See Reich, *The Funciton of the Orgasm,* 84. George refuses any consideration of Reich's energy theories after his break with the psychoanalytic establishment. In the same statement, George also performs the common reduction of the later Reich to advocacy of orgasm alone: "The ideal . . . is to achieve mental health through repeated and explosive orgasm." This error is worth correcting. Reich in *The Function of the Orgasm* describes and diagrams an energy shift in healthy living from creative, valuable *work* to *sex* and back again. Without the work there is impaired health, regardless of sexual activity, nor could the sexual contact be maintained at a vital level without its complement in work. See ibid., 247; and my article, "Toward a Dialectic of Sensuality and Work," *Paunch* 44–45 (1976): 152–70. The balance of work and sexual expression, moreover, will never be attained for most people until there is radical change in social institutions. Reich's consistent emphasis on this larger social dimension is brought out by Mann and Hoffman.

10 Heinrich von Morüngen, *The Medieval Lyric* (London: Hutchinson University Library, 1968), 180. My comments on Whitman and von Morüngen are restated from part of my earlier article, "Beginning a Reichian Approach to Literature," *Energy & Character: The Journal of Bioenergetic Research* 10 (1979): 1–12; 11 (1980): 82–85. A small portion of my comments below on *Wurthering Heights* also come from this earlier article, in somewhat different form.

11 Roger Dadoun, "Une Lecture Reichienne de Baudelaire," *Sexpol* 18–19 (1977): 88–89.

12 Paul Goodman, *Kafka's Prayer* (New York: Vanguard, 1947).

13 David Boadella, *The Spiral Flame: A Study in the Meaning of D. H. Lawrence* (1959; reprinted in *Paunch* 50–51 [1977]); Dennis R. Hoerner, "D. H. Lawrence's 'Carbon' and Wilhelm Reich's 'Core': The Biopsychological Basis of *The Rainbow*," Ph.D. diss. Hoerner's brilliant interpretation of the famous sheave-gathering scene, where Will Brangwen and Anna Brangwen engage in abortive sexual ritual, is printed in "D. H. Lawrence's 'Carbon' and Wilhelm Reich's 'Core' in *The Rainbow*," *Journal of Orgonomy* 12 (1978): : 92–99. Hoerner has gone on to offer a Reichian interpretation of *Lady Chatterley's Lover*, "Connie Chatterley: A Case of Spontaneous Therapy," *Energy & Character: The Journal of Bioenergetic Research* 12 (1981): 48–55.

14   Michael Steig, "Sue Bridehead," *Novel: A Forum on Fiction* 1 (1968): 260–66; Arthur Efron, "'A Bluer, Moister, Atmosphere': Life Energy in Thomas Hardy's *Jude the Obscure*," *International Journal of Life Energy* 1 (1979): 175–84. See also Leonore Levy, "Armoring and Human Potential in *Jude the Obscure*," *Paunch* 42–43 (1975): 149–52.

15   Michael Steig, "Bellow's *Henderson* and the Limits of Freudian Criticism," *Paunch* 36–37 (1973): 39–46.

16   John M. Bell, "Hawthorne's *The Scarlet Letter*: An Artist's Intuitive Understanding of Plague, Armor, and Health," *Journal of Orgonomy* 3 (1968): 102–15: David B. Downing, "Nathaniel Hawthorne's Poetics of Language, History, and the Body," Ph.D. diss.

17   David Kiremidjian, "Dostoevsky and the Problem of Matricide," *Journal of Orgonomy* 9 (1975): 69–81; Jerome Greenfield, "Wilhelm Reich: A New Approach to Art," *Paunch* 42 (1975): 43–58: See also John M. Bell, "Art and Orgonomy — Preliminary Considerations," *Journal of Orgonomy* 11 (1977): 226–39; Robert N. Pasotti, "The Emotional Plague in Literature," *Journal of Orgonomy* 11 (1977): 88–95, on the character structure in *Othello, Mody Dick*, Dostoevsky's *The Possessed*, and Orwell's *1984*; Joy Walsh, "Kerouac: A Reichian Interpretation," *Moody Street Irregulars: Kerouac Newsletter* 1 (1978): 3–5.

18   Arthur Efron, "The Problem of Don Quixote's Rage," *Denver Quarterly* 16 (1981): 27–46. There has also been a small amount of Reichian criticism of the drama. See John M. Bell, "Oedipus Tyrannus: Core Drama of Western Culture," *Journal of Orgonomy* 5 (1971): 65–87; Pamela Lydon Munday, "Samuel Beckett's *Waiting for Godot*," *Journal of Orgonomy*, 11 (1977); 88–95. See also Bell's forthcoming article in the same journal on Shakespeare's *The Tempest*.

19   See Arthur Efron, "Perspectivism and the Nature of Fiction: *Don Quixote* and Borges," *Thought* 50 (1975): 148–75.

20   Emily Brontë, *Wuthering Heights* (c. 1847; New York: Norton, 1972), 71.

21   See the work of Charles Konia, M.D., applying Reich's theories to current evidence on brain physiology and the central nervous system, "Brain Pulsation: Normal Functioning," *Journal of Orgonomy* 14 (1980): 103–13; "Brain Pulsation: Disturbed Functioning in Schizophrenia," *Journal of Orgonomy* 14 (1980): 223–38; "Orgonotic Functions of the Brain," *Journal of Orgonomy* 16 (1982): 110–23.

22   In a famous ploy at the opening of *Civilization and Its Discontents*, Freud first acknowledges the reality of "oceanic" feelings of energy, then protests his own complete innocence of ever having had such feelings, or of understanding them. This is followed at once by his theory — since become dogma — that oceanic feelings are nothing but echoes of early infancy and its undifferentiated state of union with the mother.

23   Wilhelm Reich, *The Impulsive Character and Other Writings*, (c. 1925; New York: Meridian Books, 1974).

24 E. M. Forster, *Aspects of the Novel* (New York: Harcourt, Brace, 1927), 144–46; David Cecil, "Emily Brontë and *Wuthering Heights*," in *Early Victorian Novelists* (London: Constable, 1935). In the Norton Critical Edition, pp. 298–305, especially p. 304: "For all its intensity, Catherine's love is sexless. . . ." And, Emily Brontë ". . . believes in the immortality of the soul *in this world*." Wayne Burns, " 'In Death They Were Not Divided': The Moral Significance of Unmoral Passion," *Hartford Studies in Literature* 5 (1973): 134–59. Both Forster and Cecil are aware of the connections between Catherine, Heathcliff, and the forces of cosmic energy, but lacking a Reichian perspective, they regard these as outside the human body or as "spiritual forces."

25 For a fine Derridean reading of the novel, which attempts to show how the whole text is "generated" out of certain subtexts in the novel, see Carol Jacobs, "*Wuthering Heights*: At the Threshold of Interpretation," *Boundary* 2 (1979): 49–71. The necessarily deliberate refusal of the deconstruction to tackle the relationship of Heathcliff and Catherine, except as textuality, is well exemplified here.

26 This is the interpretation of Burns, cited above, n. 24. For my detailed response, see " '*Paunch*' *Wuthering Heights*, and the Body," *Paunch* 40–41 (1975): 166–77.

27 The importance of the early separation and its sexual dimensions were brought out by John R. Doheny in "From PMLA to *Wuthering Heights*," *Paunch* 23 (1964): 21–34. See also the objections raised by William Empson, and Doheny's reply, *Paunch* 23 (1965): 81–94; and Empson's further remarks, and my reply, *Paunch* 25 (1966): 68–72.

28 Reich, *The Function of the Orgasm*, 239–40.

29 Contrast, for example, the acclaimed book by Sandra M. Gilbert and Susan Gubar, *The Madwoman in the Attic: The Woman Writer and the Nineteenth-Century Literary Imagination* (New Haven: Yale University Press, 1979). In some ninety pages spent on *Wuthering Heights*, the authors touch only sparingly, and disparagingly, on the relationship of Catherine and Heathcliff.

Literature Through Erich Fromm—*Rusch*

1 Erich Fromm, Afterword to *1984*, by George Orwell (c. 1949; New York: New American Library, 1961).

2 Margaret Mead, quoted in Dava Sobel, "Erich Fromm Dies in Switzerland: Psychoanalyst and Author was 79," *New York Times*, 19 March 1980.

3 Erich Fromm, *On Disobedience and Other Essays* (New York: Seabury Press, 1981) 26, 39.

4 R. S. Peters, ed., *Brett's History of Psychology*, abr. ed. (Cambridge, Mass.: M.I.T. Press, 1967), 750, 753. For a critical interpretation of the neo-Freudian, especially Erich Fromm, from an orthodox Marxist viewpoint, see V. I. Dobrenkov, *Neo-Freudians in Search of Truth* (Moscow: Progress Publishers, 1976).

5   Richard I. Evans, *Dialogue with Erich Fromm* (New York: Harper & Row, 1966) 56–57.

6   Erich Fromm, in Evans, *Dialogue with Erich Fromm*, 58–59.

7   Erich Fromm, *Escape from Freedom* (New York: Farrar & Rinehart, 1941), 27.

8   Erich Fromm, *The Anatomy of Human Destructiveness* (New York: Holt, Rinehart & Winston, 1973), 259.

9   Fromm, *On Disobedience*, 1–2.

10 Erich Fromm, *The Sane Society* (New York: Holt, Rinehart & Winston, 1955), 21–28.

11 Erich Fromm and Ramón Xirau, eds., *The Nature of Man* (London: Macmillan, 1968), 24.

12 Erich Fromm, *To Have Or To Be?* (New York: Bantam Books, 1981), 23.

13 Grover Smith, *T. S. Eliot's Poetry and Plays: A Study in Sources and Meaning* (Chicago: University of Chicago Press, 1962), 16.

14 T. S. Eliot, *The Complete Poems and Plays, 1909–1950* (New York: Harcourt, Brace, 1952), 5.

15 It may be of some interest to compare the characterization of Prufrock to this description of Eliot himself from Virginia Woolf's diary: "Tom to tea yesterday . . . how he suffers! . . . He seemed to have got so little joy or satisfaction out of being Tom . . . he revealed his passion, as he seldom does. A religious soul: an unhappy man: a lonely very sensitive man, all wrapt up in fibres of self torture, doubt, conceit, desire for warmth & intimacy." Virginia Woolf, quoted in Robert Kiely, "The Diary of Virginia Woolf," *New York Times Book Review*, 11 July 1982, 22.

16 F. Scott Fitzgerald, "The Crack-Up," in *The Crack-Up*, ed. Edmund Wilson (New York: New Directions, 1956), 79. In a discussion of Fromm's ideas on personal identity, John H. Schaar cites *The Crack-Up* as illustrative of how a person can both lose his identity and create a false one. See *Escape from Authority: The Perspectives of Erich Fromm* (New York: Basic Books, 1961), 69–70.

17 Erich Fromm, *The Heart of Man: Its Genius or Good and Evil* (New York: Harper & Row, 1964), 42, 57.

18 For a more extensive discussion of Fitzgerald and Fromm, see Frederik L. Rusch, "Marble Men and Maidens, The Necrophilous People of F. Scott Fitzgerald: A Psychoanalytic Approach in Terms of Erich Fromm," *Journal of Evolutionary Psychology III*, 1–2 (1982): 28–40.

19 F. Scott Fitzgerald, *The Great Gatsby* (New York: Scribner, 1953), 6.

20 For a lengthy discussion of Adolf Hitler as a necrophilous person, see Fromm's *Destructiveness*, 369–433. In the same book, Fromm proposed a study of necrophilia in literature: ". . . as far as literature is concerned, it (necrophilia) is too complex to be dealt with briefly; I plan to deal with this topic in a later book" (p. 36n).

21 Fromm, *To Have Or To Be?*, 135.

22 F. Scott Fitzgerald, "The Ice Palace," in *Babylon Revisited and Other Stories* (New York: Scribner, 1960), 1.

23 Erich Fromm, *The Art of Loving* (New York: Harper & Row, 1956), 2.

24 Fromm, *To Have Or To Be?*, 33.

25 Ibid., 13.

26 Erich Fromm, *Man for Himself: An Inquiry into the Psychology of Ethics* (New York: Rinehart, 1947), 75-76.

27 Arthur Miller, *Death of a Salesman: Certain Private Conversations in Two Acts and a Requiem* (New York: Viking, 1958), 30.

28 Erich Fromm, *The Forgotten Language: An Introduction to the Understanding of Dreams, Fairy Tales and Myths* (New York: Rinehart & Winston, 1951), 196.

29 J. J. Bachofen, quoted in Fromm, *The Forgotten Language*, 208.

30 An excellent example of a modern matriarchal point of view can be found in Meridel LeSueur's "Memorial": "We will journey into a spoke leading to the vortex toward the central energy of a global form, away from the linear narrative form so highly developed by the male scientific aggressive orientation of the past. It is a story of three women: mother, whore and intellectual, searching for their dead and their past. They will go to the tavern where they come together in a communal memory and illumination of their mutual history and suffering. The three women leave together, fall into the dead mine as into hell, find each other in their terrible and illumined past, draw together melded by suffering, and find the great Iowa Sox in the night and sleep in the true and mythical identity and cyclic return of all female nature." See Meridel LeSueur, quoted in Meredith Tax, "Midwestern Original," *The Nation*, 13 July 1982, 25.

Jacques Lacan and Jean Genet—*Ragland-Sullivan*

1 Jacques Lacan, "Le seminaire sur 'La Lettre volee,' " in *Ecrits* (Paris: Seuil, 1966). See the English translation in *Yale French Studies* 48 (1972): 39-72.

2 Jean Genet, *The Maids and Deathwatch*, trans. Bernard Frechtman, ed. Jean-Paul Sartre (New York: Grove Press, 1961). For documentation of the theatrical reception history of *The Maids*, see Robert M. Dandarg, "Jean Genet: Thirty Years of Criticism in France, England and America," Ph.D. diss., University of North Carolina, Chapel Hill, 1975.

3 Both Kate Millett and Jean-Paul Sartre documented the Papin sisters' crime as the source of Genet's *The Maids*. See Millett, *Sexual Politics* (Garden City, N.Y.: Doubleday, 1970), 351; and Sartre's Introduction to *The Maids and Deathwatch*, 18.

4 Jacques Lacan, *De la psychose paranoïaque dans ses rapports avec la personnalité suivi de premier écrits sur la paranoïa* (Paris: Seuil, 1975), 389-98.

5 Sartre, Introduction to *The Maids and Deathwatch*.

6 Jean Genet, *L'Atelier d'Alberto Giacometti, les bonnes suivi d'une lettre (à Pauvert), l'enfant criminel, le funambule* (Decines, France: Marc Barbezat, 1958), 144. Genet discusses with Pauvert his concept of the abolition of characters. Translations from Genet's letter to Pauvert are my own..

7 M. E. Ragland-Sullivan, "The Psychology of Narcissism in Jean Genet's *The Maids,* "*Gradiva: International Contemporary Journal* 2 (Fall 1979): 19–41.

8 Sandra M. Gilbert and Susan Gubar, *The Madwoman in the Attic: The Woman Writer and the Nineteenth-Century Literary Imagination* (New Haven: Yale University Press, 1979).

Reading One's Self and Others—*Kann*

1 Heinz Lichtenstein, "Identity and Sexuality: A Study of Their Interrelationship in Man," *Journal of the American Psychoanalytic Association* 9 (1961): 179–260.

2 See, for example, David Norton and Lawrence Stark, "Eye Movements and Visual Perception," *Scientific American* (June 1971): 219–27; and W. H. Ittelson and F. P. Kilpatrick, "Experiments in Perception," *Scientific American* (August 1951): 174–79.

3 This idea is developed in exceedingly interesting ways by Christopher Bollas in his paper "The Aesthetic Moment and the Search for Transformation," presented at a meeting of the Group for Applied Psychoanalysis at the State Univerisity of New York at Buffalo, November 1976. Another approach is provided by D. W. Winnicott, *Playing and Reality* (London: Tavistock Publications, 1971). See, especially, chapter 1, "Transitional Objects and Transitional Phenomena," 1–25; and chapter 7, "The Location of Cultural Experience," 95–103.

4 "Transactive Criticism: Recreation Through Identity," *Criticism* 18 (1976): 334–52.

5 *Washington Irving: Selected Prose*, ed. S. T. Williams (New York: Holt Rinehart & Winston, 1964): 90–107.

Describing Sonnets by Milton and Keats—*van den Berg*

1 Roy Schafer, *A New Language for Psychoanalysis* (New Haven: Yale University Press, 1976), 139.

2 "Narration in the Psychoanalytic Dialogue," *Critical Inquiry* 7 (1980): 29–54; "Action and Narration in Psychoanalysis," *New Literary History* 12 (1980): 61–86.

3 I cite the text of this poem from Milton's *Complete Poetry and Major Prose*, ed. Merritt Hughes (New York: Odyssey Press, 1957), 168.

4 For a thorough survey of critical interpretations, see the discussion of this poem by A. S. P. Woodhouse and Douglas Bush, *A Variorum Commentary on the Poems of John Milton*, vol. 2, pt. 2 (New York: Columbia University Press, 1972), 442–69.

See also Stanley Fish's remarks on this sonnet in "Interpreting the Variorum," reprinted in *Is There a Text in This Class?* (Cambridge, Mass.: Harvard Univesity Press, 1980), 147–74; N.B. 155–58.

5   I cite the text of this poem from *The Poems of John Keats*, ed. H. W. Garrod (London: Oxford University Press, 1962), 366.

Third Force Psychology—*Paris*

1   Portions of the following essay are taken from "Third Force Psychology and the Study of Literature, Biography, Criticism, and Culture," *The Literary Review* 24 (1981): 181–221; and from "Hamlet and His Problems: A Horneyan Analysis," *The Centennial Review* 21 (1977): 36–66. I am grateful to the editors of these journals for permission to reprint excerpts from these essays.

2   Other Third Force psychologists include Kurt Goldstein, Otto Rank, C. G. Jung, Erich Fromm, Rollo May, Carl Rogers, Gordon Allport, and Ernest Schachtel. For a fuller listing, see Abraham Maslow, *Toward a Psychology of Being* (Princeton, N.-J., Van Nostrand, 1962), vi—hereafter cited as *PB*. For a more complete exposition of Third Force psychology than the one presented here, see Bernard J. Paris, *A Psychological Approach to Fiction: Studies in Thackeray, Stendhal, George Eliot, Dostoevsky, and Conrad* (Bloomington, Ind.: Indiana University Press, 1974), chapter 2.

3   Karen Horney, *Neurosis and Human Growth* (New York: Norton, 1950), 15. Hereafter cited as *NHG*.

4   Maslow had hoped to illustrate his description of the self-actualizing person with some examples from literature, but he and his students were unable to find any. My students and I have so far found only two. In "I'd Rather Be Ratliff" (*The Literary Review* 24 [1981], 308–27), Marjorie Haselswerdt makes a convincing case that the sewing machine salesman in Faulkner's Snopes trilogy possesses many of the attributes that the Third Force psychologists associate with healthy human development; and I believe that Sir Thomas More as he is depicted in *A Man for All Seasons* is a self-actualizing person. Most characters in literature who choose death, as Sir Thomas does, do so for reasons I cannot admire. Sir Thomas, however, does everything that he possibly can to avoid martyrdom; but he is finally forced to choose death because he will not give up his real self. For a further discussion of Sir Thomas, see my essay in *The Literary Review*, cited above.

5   Karen Horney, *The Neurotic Personality of Our Time* (New York: W. W. Norton, 1936), 96.

6   Karen Horney, *Our Inner Conflicts* (New York: W. W. Norton, 1945) 49. Hereafter cited as *OIC*.

7   E. M. Forster, *Aspects of the Novel* (London: Edward Arnold, 1927), chapter 4. For a fuller rationale for the psychological analysis of literary characters, see my *A Psychological Approach to Fiction*, chapter 1.

279

8   I am using, with a few exceptions, the Hardin Craig text of *Hamlet*. I prefer "solid" to "sullied" in I, ii, 129; and I read III, iv, 169 as "curb the devil." Act and scene numbers will be indicated after quotations unless they are obvious from an earlier reference or from the context.

9   Norman Holland, *The Dynamics of Literary Response* (New York: Oxford University Press, 1968), 55.

10   Bernard J. Paris, *Character and Conflict in Jane Austen's Novels* (Detroit: Wayne State University Press, 1978), chapter 6. I have offered a brief analysis of Hardy's personality in "Experiences of Thomas Hardy," *The Victorian Experience*, ed. Richard A. Levine (Athens, Ohio: Ohio University Press, 1976), 233–36.

11   There will be a fuller analysis of Shakespeare's personality in the book I am currently writing—*Bargains with Fate: A Psychological Approach to Shakespeare*.

12   Bernard J. Paris, *Experiments in Life: George Eliot's Quest for Values* (Detroit: Wayne State University Press, 1965).

13   This distinction is important not only for George Eliot, but for almost all realistic novelists. Mimetic characters tend to escape the categories by which the author tries to understand them and to undermine his evaluation of their life-styles and solutions. The great psychological realists have the capacity to see far more than they can understand. Their grasp of inner dynamics and of interpersonal relations is so subtle and profound that concrete representation is the only mode of discourse that can do it justice. When they analyze what they have represented or assign their characters illustrative roles, they are limited by the inadequacy of abstractions generally and of the conceptual systems of their day. Their judgments, moreover, are often a product of their defensive needs. Psychological analysis helps us to see the character the author has actually created, rather than the one he thinks he has created, and to appreciate his genius in characterization despite his deficiences in analysis and judgment. It provides us with a sophisticated method for evaluating the author's judgments of his characters and the adequacy for life of the solutions that he affirms. Works in which the author's judgments are confused become intelligible when we see his inconsistencies as part of a structure of inner conflicts.

14   George Eliot, *Middlemarch*, ed. Gordon Haight (Boston: Houghton Mifflin, 1956), Prelude.

R. D. Laing and Literature—*Girgus*

1   Peter Sedgwick, "R. D. Laing: Self, Symptom and Society," in *R. D. Laing & Anti-Psychiatry*, ed. Robert Boyers and Robert Orrill (New York: Harper & Row, 1971), 49–50. Sedgwick continues his important study of Laing and other new-Freudians in his *Psycho Politics* (New York: Harper & Row, 1982), 107–27..

2   Elaine Showalter, "R. D. Laing and the Sixties," *Raritan* 1 (1981).

3   R. D. Laing, *The Voice of Experience* (New York: Pantheon, 1982), 43, 82.

4   Showalter, "R. D. Laing and the Sixties," 126.

5   R. D. Laing, *The Divided Self: An Existential Study in Sanity and Madness* (c. 1960; Baltimore: Penguin Books, 1965) 17. Hereafter cited as *TDS*.

6   Showalter, "R. D. Laing and the Sixties," 115.

7   Ibid., 116.

8   Ibid., 117.

9   Showalter (ibid., 119) says: "By the time he came to write *The Politics of Experience*, Laing had come to believe that schizophrenia was no more than a sociological label applied to those not adapted to a mad society by those who were."

10 R. D. Laing, *The Politics of Experience* (New York: Ballantine, 1967), 144.

11 Marion Vlastos, "Doris Lessing and R. D. Laing: Psychopolitics and Prophecy," *PMLA* 91 (1976): 250.

12 Sedgwick, "Self, Symptom and Society," 34.

13 R. D. Laing, *The Politics of Experience*, 144–45.

14 Sigmund Freud, *Civilization and Its Discontents*, trans. and ed. James Strachey (c. 1961; New York: Norton, 1962), 92.

15 Edgar Allan Poe, "William Wilson," in *Selected Writings of Edgar Allan Poe*, ed. Edward H. Davidson (Boston: Houghton Mifflin, 1956), 130. Also, see my *The Law of the Heart: Individualism and the Modern Self in American Literature* (Austin: University of Texas Press, 1979), 24–36, for an extended discussion comparing Laing and Poe.

16 Paul Tillich, *The Courage to Be* (New Haven: Yale University Press, 1952), 66.

17 Poe, "The Imp of the Perverse," in Davidson, 230.

18 Poe, "The Pit and the Pendulum" in Davidson, 180; Soren Kierkegaard, *The Sickness unto Death*, trans. Walter Lowrie, in *A Kierkegaard Anthology*, ed. Robert Bretall (New York: Modern Library, 1946), 342.

19 Poe, "The Fall of the House of Usher," in Davidson, 101.

20 Vlastos, "Doris Lessing and R. D. Laing," 246.

21 Elizabeth Janeway, "Who is Sylvia? On the Loss of Sexual Paradigms," in *Women: Sex and Sexuality*, ed. Catherine R. Stimpson and Ethel S. Person (Chicago: University of Chicago Press, 1980), 6.

22 Ibid., 8, 16, 19.

23 Cynthia G. Wolff, "Thanatos and Eros: Kate Chopin's *The Awakening*," *American Quarterly* 25 (1973): 453.

24 Kate Chopin, *The Awakening* (c. 1899; New York: Norton, 1976), 15.

25 Wolff, "Thanatos and Eros," 451, 452, 456, 457.

26 Ibid., 462, 463, 469.

27 Chopin, *The Awakening*, 113.

28 Nathaniel Hawthorne, *The Scarlet Letter* (c. 1850; New York: Norton, 1961), 45–46.

29 Ibid., 46.

30 Ibid., 140.

31 Ibid., 186.

32 See Frederick Crews, *The Sins of the Father: Hawthorne's Psychological Themes* (London: Oxford University Press, 1966).

Phenomenological Psychology—*Natoli*

1 Bernard Paris, *A Psychological Approach to Fiction: Studies in Thackeray, Stendhal, George Eliot, Dostoevsky, and Conrad* (Bloomington: Indiana University Press, 1974), 4ff., is a fairly recent defense of the view that it's proper to treat literary characters as real people.

2 Howard Kendler, "The Unity of Psychology," in *Theories in Contemporary Psychology*, ed. Melvin Marx and Felix Goodson (New York: Macmillan, 1976), 617.

3 Maurice Natanson, *Literature, Philosophy and the Social Sciences* (The Hague: M. Nijhoff, 1962), 97.

4 Maurice Merleau-Ponty, *Phenomenology of Perception* (New York: Humanities Press, 1962), xx.

5 Natanson, *Literature, Philosophy*, 97ff.

6 David M. Levin, Foreword to *The Literary Work of Art*, by Roman Ingarden (Evanston, Ill.: Northwestern University Press, 1973), xxxii.

7 For the Existentialists, the *Lebenswelt* is a central concern, one that emphasizes "being-in-the-world." Husserl's *The Crisis of European Sciences* (The Hague: M. Nijhoff, 1954) deals specifically with the *Lebenswelt*, although — as Gerd Brand points out in "The Structure of the Life-World According to Husserl," *Man and World* 6 (1973): 143–62 — Husserl's life-world is infused with his eidetic phenomenology, the "idealist" aspect of his work ignored by the Existentialists. Lee B. Brown's "World Interpretations and Lived Experience," *Monist* 55 (1971): 275–92, distinguishes *Lebenswelt* from ordinary experience and Husserl's views from those of his "followers." Maurice Natanson's "Phenomenology and the Natural Attitude," in *Literature, Philosophy* presents a view that — together with Wild's ("Man and His Life-World," in *For Roman Ingarden: Nine Essays in Phenomenology* [The Hague: M. Nijhoff, 1959]), van den Berg's (*A Different Existence* [Pittsburgh: Duquesne University Press, 1972], and *Things* [Pittsburgh: Duquesne University Press, 1970]), and Merleau-Ponty's — forms the basis of my own use of *Lebenswelt*.

8   Joseph Natoli, "The *Lebenswelt* of Lancelot Lamar," *Journal of Phenomenological Psychology* 12 (1981): 63–74, presents a detailed view of these four main areas of a phenomenological literary analysis, a view that should complement what is presented in this essay.

9   Martin Heidegger, *Being and Time* (New York: Harper, 1962).

10 William Blake, "The Sick Rose," in *Songs of Innocence and of Experience* (Paris: Trianon Press, 1967), 39.

11 William Sakespeare, *Hamlet* (New Haven: Yale University Press, 1947).

12 Joan Didion, *Play It as It Lays* (New York: Farrar, Straus & Giroux, 1970).

13 Blake, "The Garden of Love," in *Songs of Innocence*, 44.

14 Blake, "The Human Abstract," in *Songs of Innocence*, 47.

15 Blake, letter to Dr. Trusler, in *The Poetry and Prose of William Blake* (New York: Doubleday, 1970), 677.

16 Joseph Natoli, "Fiction as Pathography," *Journal of Phenomenological Psychology* 13 (1982): 73–84, presents a fuller description of pathography in fiction as well as an earlier version of my analysis of *Play It as It Lays*.

17 Van den Berg, *A Different Existence*, 44.

18 Didion, *Play It As It Lays*, 124.

19 Ibid., 72.

20 Ibid., 78.

21 Ibid.

22 Ibid., 21.

Constructivist Interpretation—*Herring*

1   Bernard J. Paris, *A Psychological Approach to Fiction* (Bloomington: Indiana University Press, 1974), uses Karen Horney's theories as an interpretive guide.

2   Edward Chace Tolman, *Collected Papers in Psychology* (Berkeley and Los Angeles: University of California Press, 1951).

3   Some important works in attribution theory include Fritz Heider, *The Psychology of Interpersonal Relations* (New York: John Wiley, 1958); Edward E. Jones et al., *Attribution: Perceiving the Causes of Behavior* (Morristown, N.J.: General Learning Press, 1972); and John Harvey et al., *New Directions in Attribution Research*, vols. 1 and 2 (Hillsdale, N.J.: Lawrence Erlbaum Associates, 1976, 1978).

4   Thomas Lidz, *The Origin and Treatment of Schizophrenia* (New York: Basic Books, 1973), 22, 53.

5   J. B. Rotter, *Social Learning and Clinical Psychology* (Englewood Cliffs, N.J.:

Prentice-Hall, 1954); and George A. Kelly, *A Theory of Personality* (New York: Norton, 1963).

6   Jean Piaget and Barbel Inhelder, *The Psychology of the Child* (New York: Basic Books, 1969), provides a useful summary of the ideas used here.

7   Although Piaget's interpretations have a fundamental relevance here and a basic similarity to the ideas of other cognitive psychologists, differences do exist. Ulric Neisser, *Cognition and Reality* (San Francisco: W. H. Freeman, 1976), 67–68, interprets these findings about objects as reflecting undeveloped skills of attention and articulation, for example.

8   Jean Piaget, *Structuralism*, trans. C. Machsler (New York: Basic Books, 1970), 119.

9   Jerome S. Bruner, *The Process of Education* (Cambridge, Mass.: Harvard University Press, 1960), 7.

10   Neisser, *Cognition and Reality*, 20–24.

11   Jerome Bruner, *Toward a Theory of Instruction* (Cambridge, Mass.: Harvard University Press, 1966), 41.

12   Kelly, *A Theory of Personality*, 9.

13   Nathaniel Hawthorne, *The Scarlet Letter*, in *The Centenary Edition of the Works of Nathaniel Hawthorne*, vol. 1, ed. William Charvat (Columbus: Ohio State University Press, 1962).

14   Carol Johnson, *Reason's Double Agents* (Chapel Hill: University of North Carolina Press, 1966), 2–37, offers an insightful discussion of the movement away from reason as a characteristic of literature.

15   Albert Ellis, "Rational-Emotive Therapy," in *Current Psychotherapies*, ed. Raymond J. Corsini (Ithaca, Ill.: F. E. Peacock, 1979), 1185.

16   William Shakespeare, *King Lear*, ed. Alfred Harbage (Baltimore: Penguin Books, 1970).

17   Frank Kermode, *The Sense of an Ending* (c. 1966; New York: Oxford University Press, 1979), 31, calls comfort the purpose of a literary work, although Kermode is not a psychological critic. Frank Lentricchia, *After the New Criticism* (Chicago: University of Chicago Press, 1980), provides a thorough discussion of the critical conceptions of literature that devalue or deny its cognitive possibilities.

18   Henry James, *The Portrait of a Lady* (Boston: Houghton Mifflin, 1882).

19   Jerome Rothenberg, "The Unconscious and Creativity," in *Psychoanalysis, Creativity and Literature*, ed. Alan Roland (New York: Columbia University Press, 1978), 144–61.

20   John Berryman, *The Dream Songs* (New York: Farrar, Straus & Giroux, 1969).

21   William Shakespeare, *Macbeth*, ed. G. K. Hunter (Baltimore, Penguin Books, 1967).

22 Norman Holland, *The Dynamics of Literary Response* (New York: Norton, 1968), 106-14.

23 John Crowe Ransom, *The World's Body* (New York: Scribner, 1938), 301-2.

An Empirical Approach—*Lindauer*

1 Empirical and scientific (-method, -techniques, -procedures) and empiricism are terms that will be used interchangeably. (There are other meanings, as in "dust bowl" [dry] empiricism.) Technical details, impossible to cover in one chapter, are discussed in numerous texts. See especially E. R. Babbie, *The Practice of Social Research*, 2d ed. (Belmont, Calif.: Wadsworth, 1979); and C. Selltiz, et al., *Research Methods in Social Relations*, 3d ed. (New York: Holt, Rinehart & Winston, 1976).

2 Reviews of the outcomes of empirical research in the psychology of literature (i.e., content rather than method) are found in M. S. Lindauer, *The Psychological Study of Literature* (Chicago: Nelson-Hall, 1974); and M. S. Lindauer, "Psychology and Literature," in *Psychology and Its Allied Disciplines*, ed. M. H. Bornstein (Hillside, N.J.: Lawrence Erlbaum Associates, in press). The phrase "psychology of literature," as used throughout this chapter refers to all related aspects of literature, i.e., the work, author, and reader.

3 F. C. Crews, "Literary Criticism," in *The New Encyclopaedia Britannica*, 15th ed. (Chicago: Encyclopaedia Britannica, 1978), 10:1037-41; H. J. Eysenck, *Sense and Nonsense in Psychology*, rev. ed. (Baltimore: Pelican, 1958), 308-39; Lindauer, *Literature*, chap. 4; M. Peckham, "Psychology in Literature," in *Literary Criticism and Psychology*, ed. J. P. Strelka (College Park: Pennsylvania State University Press, 1976), 48-68; Strelka, *Literary Criticism*.

4 N. Kiell, ed., *Psychoanalysis, Psychology, and Literature: A Bibliography* (Madison: University of Wisconsin Press, 1963).

5 J. Hospers, "Implied Truth in Literature," *Journal of Aesthetics and Art Criticism* 19 (1960); 37-46; J. Bronowski, "Science, Poetry, and Human Specificity," *American Scholar* 43 (1974): 386-404; M. S. Lindauer, "Psychology as a Humanistic Science," *Psychocultural Review* 2 (1978): 139-45.

6 A technique that captures the readers' ongoing reactions is used by E. Klinger, "The Flow of Thought and Its Implications for Literary Communication," *Poetics* 7 (1978): 191-205.

7 Lindauer, *Literature*; P. L. Bodman et al., "What's In a Name? Evaluations of Literary Names in Context and in Isolation," *Poetics* 8 (1979): 491-96.

8 Professional poets were used by C. Patrick, "Creative Thought in Poets," *Archives of Psychology* 9 (1935), 178. Both students and others were used by F. Barron, *Artists in the Making* (New York: Seminar Press, 1972); and J. W. Getzels and M. Csikszentmihalyi, "From Problem Solving to Problem Finding," in *Perspectives in Creativity* ed. I. A. Taylor and J. W. Getzels (Chicago: Aldine, 1975), 90-116. See

also M. S. Lindauer, "Imagery and the Arts," in *Imagery*, ed. A. A. Sheikh (New York: John Wiley, in press).

9   O. R. Holsti, *Content Analysis for the Social Sciences and Humanities* (Reading, Mass.: Addison-Wesley, 1969).

10   Content analysis is frequently used in cases of disputed authorship (Lindauer, *Literature*). Similar forms or expressions in a work suggest a single author, or an identification with works whose authorship is not in dispute. In C. Martindale's *Romantic Progression* (New York: Halstead-Wiley, 1975), computer-assisted content analysis was used to reveal unconscious childhood regression in early French and English poets. Content analysis is also widely used in sociology, e.g., social trends are revealed by short stories in mass-circulation magazines.

11   G. W. Allport, *Personality* (New York: Holt, 1937).

12   P. O. Davidson and C. G. Costello, *N = 1: Experimental Studies of Single Cases* (New York: Van Nostrand, 1969). While a single author may be studied, all of his written works, including letters and diaries, would have to be included. R. R. Sears et al., "Content Analysis of Mark Twain's Novels and Letters," *Poetics* 7 (1978): 155–75.

13   Whether to use the same or different sets of subjects for each condition (the so-called matched or independent groups design, respectively) is a complicated design and statistical question. For example, suppose a study had several short stories to be read, and several scales with which to rate them. It would seem more efficient to have the same group of subjects read all the stories and do all the ratings. Time would be saved in not having to find and train different sets of subjects for each story and set of ratings. Yet the usual recommendation is to use different sets of subjects for each story and set of ratings. One reason is to avoid the effect of the previous reading or rating on subsequent tasks.

14   Three standard measures are the formulas of R. Flesch, "A New Readability Yardstick," *Journal of Applied Psychology* 32 (1948): 221–33; the test by G. W. Allport et al., *Study of Values*, 3d ed. (Boston: Houghton Mifflin, 1969); and the scales of C. E. Osgood et al., *The Measurement of Meaning* (Urbana: University of Illinois Press, 1967).

15   Another troublesome characteristic of the correlation statistic is its literal meaning. Consider the correlations (symbolized as r or *rho*) $r = -.40$ and $r = .35$ (positive signs are not shown but understood). First, the number itself (which is not a percentage) is independent of its sign. This number — which can range from 0 to 1 — indicates the degree of relationship ($-.40$ is slightly higher than .35, and both values can be described as "moderate"). Second, the sign indicates the direction of the relationship. The value $-.40$ describes a negative or inverse relationship, in which like and unlike go together, e.g., high IQ and little reading of good books, and low IQ and much reading. A positive sign (.35) means that like goes with like (high IQ and much good reading, and low IQ and little reading). Correlations, like other statistics, (What is the sign between high IQ and much "poor" reading?) may or may not be statistically significant, i.e., have a value greater than zero (or larger

than another correlation). i.e., have a value greater than zero (or larger than another correlation). E.g., $r = .32$, $p < .05$, is statistically significant, while $r = .87$, $p > .05$, is not.

16 That quality was attributed to the psychologist (and philosopher) William James. The Goethe Prize was received by Freud for the quality of his writing.

17 Kiell, *Psychoanalysis*.

18 For exceptions, see D. W. MacKinnon, "IPAR Contribution to the Conceptualization and Study of Creativity," in Taylor and Getzels, *Perspectives*, 60-89; Martindale, *Romantic*; A. Rothenberg, *The Emerging Goddess* (Chicago: University of Chicago, 1979).

19 Davidson & Costello; E. J. Webb et al., *Unobtrusive Measures* (Chicago: Rand McNally, 1966).

20 But see H. Gardner, *The Arts and Human Development* (New York: John Wiley, 1973).

21 The students who did the research (in alphabetical order) are Loren S. Burch, Ann Henderson, Gregory R. Lattau, Beth Maess, Deborah Sitterly, and Clifford Tambs.

22 In order to emphasize methodology rather than content, the background, results, and discussion in each study are only briefly mentioned or omitted entirely. The methodological details ordinarily found in published reports have been edited for reasons of space. For these and other reasons mentioned in the text, the reader's critical evaluation should be tempered.

23 This work was chosen, in part, because it is brief (it lasts only about one hour). The possible role of other factors (e.g., fatigue and interactions with other members of the audience) was therefore minimized. The brevity of the measures also made them less likely to intrude on the theater experience. The Adjective Checklist is found in M. S. Lindauer, "Aesthetic Experience," in *Psychology and the Arts*, D. O'Hare (Sussex, England: Harvester, 1981), 28-75; the semantic differential scales are from Osgood.

24 This is an interaction effect, since the choice of words depended upon when the test occured. Its statistical significance is indicated as $F(3, 18) = 5.40$, $p < .01$. Of relevance to the reader of this chapter is the p-value of this F-statistic. It means that the effect could occur by chance in less than one out of 100 times, an event so unlikely (at least in the social sciences) that it is justifiable to consider it as *not* due to chance. Instead, it is likely to be a consequence of the treatment whose numerical effects are represented by the statistic.

25 Most studies can be faulted for their artificial sampling of subjects, measures, and treatments. This study is no exception. The way the measures were administered is also problematic. By using the same tests twice, over so short a period of time, the possibility is raised that subjects' memories of their last ratings — rather than their actual experience of the event — were being measured. Also troublesome is the

combined theatrical and musical aspects of an opera. Any effect may be due to one or the other aspect, or both. One might also have wished that additional subjects could have been tested over a longer period (a day or even an hour later). This would indicate the duration of the effect. But the biggest source of ambiguity is the absence of a control group. A similar set of subjects should have taken the same tests twice, with the interval between (comparable to the performance of the opera) filled with a neutral activity (or left empty). The sources of the control group would establish whether changes in the theater group's checklist would have occurred anyway, even if they hadn't been present for the opera. (Perhaps they got better at taking tests?)

26   Lindauer, "Aesthetic Experience."

27   Flesh, "Readability."

28   One aspect of this study has been published elsewhere. See Lindauer, "Psychology and Literature," in press.